Charlotte Mary Yonge, Albert Du Boys

Catharine of Aragon and the Sources of the English Reformation

Vol. 1

Charlotte Mary Yonge, Albert Du Boys

Catharine of Aragon and the Sources of the English Reformation
Vol. 1

ISBN/EAN: 9783337295479

Printed in Europe, USA, Canada, Australia, Japan

Cover: Foto ©ninafisch / pixelio.de

More available books at **www.hansebooks.com**

CATHARINE OF ARAGON

AND THE SOURCES OF

THE ENGLISH REFORMATION

BY

ALBERT DU BOYS

EDITED FROM THE FRENCH, WITH NOTES

BY

CHARLOTTE M. YONGE

AUTHOR OF
"THE HEIR OF REDCLYFFE,"
&c., &c.

IN TWO VOLUMES.

VOL. I.

LONDON:
HURST AND BLACKETT, PUBLISHERS,
13, GREAT MARLBOROUGH STREET.
1881.

All rights reserved.

EDITOR'S PREFACE.

MONSIEUR DU BOYS looks at the history of Henry VIII. from a different point of view from that of an Anglican, and there are many of his conclusions to which we cannot assent. Nevertheless, it has been thought well to translate his book, as an ably drawn-up compendium of the documents relating to the dissolution of the marriage of Catharine of Aragon. The documents cited therein have been taken direct from the original (when English), not re-translated from the author's rendering, which is not always perfectly exact. Sundry incidental errors have also been corrected, such as are always apt to be found when great attention has been paid to a single period without proportionate pains being taken with general history.

M. du Boys cannot be expected to realise that

though Clement VII. was quite right in the individual case of Henry and Catharine, since all evidence went to prove that the marriage with Arthur had been only nominal, yet he was bearing the penalty of the laxity of former popes in tampering with holy wedlock.

The theory was a just one that an impediment according to the Scriptural law could never be set aside; but that one which had been decreed by the Church (such as cousinship, former betrothal, or sponsorship), the Church, in cases where it was thought expedient, had power to remit by dispensation. In point of fact, in order to gratify kings or serve their policy, the Divine law had been disregarded in some of these dispensations, and the most futile pretexts had been allowed for the dismissal of a wife. On the one hand, Catharine's own sister Mary was the reigning wife of the undoubted husband of her deceased sister, Isabella, and in the next generation, Philip II. actually took his own niece as his fourth wife; while, on the other, the history of Spain alone is full of cruel and unmerited divorces; and Henry VIII.'s own contemporary, Louis XII., had been permitted to discard the unfortunate Joan of France with far less shadow of excuse than Henry could show for putting away Catharine. She was childless, and Anne of Brittany was a duchess in her own right,—that was all. Moreover, being an orphan French Princess, she had no one to take her part but the poor, who shouted, after hearing the bull annulling the marriage, " There go Caiaphas, Annas, and Herodias, who have ,condemned our holy queen!"

Surely this may account for the belief entertained by Henry, Wolsey, and Gardiner that the difficulty lay, not in the conscientious scruples of Clement, but in the strength and power of Charles V. We need not ask whether, if the wife had been obscure and friendless, the bull would not have been granted as a trifle in which the pope was ready to oblige his Majesty.

Henry and his statesmen evidently expected that so it would be, and were angered at the resistance. Wolsey acted out of policy, thinking Anne Boleyn too obscure to be the object of a lasting passion, and hoping for a useful foreign connection. Gardiner appears to have been actuated by the strong desire to do his utmost as an agent. It is curious to look at that remarkable scene when he threatened the pope with the secession of England in connection with his conduct when reproached by Queen Mary's victims. Then he confessed his error; and on his death-bed he declared that he had sinned like Peter, and hoped that he was repenting like Peter.

That the rupture with the Roman Church was by no means the Reformation in England, M. du Boys does not understand, nor does he see that Wolsey and Warham had already been meditating an inquiry into the state of the monasteries. Still less does he acknowledge that the Council of the Church was as honestly desired by Henry as by Charles V., and that it was staved off by the Italian cardinals because of their corruptions, and by Clement VII. on account of his own illegitimate birth, Francis I. assisting them out of hatred to the emperor.

The truth was that, but for the violence of Henry in breaking with the Continental Church, the English clergy would have been present at the Council of Trent, and added weight to the reforming party, as they had done at Constance, so that a really efficient reform might have taken place. The persons who had become imbued with the doctrines of Luther and of other reformers naturally rejoiced in the separation from Rome; but, as long as Henry lived, they found that this by no means meant toleration of any teaching save that of the Roman Communion. No changes either of doctrine or ritual (except the use of vernacular Lessons and litany) were made until the ensuing reign. The destruction of fraudulent relics and of the monasteries (though shocking to a devout Roman Catholic) was not connected with any church doctrine. Erasmus and More had been as much shocked by the absurd exhibition at Canterbury as the staunchest Protestant could be.

M. du Boys has thus written the history of the causes of the English separation, but he has not written the history of the Reformation of the English Church. This was indeed rendered possible by the breach with Rome; but it had not yet begun when he closes his history with the retribution upon Anne Boleyn. He has shown how, whatever was the effect on England, her fascination was utterly fatal to the once noble, generous, and pious nature of Henry VIII.

C. M. YONGE.

DEDICATION.

MY LORD,

Your Eminence having vouchsafed your permission allowing me to dedicate to you my work on Catharine of Aragon, this book has the peculiar good fortune to appear under the auspices of the famous name of Cardinal Newman.

On a late solemn occasion, Your Eminence made a strong protest against the pretended equality of all forms of Christianity in the sight of God, as well as the most various demonstrations of the religious sentiment. But, on the other hand, you allowed that in the state of modern society, especially that of England, a government cannot exact information as to his belief or form of worship from every individual before granting him the rights of citizenship. Such political neutrality has become a necessity of the period.

At the same time, you stated that persuasion is the only means that can be employed for the restoration of unity in a divided country, and thereupon quoted the words of Scripture, *Mansueti hæreditabunt terram.*

The English Church was established by an exactly contrary process. Violence was used by its founder, not for the preservation of unity, but for its destruction. I have collected some fresh information concerning the melancholy origin of that Church. The schism that gave it birth was thrust upon the nation by government with the exercise of violence almost unexampled in our modern times.

No one has more ably shown than Your Eminence how the divine direction in Anglicanism has gradually given place to a kind of purely civil constitution.

In the attempt to cast a little more light on the sources of this work of darkness, I shall endeavour to give the present generation grounds for estimating the value of this Cæsarian religion, only propagated by treading under foot the most noble and lofty souls of England, and by punishing as crimes of high treason the most lawful resistance of conscience, the inviolable sanctuary that no human hand should violate.

I believed that I should act in accordance with the views of 'Your Eminence by giving prominence to the heroism of some of the martyrs who then adorned the Catholic faith in England.

I am, with respect,
Your Eminence's most obedient servant,
ALBERT DU BOYS,
LATE MAGISTRATE.

LA COMBE, *July* 25, 1879.

REPLY

OF

HIS EMINENCE CARDINAL NEWMAN.

THE ORATORY, *July* 28, 1879.

SIR,

I thank you for the compliment you pay me in proposing to dedicate to me your work on Catharine of Aragon.

Certainly, as you say, the Anglican Church became the established religion by the application of tyrannical force. I trust that now there are very few of its members who wish to use such means of upholding it, or would profess or act upon the principles of Cæsarism.

I am, sir,
Your faithful servant in X°
JOHN ST. CARD. NEWMAN.

PREFACE.

I.

HISTORY would be unworthy of its mission if it confined itself to recording the results of great occurrences without informing us of the concealed springs that set them in motion, or giving us its stern teaching respecting the morals of the men who took part in them.

The men of the present century are more than ever anxious to obtain the instructive and characteristic particulars which cast so great a light on the weaknesses and passions of man. We are therefore, so to speak, more on the watch for any fresh information exhumed from the dust of our own archives, or from those of neighbouring countries, and the attention of the more intelligent public is sure to be attracted if such information be placed within its grasp.

We have thought it desirable to gratify this contemporary inclination by writing the life of Catharine of Aragon from documents previously unpublished, and lately brought out in England, bearing on the reigns of Henry VII. and Henry VIII.

The life of Catharine of Aragon reaches back to the commencement of the glorious reigns of Ferdinand and Isabella. The second portion of Catharine's career was implicated in all the disturbances of the sixteenth century, in the rivalry of Francis I. and Charles V., in the vicissitudes of the papacy, and in the greatest event of modern times, namely, what is called the Reformation, and which was, in fact, the rending of the seamless vesture.

In England schism had a peculiar origin. It owed its birth to an impure passion of King Henry VIII.; for the satisfaction of that passion he chose to break the indissoluble bonds that united him to the noble daughter of the great Queen Isabella of Castille, aunt of the Emperor Charles V., and to bid defiance to the thunders of the Vatican.

The history of this suit of nullity of marriage, or of divorce, perhaps the most memorable of the kind that has ever been argued in the world, has received new and unexpected revelations from the documents that have just been made public. Therein may be seen the weaving of unheard-of plots against an unhappy princess who at one time seemed entirely deserted, and who was even invited to go to Rome, and to give up her own cause. Her haughty and noble bearing during the progress, and especially at the end of the suit was already attested by history. When still better known it will excite admiration of her individual self. On another side we shall show how consistently Charles V. was able to maintain the honour of his nation, his blood, and his race, without exclusive regard to politics. Lastly, it will be seen how the sovereign pontiff had to resist the detestable pressure of the agents of Henry VIII.; and Orvieto in some respects may remind us of Anagni.* Clement VII. in his turn saved the honour of the papacy, possibly with less firmness than Boniface VIII., but with less obstinacy. At last, amid the members of his consistory on whom the acts of corruption had been vainly tried, he pronounced in favour of the indissolubility of the marriage tie, one of those decrees that re-echo loudly throughout history.

Henry VIII. replied to the sentence of the Church by separating his kingdom from the Church; and this was the miserable origin of the still existing schism.

II.

Some historical notes appear to us to be requisite before actually entering upon the life of Catharine of Aragon.

The interest of the life of that princess turns upon her two marriages, the histories of which are closely

* The scene of the contention between Boniface VIII. and Philip the Fair. (Ed.)

vol. i.   *b*

connected together; for the second was only impugned, and, in fact, was only made liable to attack, by the fact of the first having taken place.

Besides, the manners and politics of the time must be considered. Royal marriages were then affairs of state far more than family matters. In some countries, where the sovereigns were able rulers, they became methods of aggrandisement more secure and less sanguinary than conquests by force of arms. The Austrian motto may be remembered:

Tu felix, Austria, nube!

They were also considered firm, nay, almost indissoluble, pledges of alliance between dynasties.

The marriage of Catharine of Aragon with Arthur, Prince of Wales, was preceded by very important negotiations. It may be said to have had more distinctly a political bearing than most of the princely marriages contracted about the same time.

Catharine of Aragon's second marriage was the occasion of events still more strange than arose from the first, and of complications, we might even say intrigues, of much greater variety.

Thus, between Ferdinand of Aragon on one side, and Henry VII., King of England, on the other, diplomacy, properly so called, had a very considerable part to play.

In the collections before alluded to have been gathered all the despatches and letters of the sovereigns of each country, and their ambassadors, relating to these diplomatic and matrimonial negotiations. These various documents had hitherto been unpublished.*

Laying stress chiefly upon these new documents, we have thought it needful to study and explain, in an introduction of no great length, the characters of three great historical personages, Henry VII. of England, Ferdinand of Aragon, and Isabella of Castille. Indeed it was they who gave the first impulse

* The first of these collections is entitled "Calendars of letters, despatches, and state papers relating to the negotiations between England and Spain, preserved in the archives at Simancas and elsewhere," five vols., royal 8vo. We say five volumes by including a supplement to vol. ii. " London, Longman & Co." The second has for title "Letters and papers, foreign and domestic, of the reign of Henry VIII., preserved in the public record office, the British Museum, and elsewhere in England, arranged by J. S. Brewer, M.A. London, Longman & Co. Four volumes 8vo. have appeared, and these publications will be continued. The learned Bergenroth published the three first volumes of the former of these collections, including the supplement, having spent two years at Simancas inspecting the archives; he there contracted an incurable fever, and shortly afterwards died of it at Madrid. The Spanish savant, Gayangos, edited the third and fourth volumes of this collection. As to the second, three volumes of documents, abridged, set in order, and catalogued, were. first published by Longman. In 1875 there appeared a fourth volume, with a long and learned introduction by Professor Brewer, editor of this collection. This writer has given proof of much sagacity, and even impartiality, in the review of the documents he edited. He is a distinguished member of the English High Church. We have also placed under contribution a third calendar, that of Rawdon Brown, who has given us the despatches and reports of the Venetian agents from the commencement of the reign of Henry VIII. to his condemnation by the Court of Rome. Lastly, we have made use to the utmost of our power of the manuscript of Archdeacon Harpsfield, lately published by the Camden Society, an edition of only two hundred copies.

to this profoundly tragical drama by devising the idea of these two marriages, the first of them so short in duration, the second so fruitful of various events. We are therefore about to trace a sketch of the portrait of the first of the Tudors, Henry VII., and the two Catholic sovereigns who accomplished the union of the whole Spanish peninsula under one sceptre.

CONTENTS

OF

THE FIRST VOLUME.

HISTORICAL INTRODUCTION 1

PART I.—THE TWO MARRIAGES AND CORONATION OF CATHARINE OF ARAGON.

CHAPTER I.

Birth of Catharine of Aragon—Her Childhood spent in Camps and the Palace of the Alhambra, Grenada—Negotiations for the Marriage between Catharine of Aragon and the Prince of Wales—Isabella's Letter—Latin Correspondence between Arthur and Catharine 33

CHAPTER II.

Catharine's Arrival at Plymouth—Her Warm Welcome—Difficulties of Spanish Etiquette removed by the Authority of Henry VII.—Renewal of the Promise of Betrothal—Baynard Castle and the Alhambra—Catharine's Marriage celebrated at St. Paul's, London—Tournament and Symbolical Representations—Stage Appearance of Alphonso the Wise—Arthur and his Court at Ludlow Castle in Shropshire—His Death—What was the Cause of it?—His Monument at Worcester—Cruel Situation of the Young Widow 49

CHAPTER III.

Grief of Queen Elizabeth, Catharine's Mother-in-law—Isabella Wishes to recall her Daughter to Spain—Ferdinand desires to Marry her again in England to the new Prince of Wales—The Young Princess at first appears not to favour this Union—Henry VII. proposes to marry her Himself—Indignant Reply of Isabella—Renewal of Negotiations—Treaty of Marriage arranged between Catharine and her Brother-in-law, Henry, Prince of Wales—The Pope's Bull—The Betrothal—Death of Isabella of Castille—Pecuniary Wranglings between Ferdinand and Henry VII.—Catharine is held by the Latter as a Living Pledge—Protest of the Prince of Wales against his Betrothal to Catharine—Henry VII. wishes to Marry the Queen-Dowager of Naples—Remarkable Negotiations on this Matter 59

CHAPTER IV.

Opposition of a Divine to the Betrothal of Henry, Prince of Wales, and Catharine—Henry VII. seems to have Serious Thoughts of a Marriage with the Queen-Dowager of Naples—Remarkable Negotiations entered upon Through the Medium of Catharine—Matrimonial Catechism—The Queen declares that she will not marry again—Destitution of Catharine—Doña Juana and the Archduke Joseph in England—Henry VII.'s Exercise of Constraint to keep them in England—He does not allow Freedom of Communication between Catharine and Juana—The Archduke's Departure—Urgent Letter from Catharine to her Father, Ferdinand—Catharine's Sufferings—Troubles connected with Royal Marriages . 79

CHAPTER V.

Why does not Ferdinand pay Catharine's Marriage Portion?—Puebla himself comes at last to pity this Princess—Death of the Archduke Philip the Fair—Henry VII. asks the Widow Juana in Marriage—Ferdinand makes Delays, but gives Hopes—Henry VII. is satisfied, and treats Catharine better—She serves him as a go-between in his Matrimonial Negotiations—Under Henry's Influence, she writes a very Strong Letter in favour of this Marriage—Subtlety and little Dissimulations of the Princess required by the Necessities of her Position— The Treaty of Marriage between Henry VII. and Juana absolutely comes to an End—This Check makes Catharine's Wretched Condition still worse—Ferdinand's Great Anger with Henry VII., for he neither will marry her to the Prince of Wales, nor let her go back to Spain—Ferdinand is on the point of declaring War against England, when he hears of the Death of Henry VII. 100

CHAPTER VI.

Clerical Education of Henry VIII.—A Stop to all Misunderstanding between Ferdinand and England—The New King's Council recognize the Validity of the Bull of Dispensation of Pope Julius II.—Marriage and Coronation of the Queen—Popularity of Henry VIII.—Restrictive Explanations given by Henry of his Coronation Oath—Affectionate Correspondence of Henry and Ferdinand—Dexterity and Diplomatic Artifices of Ferdinand—Henry VIII. goes to Fight in France —Catharine Regent—The Victory of Flodden—Coolness between Henry and Ferdinand—Marriage of Henry's Sister to Louis XII.—Presents of Ferdinand to Henry, and Reconciliation of the Two Kings—Charles V.'s Voyage to England —Work of Henry VIII. against Luther—He Receives the Title of Defender of the Faith—Portrait of Henry VIII., by a Venetian Ambassador 125

PART II.—DIVORCE OF HENRY VIII. AND CATHARINE OF ARAGON. SUFFERINGS AND DEATH OF THAT PRINCESS.

CHAPTER I.

How was the First Idea of the Divorce conceived by Henry VIII.?—Fears of Fresh Civil Wars, if the King had no heir, by the Lords and Grandees of the Realm—Cooling of King Henry VIII.'s Affection for the Queen after Fifteen or Sixteen Years of Marriage and United Life—Excuses given for Henry VIII.'s Conduct by his Apologists—Falseness of these Excuses—Tardy Scruples of Henry VIII.—Theology and Policy furnish him with Pretexts after the Deed . . 156

CHAPTER II.

Was Henry VIII.'s Conduct Exemplary during the First Years of his Marriage?—Did the Real Piety that he professed preserve him from all Moral Failings?—What is to be thought of the Business of Compton, lately made public in the Diplomatic Correspondence of Louis Carroz?—Was not this Strange and Mysterious Adventure the real Origin of Henry VIII.'s Hatred for Buckingham?—The King's Connection with Elizabeth Blount—Recognition of his Natural Son the Duke of Richmond—Honours heaped upon the Young Duke even before he was out of his Childhood . . . 163

CHAPTER III.

Henry VIII.'s Love-affair with Elizabeth Blount—Almost Royal Homage paid to her Son, the Young Duke of Richmond—Increasing Coolness of the King to Catharine . . 173

CHAPTER IV.

Picture of the Court of England by Erasmus during the Youth of Henry VIII.—Origin and Social Position of the Boleyns—Their Morality and that of their Society—Anne Boleyn at the Court of France—Her Sister Mary Mistress of Henry VIII.—Anne recalled to England—Her Portrait—Her Success at Henry's Court—Plots contrived against Catharine by Anne Boleyn and her Family 179

CHAPTER V.

Wolsey and Longlands were the Originators of the King's Doubts and Scruples as to the Validity of his Marriage—Judicial Farce contrived between Wolsey and Henry VIII. concerning the Pretended Nullity of Marriage with Catharine of Aragon—This Farce remains a Secret and without Result—Capture and Sack of Rome by the Imperial Army—Henry VIII. and Francis I. try to renew and strengthen their Alliance against the Emperor—The first Notion of Divorce falsely attributed to the Bishop of Tarbes—Matrimonial and other Negotiations between France and England—Proposed Marriage of the Princess Mary to Francis I., or his Second Son, the Duke of Orleans—Difficulties are raised in the Clauses of the Treaty between Wolsey and the French Ambassador—Conclusions of the Treaty—Solemn Reception and Festivities at Greenwich Palace 195

CHAPTER VI.

Perfidious plans of Cranmer—Catharine claims her Defence—Arrival in London of Mendoza, the Spanish Ambassador—He is long prevented from seeing the Queen in private—Wolsey goes to France—Mendoza takes advantage of it to communicate more easily with Catharine—Unpopularity of Wolsey, Popularity of the Queen—Catharine's Letter to Charles V.—Mendoza discovers and announces the preparations for the Divorce Suit—Consultation of Divines and their Evasive Answer—Cruel Conversation of the King with Catharine—Mendoza informs the Emperor of this Domestic Scene—Charles V. takes his Aunt's Side with Henry VIII., and at the same time uses influence with the Pope in her favour—Insidious Advice of Gardiner to Mendoza—Affectionate Letter of Charles V. to his aunt—Catharine endeavours to prepare her defence 214

CHAPTER VII.

Cardinal Wolsey's Double Mission—His Splendid Train—His Meeting with Archbishop Warham, and afterwards Fisher, Bishop of Rochester—He works for the Divorce and against Catharine—Wolsey's Prayer at the tomb of Saint Thomas of Canterbury—Expedients proposed in his Correspondence with Henry VIII.—Wolsey in France—Charles V. seems to treat him gently—Wolsey at the Court of Francis I.—The Hand of the Princess Mary is promised to the Duke of Orleans—The other Clauses of the Treaty of Alliance are also settled and signed—Wolsey at last opens the Question of Divorce—But Queen Louise of Savoy will not leave him any Hopes of the Eventual Marriage of a Daughter of France with Henry VIII. 238

CHAPTER VIII.

Wolsey in England—Henry VIII.'s Theological Treatise against the validity of his marriage—Clement VII. a Prisoner in the Castle of Saint Angelo—Henry sends him his secretary,

Knight, who fails in his Mission—Wolsey resumes the conduct of the business, and gives Instructions and a fresh Commission to Casale living in Italy, and then to Fox and Gardiner; they go from England, and find the Pope escaped from the Castle of Saint Angelo and gone to Orvieto—Destitution and Isolation of Clement VII.—Curious Letter given by Wolsey to Fox and Gardiner—Violent scene between Gardiner and the Pope—He obtains the Conditional Dispensation he had requested, but the terms of the Commission are reviewed, and do not give an absolute power without appeal to two Legates sent to determine the matter of the Divorce—Cardinal Campeggio, as Legate and Member of the Commission or Ecclesiastical Court, is united to Wolsey—Wolsey protests before Fox that he will judge conscientiously whatever may happen 253

CHAPTER IX.

The Two Kings' Defiance, and the Emperor's Reply—Policy and Attitude of Wolsey before the Arrival of Cardinal Campeggio—The Appointment of the Abbess of Wilton—Discontent of Henry VIII., and his Correspondence with Wolsey on this Business—The Sweating Sickness—Henry's Momentary Return to Catharine—His Letters to Anne Boleyn, and hers to Wolsey 287

HISTORICAL INTRODUCTION.

SECTION I.—HENRY VII., KING OF ENGLAND.

RICHARD III. thought he had secured his own triumph by the murder of his nephews, after the entire destruction of the direct line of the House of Lancaster.

But the partisans of the red rose derived fresh strength from the very hatred excited by the base and cruel king; they were determined to find a fresh representative of Lancaster to become their chief and avenger. They succeeded; the required person was found in the Earl of Richmond, the descendant of a bastard of this House of Lancaster, whose legitimate line seemed to have been exhausted by the interminable civil wars.* He was recalled from exile in

* In virtue of letters patent of Richard II., confirmed by Parliament, John of Gaunt, Duke of Lancaster, had caused his natural children to be legitimated, but in their case there was added to the deed a clause of exclusion from all claims to the throne of England.

VOL. I. B

France, that he might undertake the conquest of the throne of England.

Thus, in the eyes of the enemies of the House of York, the Earl of Richmond was only a king for expediency's sake; but such as he was, he succeeded in gaining the victory of Bosworth over Richard III. Thus at first the Lancastrian claimant had the judgment of God on his side, and soon afterwards the Parliament recognised him as legitimate sovereign; thenceforward he entitled himself "King by the grace of God," and caused himself to be solemnly crowned by the Archbishop of Canterbury.

Margaret, the mother of Henry VII., was the last survivor of the direct line of Beaufort. Her husband, Edmund Tudor, was the son of Owen Tudor, a Welsh gentleman who had married Catharine of France, widow of Henry V.

He afterwards married, according to a promise made even before his coming to England, the Princess Elizabeth, who, after the violent death of her two brothers, was, as the daughter of Edward IV., the representative of the elder branch of the House of York.

There is not much evidence respecting the appearance and physical qualities of Henry VII. It appears that he was of middle stature, and did not enjoy vigorous health. Foreign diplomatists, who were in personal communication with him, said that he had a good deal of expression and much play of countenance. His long sojourn in Brittany and France had given him great facility in the use of the French language; he spoke it very well to the end of his life. It is stated that his air and manners were those of a Frenchman rather than of an Englishman. He wrote with equal ease in both languages.

English historians have not denied the defects of this prince; but they have extolled his mercy and clemency.

Placed in history between the monster Richard III. and the tyrant Henry VIII., he owes much to this juxtaposition. The comparison could not be otherwise than favourable to him.

The best thing that can be said of him is that his thirst for gold was greater than it was for blood.

He was very willing to accord a certain measure of forgiveness to the vanquished Yorkist nobles for their defence of the sovereign to whom they had promised fidelity. He did not condemn them to the fearful death of a traitor. It must be owned that this was a kind of innovation in the long list of political reprisals in England. But these lords were constrained to submit, and place themselves, as the phrase ran, at the king's mercy, and this was granted to them by a magnanimity which only seized their property.

It is true that Henry VII. was not so indulgent in the instance of the Earl of Warwick, son of the Duke of Clarence, and the last scion of the younger branch of the House of York. This young prince, who might have become a dangerous claimant, had been confined in the Tower of London. Weary of a captivity that seemed likely to be interminable, the young prince attempted to escape. This innocent attempt was construed into a crime of high treason. The unhappy prince was condemned to death. Henry VII. signed the sentence, and the execution took place.

The private life of this king was free from irregularity, but he showed little consideration, and evinced little affection towards his queen, Elizabeth—at least, during the early part of his married life. The Prior of Santa Cruz says that he considers this princess as the most noble woman of England, and that she was condemned to the most mournful and wretched existence; only he implies that the cause of this was not tyranny and oppression by the king himself so much as by his mother, the Countess of Richmond, a haughty and imperious person.*

King Henry had few friends among the higher ranks of English society; his tastes did not range so high. He showed a real friendship for the Spanish envoy, Doctor Puebla, who was intimate with hardly any person in England but the king.

* She was a charitable and pious princess, a patron of letters; but such virtues are not inconsistent with a temper hard to deal with. Indeed, a person may be a combination of most eminent qualities, and yet a bad mother-in-law.

Henry VII. was selfish and avaricious. Like misers and professional usurers, he buried his gold, or hid it carefully in a chest. Nevertheless, on the occasions of his solemn receptions, he sometimes displayed magnificence and ostentation.

This prince showed great vigilance and real dexterity in the defence of his crown against constant insurrections; but he did not exhibit the same superiority in his foreign policy.

He did not love war, yet, notwithstanding all his dexterity, he allowed himself to be repeatedly drawn by Ferdinand into hostilities with France, without obtaining any advantage from them.

His especial deficiency was in generosity and largeness of mind. He always had a smack of the adventurer and *parvenu*. His captious pettiness is betrayed in his correspondence, as well as his complete want of frankness and sincerity. Numerous proofs of his political duplicity will appear in the account of his negotiations with Spain, and of his conduct towards Catharine of Aragon. In our opinion an indelible stain is attached to his memory by his crafty and persistent harshness towards that unhappy princess.

SECTION II.—ISABELLA OF CASTILLE, QUEEN OF SPAIN.

THE proclamation of the claims of Isabella to the

crown of Castille, and her accession to the throne in 1474, were hailed with great joy by the Spanish nation, who were heartily disgusted with the spectacle of immorality presented by King Henry IV. and his Court.

This feeble monarch lived under the same roof as his queen for a long time without ever suspecting that one of his courtiers, Beltran de la Cueva, was enjoying all the privileges of her favoured lover.

If questions of political law were dealt with according to maxims borrowed from Roman jurisprudence, slaying the spirit of them while interpreting them according to the letter, this matter might be reduced to the dimensions of a civil suit, and it might be pleaded that Isabella was a usurper, and that the true heiress of the crown was Doña Juana, daughter of Henry IV.* But though this lady was born on the steps of the throne, and was not volun-

* There is in existence a very curious memorandum concerning the illegitimacy of the birth of this princess. It was prepared to prove the suitability and desirability of a marriage between Charles V. and the Princess of Portugal. Doña Juana, called la Beltraneja, was then still alive, confined in a convent near the banks of the Tagus. Several years before, Alphonso, King of Portugal, had chosen to take up her cause. He was conquered, and died soon after. But there was some black spot in the business that still excited uneasiness in the minds of the Castillians. It was thought that a marriage would be very politic which would give Charles V. or his heir all possible claims to the inheritance of the throne of Portugal, and hinder any claim being set up in that country to the crown of Spain for the Beltraneja. See Calendar of State Papers, vol. ii, pp. 396, 397. The memorandum gives conclusive proofs of the illegitimacy of Doña Juana.

tarily disavowed by the king, it was immediately evident that she was most decidedly rejected by public opinion. It is well known that the nickname of "Beltraneja"—that is to say, daughter of Beltran de la Cueva—was instantly bestowed on her. This was the contemporary opinion, and it was confirmed by posterity and history.

The Spanish people were too proud to continue to put up with royalty thus dragged through the mire.

The movement in favour of Isabella, that pure and austere young princess, owed its origin to a reaction of all that was honourable against all that was corrupt, of all that was noble against all that was vile. This impulse became so strong that Henry IV. himself was obliged to yield to it to avoid the danger of losing his crown and his life. The assembly of the nobles of Castille, meeting at Toro de Guisando, declared that Isabella was his heir presumptive, and must be proclaimed Princess of the Asturias.

Isabella had already, with firm, wise gentleness, repulsed the premature offer of the throne of Castille that had been made to her. On that occasion she had contented herself with obtaining a recognition of her freedom and complete independence in the choice of a husband. And, as is well known, she profited by this permission to marry Ferdinand of Aragon, in spite of the opposition of her brother, Henry IV.

As long as that prince lived, she paid most scrupulous respect to his powers and rights. But, as soon as he was dead, she seized the reins of government in a firm grasp, in faithful execution of the sort of compact she had made with Castille. In her youth she had undergone many strange adventures and reverses, and had throughout evinced great dexterity and infinite tact. After various romantic adventures she had married the Infant Ferdinand of Aragon, and placed him beside her on the throne of Castille, thus putting herself into a position of difficulty and delicacy. She had given a share of her power to her royal spouse, a share which he always thought less than his due. It needed all the graces, and the charms, and the tact of Isabella to lull the umbrageous jealousy of Ferdinand. She succeeded in making him understand that any division of power between them could be but nominal, since their interests were in common, and their principles and ideas exactly identical, but at last she thoroughly convinced him that they would always proceed together in perfect and affectionate unity,

Isabella effected a complete change in the evil customs that had prevailed in the court of the two kings, her predecessors. A strong vigour and esteem for authority took the place of the spirit of anarchy and revolution; perfect decorum prevailed instead of scandalous licence, and for the former rudeness of manners was substituted that refinement of morals and habits which renders strength polished, and even audacity deferential. She took advantage of the disposition of her Spanish people, who still remained the most chivalrous in Europe, to exercise over them an influence only belonging to her sex, and of her sex, only to persons, like herself, endowed with supreme dignity of demeanour, language, and tone, even in the expression of the countenance, the certain reflection of the mind.

We have a portrait of Isabella before us; it is an engraving after an obscure master. The picture was, a few years ago, in the palace of Don Blas at Madrid. On a comparison of this portrait with that by the first master of colour of the sixteenth century, Titian—which we have seen and admired in the gallery at Augsburg, in Germany—this is the idea that may be formed of Queen Isabella.* She must have been of rather less than middle height, and remarkable for her fine figure. Her hair was a light chestnut, and shone with a slight touch of gold; her eyes were dark blue, and sparkled with a bright expression of intelligence and resolution, softened with heavenly sweetness. In the engraving we have mentioned she is represented in a high dress,

* The splendid colouring of the noble Venetian exalts the fine complexion and beautiful features of the great queen. Titian cannot have painted this portrait, to the order of Charles V., till twenty-five or thirty years after Isabella's death; but it is most probable that it was composed from portraits made of that princess during her life.

her head covered with a veil encircling the whole face; she holds a breviary in her hand. At first she seems to bear some resemblance to Giotto's virgins, whose pure and lofty expression has a certain religious severity. But a more attentive examination seems to show that the Queen of Spain's meditations are more bent upon the duties of royalty than the glories of heaven. There is something determined in her expression, announcing a positive and tenacious will. The serenity, the reserve, the self-contained dignity, so visible in her attitude and all her features, are evidences of her moral strength, and inspire the beholder with involuntary and profound respect.

The expression of resolution in the features of this portrait of Isabella is not deceptive; determination was the basis of her character, but it did not exclude grace and kindness.

She never yielded to popular insurrection.* But above all things did she strive with inflexible severity against the usurpations of the grandees of Castille, applying the laws to them just as she would have done to the least among her people.

"The chiefs of the Houses of Cadiz and Medina Sidonia," says the latest of Spanish historians,† "the

---

* Her presence of mind and indomitable courage on the occasion of the terrible insurrection at Segovia are well known.

† La Fuente, Historia General de España, pt. ii, lib. v, pp. 111, 112, second edition, Madrid, 1869.

Guzmans, the Poncé de Léon, the Aguilars, and Porto Carreros, who kept the whole country in a state of trouble and disturbance, must have experienced astonishment akin to stupefaction, when they saw this young queen intrepidly enter Seville, receive the acclamations of the people, and administer justice with a calmness as imperturbable as if her rule had long been established in the country. Of these independent lords, who seemed so formidable, some restored to the crown the property that had been given in pledge to them, others presented themselves before the queen to excuse their past conduct, and promise to be more peaceable and submissive for the future."

It was Isabella who gave the greatest encouragement and legal sanction to the Santas Hermandades, those popular institutions which had originated in the towns of Castille for the restraint of the disorders and robberies that prevented any sense of security. It was one of her special characteristics to be perfectly impartial, and to allow no consideration to interfere with strict justice, a greater merit in princes than clemency. Her judgment may sometimes have erred, but, when once she had taken up a really clear view in a matter of justice, nothing would sway her aside from it.

Thus a Knight of Galicia named Yanez de Lugo, who had committed a crime, begged to be excused from prosecution, offering for his letters of pardon the sum, enormous for that time, of forty thousand doubloons of gold. Isabella was much in want of money, and her councillors pressed her strongly to accept it; but she was inflexible in her refusal.*

Here is another specimen of her severity even towards the persons of her Court, and of what may be called her passion for justice.

One day in the guard-room of her palace at Valladolid, a quarrel arose between two young men, Ramiro Nuñez de Guzman, Lord of Toral, and Frederick Henriquez, son of the Admiral of Castille, who was uncle to King Ferdinand. As soon as the queen was informed of this dispute, she gave a safe conduct to the Lord of Toral, to protect him till a reconciliation should take place. However, Don Frederick, in spite of the royal protection, took with him three of his companions, lay wait for his enemy at night in the streets of Valladolid, and treacherously beat him with a stick.

The moment Isabella heard of this ambuscade and violation of her safe conduct, she mounted her horse in the midst of a dreadful storm and torrents of rain, and galloped away to the Castle of Simancas, then occupied by the admiral, father of the culprit; her guards could hardly keep up with her, and she reached the fortress before them. She immedi-

---

* Pulgar, Reges catolicos, pt. ii, cap. xcv. L. Marinœo, Cosas memorabiles, fol. 180.

ately summoned the admiral to deliver up his son to her, but he asserted that Frederick Henriquez was not within the walls of the castle, whereupon she caused all the keys to be delivered to her, and examined all the rooms, and every corner of the dungeons; and, as her search proved fruitless, she returned to Valladolid. Next day, either in consequence of the fatigue, or the disappointment she had experienced, she was obliged to remain in bed. Being asked what ailed her, she replied, "My body is bruised all over by the blows given by Frederick to Guzman, in despite of my safe-conduct."

The admiral saw that it was undesirable to withdraw his son from the queen's justice, lest he might himself incur disgrace. Two days afterwards, therefore, he sent him to the palace at Valladolid in the custody of his uncle, the Constable de Haro, who interceded with Isabella for the culprit. The queen would not allow herself to yield to their supplications; she thought it absolutely necessary to make an example. She therefore gave orders to the alcaldés to publicly lead the young man across the grand square of Valladolid, and to keep him in solitary confinement in a narrow cell. At last, on the entreaty of the king, who was nearly related to the young prisoner, she consented to commute his imprisonment for an exile of several years to Sicily.*

With a like sense of justice, taking a different

* Prescott, Ferdinand and Isabella, vol. i, pp. 175, 176.

direction, when she thought any eminent person peculiarly marked out by merit for high office, she guarded herself against all influence, and even the bias of her own affections, so as not to betray that first duty of royalty which consists of making the best possible choice for the public welfare. Thus, when the metropolitan see of Toledo was vacant, instead of the young Don Alphonso of Aragon, who was already Archbishop of Zaragoza, and was warmly recommended by Ferdinand himself, she chose that pious and austere monk who is known as Ximenes.

But it was in the part she took in the Moorish war that the great qualities of this queen were chiefly displayed. She understood better than anyone what was wanting in the Spanish knights, who daily performed the most heroic exploits, but who, contented with the glory acquired by their prowess, would have on the morrow abandoned all that had been gained and sought merely repose after victory. It was owing to her that the war became something more than a course of adventures; she brought into play foresight, perseverance, combination, and regularity of operations.

Thus she would not allow the capture of Alhama, that great blow to the Moors, to be rendered a mere barren feat of arms by the retreat of the army which had planted the banner of the cross upon these towers hitherto deemed impregnable. This place was certainly so distant from the other strongholds occupied by the Christians as to be exposed to continual attack from the enemy, but she viewed it as the first post to be held upon the road to Grenada. Dating from this time, it was she who undertook the raising of recruits and collecting of food and stores. Nothing could withdraw her from her one aim, the capture of Grenada and the conquest of the Moors.

· One day Ferdinand declared that he intended to apply the resources of his little kingdom to the extension of the frontiers of Aragon, not of those of Castille, even announcing that he should set off to reconquer Roussillon. On this, Isabella declared war against the infidels, and she was actually preparing to do so when Ferdinand returned. Fortunately for his fame, the Cortes of Aragon had refused him a subsidy.

While the Spaniards were besieging Baza their ammunition failed, and the treasury was exhausted; the queen pledged her jewels and personal ornaments to supply the needs of war.

Nevertheless, the Spaniards were discouraged, and were gradually giving up the siege, as it became protracted, when the queen herself appeared in the camp, accompanied by Cardinal Mendoza and a brilliant escort. On the spectacle of this numerous cavalcade issuing from the valleys, and at the sound of the enthusiastic acclamations of the Spanish army, the inhabitants of Baza, struck with dread and astonishment, offered to capitulate.

Again at the siege of Malaga she ran personal risks. She watched above all things over the soldier's welfare; they called her the mother of the camps— *mater castrorum*. She it was who was the first to establish ambulances and military hospitals; she often personally superintended the care of the sick and wounded.

Under her strict superintendence the moral discipline of the camp was excellent; gambling, vice, nightly revels, oaths, and licentious talk were alike prohibited, yet all the time this austere queen continued to be most popular among the gentlemen of every degree, and even among the soldiery. The tents were left open, and no thefts took place. On Sundays and holidays divine service was regularly celebrated. Not only was this war in Isabella's eyes a crusade which must be carried on, but the observance of religious ordinances was moreover a means of maintaining morality among the soldiery and supporting military discipline.

When Grenada itself was besieged, Isabella used the same means, rendered still more perfect by experience, and with redoubled vigilance and activity; she herself fixed the route of the convoys, distributed the stores, and encouraged with gracious words the warriors who approached her. When almost all the tents had been consumed in a single night by a terrible conflagration, she caused stone buildings to be raised with incredible rapidity in the stead of these frail canvas shelters, so that a town stood where a camp had been planned in the form of a cross. It was proposed to call it Isabella, but she modestly refused, and by her wish the name of Santa Fe was given to this city built under the protection and in the honour of the God of Sabaoth.

When Grenada capitulated, it was universally allowed that the chief of the success was owing to her who had made it the business and passion of her life, to her who had been the soul of the enterprise for many long years—to the great Queen Isabella of Castille.

Isabella was free from the bigotry imputed to her by certain Protestant writers. Her religion was undoubtedly severely exact and faithfully carried out, but she was always large-minded and devout. The remnant of her correspondence with her directors, especially Talavera, displays in its fulness her admirable spirit.

It is untrue that narrow prejudice had sealed her heart against pity. It was with great difficulty that she was induced to accept the idea of the Inquisition; and, when the bull for its foundation had been obtained from Sixtus IV., she delayed its publication and execution, while making trial of gentler means of conversion with the Judaisers and New Christians. She agreed on this point with Cardinal

VOL. I.   C

Mendoza, who had drawn up a catechism for the special use of this class of Christians not as yet established in the faith, and had ordered it to be taught and explained throughout his diocese.* But when she was shown that all zealous efforts failed in shaking indomitable persistence, when learned doctors and prelates highly esteemed in the Church assured her of the necessity of establishing a special tribunal for crimes against religion, the perpetual occasion of sedition and tumults, then Isabella gave way, thinking it her duty to submit to the authorities whom she was accustomed to regard as the safest guides of her conscience. We may further observe that this was one of the occasions when Isabella yielded her opinion to that of her royal husband.

Moreover, a feeling as much national as religious was impelling Spain to unity of faith at the same time as to political unity,† being in a manner the consequence and the completion of the splendid victory over Islam, and the desire to efface all traces of that faith from the soil of the Peninsula. On the other hand, Isabella's attentive and vigilant humanity is proved by the witness of Las Casas, the apostle of the poor Indians.

It was Isabella who appreciated Christopher

* Historia de España, by La Fuente, part ii, lib. iv, p. 137.
† See the wise reflections on this subject by M. de Pidal in his excellent history of the dissensions of Aragon.

Columbus, and who upheld him against the prejudice of the courtiers, and of King Ferdinand himself, as well as against the calumnies and persecutions of his slanderers. She was high-minded enough to comprehend the spirit of that great man, who was so cruelly misunderstood by others in his lifetime.

Her affections were unshaken in their fidelity. She never would part with Beatrice de Bobadilla, who had been devoted to her during the times of isolation and desertion in her youth; and she treated with the like favour Cabrera, Marquis of Moya, who had rendered her great services at the same time, and who became the husband of Beatrice.

She had early learnt to speak Spanish with elegance, but she had had so few opportunities of intellectual improvement in her earlier years that her education was very incomplete, until she laboured to supply her deficiencies with an energy most meritorious in her situation. Tearing herself from the whirl of occupation in the Court, and avoiding as much as possible absorption in business, she daily devoted some hours to study. Thus she learnt Latin, the language of the Church as well as of science and diplomacy, and she was afterwards able to write in Latin to her confessor. She likewise studied several living tongues.

Her example made study fashionable among the ladies about her. The Court, hitherto so frivolous, seemed to have adopted serious literary tastes, and, step by step, these tastes were transmitted throughout the nation, and thus it may be said that in this respect, as well as in morals, a complete transformation was effected by the influence of one woman during a reign also distinguished by generous undertakings. It is evident that such a princess as Isabella could not but exercise a strong influence on the education of her daughters. Her son, Don Juan, was brought up among boys chosen from the Castillian youth. He was grounded in all the branches of human knowledge, and profited admirably by the lessons he received; but he died in early youth, just as he had inspired the Spaniards, over whom he was to have reigned, with the most brilliant hopes.

As for the princesses, his sisters, they received instruction from the learned and pedantic Peter Martyr, who thus boasts of them:

"I was the literary foster-father of almost all the princes, and of all the princesses of Spain."

Erasmus, who much admired the education bestowed on the Spanish Infantas, gave the epithet of "learned" to the youngest of them, Doña Catalina, or Catharine, the same whose history we have undertaken to write.

Alike in the government of her people and in the education of her children, although Isabella had the widest and loftiest aspirations, in practice she guided the carrying out of her plans to some sense. There was nothing visionary or Utopian about her. No doubt she thought of more reforms than she had time to execute, but she completely succeeded in those she actually undertook. Thus the reform in the religious orders which she attempted in concert with Ximenes was a work carried on with a steady gentleness full of ability. She restored cloistral seclusion and observance of discipline in all the nunneries which she visited by mingling persuasion with authority. Neither did Ximenes tolerate the existence of laxity in monasteries for the other sex, but suppressed several. The members of some brotherhoods actually revolted against the requirements of their reformers, broke from the cloister, and threw away their frocks and cowls on the bushes in the roads, so much less successful was the iron hand than the velvet hand.

No one can guess at all the reforms Isabella would have effected had she lived longer. When we see what she did in a thirty years' reign, we are amazed, and wonder what she might have arrived at if the fifteen years of Hezekiah had been granted her. But Isabella never seems to have wished for that fresh lease of life, that respite or that favour which was accorded to the King of Judah, and never entreated Divine power for it. On the contrary, we are told that, remarking the tears shed round her death-bed, she said, "Weep not for me, and lose no time in useless vows for the restoration of my health, but rather pray for the salvation of my soul." We are also told that she received the sacraments with tender devotion, but that, when extreme unction was administered, she objected to having her feet uncovered according to the usual custom, thus showing even to her last sigh those instincts of modesty which, without detracting from her masculine courage and manly resolution, had always betrayed her peculiar feminine delicacy.

She expired on Friday, the 26th of December, 1504, in the fifty-fourth year of her age. As the Spaniards adored their good and great queen, her death caused throughout the Peninsula a grief almost amounting to despair.

Shortly before her death, Isabella had drawn up, with her own enfeebled hand, a very detailed will,* in which, with admirable wisdom, she had provided for the interests of Spain and of her family.

If we have sketched at some length the details of this admirable figure, it is because it seemed needful to know the mother in order to explain the daughter. After having studied Isabella of Castille, it will be easier to understand Catharine of Aragon.

* The autograph of this will is preserved among the manuscripts in the royal library at Madrid. At the head of the list of executors stand the names of Ferdinand and of Ximenes de Cisneros. Faithful in friendship to the last, the queen warmly commends to her executors, especially to the king, the Marquisa de Moya, Beatrix de Bobadilla.

SECTION III.—FERDINAND OF ARAGON, KING OF SPAIN.

We would not have King Ferdinand become lost in the brilliancy of the rays that, like a dazzling aureole, encircle the brow of Isabella. If he had possessed a less illustrious companion of his life and throne, he would hold a much higher place in public opinion. Besides, he survived the queen, and for several years had to stand alone in the government of the dominions so disproportionately increased. His individuality, which was never lost during the former part of his life (whatever may be said), became much more evident in his latter years. We must take account of the various phases of this prince's life in the character we are going to sketch; and though we may be obliged to be hard upon his memory, we shall always try to be just.

Ferdinand was scarcely eighteen years old when, urged both by the dexterous calculations of his father, and by his own chivalrous aspirations, he set forth to accomplish that almost clandestine marriage with Isabella, which, while seeming a feat of knight-errantry, was in effect a grand stroke of policy. To obviate delays to a wedding where haste was needful to prevent the encountering of invincible obstacles, Ferdinand of Aragon brought to his betrothed a forged and fictitious papal bull of dispensation for marriage, thus causing the Princess Isabella violent remorse, almost amounting to despair, on afterwards learning this unjustifiable artifice. She could not rest till she had obtained from Pope Sixtus IV. a bull relieving her from all previous blame, and a fresh dispensation authorising her to contract the marriage more regularly, and, in consideration of her good faith, decreeing the legitimacy of the children already born.

If the heir-presumptive of Aragon had thus deceived his own wife, it is no wonder that, as king, he often deceived the various sovereigns with whom he maintained diplomatic relations.*

Certainly he was not more deficient in openness and sincerity in politics than were most of his contemporaries,† only he was more adroit than most of them.

To this acuteness he added indefatigable activity, both physical and moral, doing everything himself, and, according to the expression of one of the time, taking his repose in action.

Skilled in all bodily exercises, dexterous in the use of the lance, and in controlling a restive horse, he had all the endowments of a complete cavalier. Even in the command of armies he had given proof

---

* Learning that Louis XI. complained that he had twice been deceived by him, Ferdinand exclaimed, "He lies, the rogue, I have deceived him more than ten times."

† "Deceit regarded as a legitimate means of success, did not cause any feeling of shame, no more than theft among the Arabs." Cantù, Italian History, Trad. Franc. by Lacombe, vol. vii, p. 188.

not only of great courage, but also of real military capacity.

Nevertheless what constituted his especial superiority was the instinct of government and political foresight. In Spain itself, where the ideas and traditions of the middle ages still seemed in full force, Ferdinand ventured to run counter to them by opposing the separation and partition of provinces. Like a sovereign of the present day, he was continually advocating, even for neighbouring states, the same system of union. For example, he maintained that Scotland should as soon as possible be fused into England; but he further desired that the kingdoms thus enlarged should be compact, and formed of contiguous provinces. Therefore he did not approve of the entirely artificial union of Austria and Germany with the Spanish peninsula; but, on the other hand, when there was a proposal of re-establishing the Kingdom of Aragon for Ferdinand, the younger brother of Charles V., although the young prince was his favourite grandson, Ferdinand the Catholic flatly refused to hear one word about this mischievous project. "Aragon and Castille have been joined beneath the same sceptre, and must remain welded together for ever."*

* Instruction to Pedro de Quintana, Archives of Simancas, tratados con Inghilterra, Legais, vol. iv, p. 87. See also in the Calendar, vol. ii, the letter to Armengol, p. 160, September 22nd, 1513, and that to Ferdinand de Lanuza, p. 187, December 20th, 1513.

According to several distinguished Spanish authorities, the Inquisition, which Isabella regarded principally from the religious point of view, must have been, in Ferdinand's hands, a powerful means of centralisation of the royal house. That prince foresaw that such a tribunal would touch the great as well as the small, that it would set the example to ordinary justice of showing no respect of persons, and that the mightiest nobles would be called to account by judges giving sentences in the name of God, before whom all men are equal.

Thus was this king, at the close of the middle ages, led by modern ideas to the establishment of the Inquisition.

Prudent and moderate in everything, he disliked wars too long protracted, and over-excessive conquests. His system was, that it was first necessary to consolidate each moderate acquisition of his arms before going further, thus giving time to the victorious troops to rest while making fresh preparations, so as afterwards to renew the war with greater success.

He it was who inaugurated a method entirely different from that of Louis XI., and certainly nobler and more honest, and put an end to all the machinery of espial and corruption in operation in foreign Courts, and substituted for it the system of ambassadors,* with a recognized character and credentials, and an established position.

* According to some authors, the very word ambassador is

Although possessing good sense and business capacity, Ferdinand was illiterate. Some Spanish authors, even some of great authority, have expressed a doubt whether he could sign his name. Nothing is more unfounded than such a doubt. Not only could Ferdinand give his signature, but whole autograph letters, written by him in pure Castillian, have lately been discovered.* In some of them, addressed to Isabella, there is very affectionate language, and great delicacy of feeling. There is one that seems to us so remarkable as to be worthy of full quotation.†

"MI SENORA,

"Now at least it is clear which of us two loves best. Judging by what you have caused to be written to me, I see that you were happy, while I was losing my sleep, and messenger after messenger brought me no letter from you. The reason why you do not write is not because there is no paper to be had, or that you do not know how to write, but because you love me not, and disdain me. You are living at Toledo, I am living in small villages!

derived from the Spanish word *embiar*, to send. See Prescott, Ferdinand and Isabella, vol. i.

* There are several of these letters at Simancas, in the possession of the Duke de Frias, at Madrid, and in the collection of manuscripts in the library at Madrid. Bergenroth says he saw and read a large number there. Introduction to 1st vol. of the Calendar, p. 36.

† Bergenroth. Calendar, vol. i, 1485-1500, p. 36.

Well, every day I direct the vows of my old affection to you. Doubtless you do not wish to be my dream. Such a sin would be too heavy on your conscience.

"Write to me, and let me know how you are. There is nothing to say about the affairs which keep me here, except what Silva will communicate to you, and what Ferdinand Pulgar has told you. I beg you to believe Silva. Do write to me.

"The affairs of the princess * must not be forgotten. For God's sake remember her as well as her father, who kisses your hands, and is your servant,

"THE KING."

This letter shows that, if the married pair had loved one another passionately in the earlier years of their advancement to the throne, there were still some considerable remains of it in the maturity, and even in the decline of their age.

Isabella's firmness in sustaining her personal rights as Queen of Castille, compelling the compliance of such a proud and haughty man as Ferdinand, must certainly have been the cause of some clouds between them. But when once it had been fully established that the great crown, *corona*, was the queen's right, and that the little crown alone, *coronilla*, was the portion of the King of Aragon, Isabella,

* No doubt the Princess Catharine. The letter bears no date, but it seems to belong to the latter part of the fifteenth century.

as may be seen by a passage in the letter just quoted, continually conferred with her husband on all business of any importance. Thus, when she had fully established her authority, she made skilful concessions to Ferdinand, and succeeded in being loved as well as respected.

However, although the affection shown by the Catholic king for Queen Isabella was both sincere and constant, he had four natural children by three different mothers. Yet his loose morals were combined with habits of devotion with scandalous inconsistency, as common among princes at that period as was chicanery in political negotiations, accompanied by the most lofty pretensions to honour and chivalrous loyalty.

It was characteristic of the national spirit and prejudices of the Spaniards of the period that, though indulgent to these derelictions, they were extremely scandalised at the marriage that Ferdinand contracted, very soon after Isabella's death, with Germaine de Foix, niece to Louis XII., a young princess who might have been his daughter. It is true that this union was, on his side, a stroke of policy which obtained him the relinquishment of the claims of the French royal family to the crown of Naples. But to establish indeed these rights, so clearly recognized in word, Ferdinand and his successors were several times obliged to assert them sword in hand.

We ought here to present the outward portrait

of this prince, but the artist who represented him has left us two pictures not resembling each other. Nevertheless there is a concurrence of testimony to show that he had a fine countenancee, but wore a kind of cold, perpetual smile, which served to conceal his strongest feelings. For, says Pulgar, "neither anger nor pleasure, nor any of the most intense emotions of the soul made the smallest change in his face." John Stile, who was ambassador of the King of England in 1509, writes that this prince squinted with the left eye, and lisped in consequence of the loss of a front tooth.* It seems that Ferdinand was at this time very well preserved, and felt full of life and vigour.

Yet he did not attain to an advanced age ; and was only sixty-four when he died. He had reigned almost two-thirds of his life over Castille as well as over Aragon.† He was much regretted by the subjects of

* Bergenroth. Calendar, vol. i, p. 35. (Ed.)
† As he mounted the throne of Castille four years sooner, the calculation is that he reigned forty-one years over that country, and thirty-seven over Aragon. He died January 23rd, 1516. He desired to be buried at Grenada, in the monastery of the Alhambra, by the side of Isabella, as if to renew his union with her in the grave.
Note. Calendar, 1509. Brewer, xxxi. The portrait of Ferdinand, as drawn by contemporaneous and independent writers, is scarcely more flattering. Peter Martyr, who was in constant attendance upon him at Valladolid, ridicules his uxoriousness, in common with the rest of the world, and Machiavelli, with equal truth, condemns his suspicious and niggardly disposition. His ungenerous or timid policy had estranged from his councils the

his little hereditary kingdom, but not so much by the Castillians. And yet he had contributed to the greatness of the whole of Spain, and, with Isabella's help, had raised her to the rank of a first-class kingdom.

Nevertheless, he had not the [prestige that seems always attendant on true, practical genius. In that respect he needed Isabella to supply what he lacked, and, when she was gone, a terrible blank in the Government of Castille made itself felt.

Perhaps it is well here to give a list of the children of Ferdinand and Isabella.

The eldest of the infantas, called Isabella after her mother, was born at Duênas in 1470, and much resembled her in mental qualities and intelligence. Her first husband was Don Alphonso, heir of the crown of Portugal. A few months after the marriage, she lost this young husband to whom she was much attached. She was then asked in marriage by Don Emmanuel, who had recently mounted the throne at Portugal; at first she refused this alliance, but at last yielded to the persuasions of her royal lover and perhaps of her mother. She had scarcely been girt with the crown when she died from a violent attack of illness in the month of August, 1498.

The second of the children of Ferdinand and Isa-

ablest of his nobility. In his single hand he still grasped all the administrative functions of the State, which had long since outgrown his powers.

bella was, as before mentioned, Don Juan, Prince of the Asturias, who was born at Seville in 1478. A double marriage was arranged on the one side between this prince and Margaret of Austria, daughter of the Emperor Maximilian, on the other between the Archduke Philip the Handsome, son and heir of the Emperor, and Doña Juana, second daughter of Isabella, born at Toledo in 1479.

In 1497 the Prince of the Asturias died when nearly twenty years old.

The Princess Juana had several children by Philip the Handsome. Queen Isabella in joke called her her little mother-in-law, because of her likeness to Ferdinand's mother. It is well known that Juana, during her married life and in her widowhood, showed signs of mental aberration. She died in 1555, at Tordesillas, at the age of seventy-six years.*

The Princess Mary, born at Toledo in 1482, was third daughter of Isabella, and married in 1500 her brother-in-law, Don Emmanuel, King of Portugal.

The Infante Doña Catalina or Catharine, whose whole life is described in this volume, was the fourth daughter and fifth child of Ferdinand and Isabella; she was born at Alcala de Henares in 1485.

* Some authors say seventy-three years, but they are those who suppose that she was born in 1482, confounding her with her sister Mary. She was confined as insane and harshly treated for more than forty years of her life.

CATHARINE OF ARAGON.

PART I.

THE TWO MARRIAGES AND CORONATION OF CATHARINE OF ARAGON.

CHAPTER I.

Birth of Catharine of Aragon—Her Childhood spent in Camps and the Palace of the Alhambra, Grenada—Negotiations for the Marriage between Catharine of Aragon and the Prince of Wales—Isabella's Letter—Latin Correspondence between Arthur and Catharine.

CATHARINE of Aragon came into the world at Alcala de Henares in 1485. Alcala was then a little, unimportant town.* How then did it happen that Isabella of Castille should there have given birth to her youngest child?

The queen, whose indefatigable activity in the

* It was not till 1498 that Ximenes founded a university there which became celebrated, and gave the town some importance.

VOL. I.   D

Moorish war has been described, wished to make her presence occasionally felt in the north of her kingdom. About the end of November, 1485, leaving the army engaged in the siege of the ancient and very strong town of Ronda, where the Moors were making a valiant defence, she set out for Toledo, then the metropolis of Spain, where she reckoned on keeping her Christmas, a few days before her confinement. But on the way, at Alcala, she was surprised by the pains of childbirth, and brought into the world, before her time, Doña Catalina, or Catharine, the last of her children.

A very few days afterwards she learnt that the citadel of Ronda had surrendered to Ferdinand.

At the beginning of the spring of the year 1486 Isabella returned to Andalusia, and pursued the laborious work she had undertaken, namely, the subjugation of the Arabs, and the victory of the cross over the crescent.

The first years of Catharine's life were spent in camps. She was before the walls of Grenada when the tents of the Spanish army were destroyed by fire. She lived in Santa Fè, the town that took the place of the camp after its destruction and disappearance in the flames. She was little more than six years old when the city of Grenada surrendered to Isabella.* Then the Alhambra became the abode of Catharine, and her hours of recreation

* She was born in 1485. Grenada was taken in 1492.

were spent among the pomegranates, orange-trees, and gushing fountains in the delicious thickets of the Generalife.

We speak of the young princess's hours of recreation; for already had a portion of her time been devoted to study. Beneath the tents, as well as beneath the ceilings of the Moorish palaces, did Isabella add the care of the education of her daughters to all her other labours.

She also, from their childhood, had been devising princely alliances to be contracted for them at some future time; and even before her entrance into Grenada she had been making arrangements for Catharine's future marriage.

When a matrimonial union between Catharine, Princess of Castille, and Arthur Tudor, Prince of Wales, was first discussed, the one was not three years old, the other, at eighteen or nineteen months, was hardly out of his nurse's arms.

In the ordinary ranks of society such distant projects of union are sometimes formed, but they are made conditional upon the suitability of the parties chiefly concerned, who are one day to belong to each other; and the fulfilment of these plans, conceived so long beforehand, very seldom takes place.

In the marriages of princes one question is necessarily felt to be pre-eminent, namely, political interests. The persons united by premature betrothal are not allowed to put forward personal objections nor to mention any instinctive repugnance. They must needs bend to the will of kings and governments as to the decrees of fate. From the very opening of life they are made to feel the burden of those golden but weighty fetters which are the heritage of the great.

It was with the greatest delight that Ferdinand received the first overtures made him by the English Cabinet for this matrimonial alliance, because he was desirous of detaching King Henry VII. from France, though that prince, unlike almost all other Englishmen, was, as we have before stated, favourably disposed towards that country. His residence at the Court of Charles VIII. had made him much more French than was agreeable either to the Spanish monarch or to the British nation itself.

It was then desirable to put into Henry Tudor's political scales such a counterpoise as might prevent his inclining toward the rivals and enemies of Spain. This counterpoise was to be the marriage of an infanta of Castille with the heir-presumptive of the crown of England.

In reply to the overtures of Henry VII. Ferdinand and Isabella sent ambassadors to England to treat of the conditions on which this marriage could take place.

These ambassadors were Doctor Puebla and Juan de Sepulveda.

It was strange that the first difficulties to be encountered were pecuniary. Henry VII. was covetous, Ferdinand showed himself avaricious. The English commissioners* asked why, as the money was not to come out of the strong boxes of the king and queen, but out of the pockets of their subjects, they should not be more liberal.†

Certainly there was neither delicacy nor generosity in this language. The Spanish ambassadors could not boast of any more loftiness or disinterestedness; while the English demanded four times more, they offered four times less. Besides, they said there was a risk to be taken into the account, namely, that the Princess Catharine was to enter a family newly seated upon the throne of England, not very firmly rooted there, that might be overturned by one of the revolutions so frequent in Great Britain during the last century and a half.‡

However, the Earl of Richmond, the representative

---

* Richard Fox, Bishop of Exeter, and Giles, Lord Daubeny. See Bergenroth, Calendar, vol. i, p. 7. Puebla to Ferdinand and Isabella.

† The marriage portion was fixed at 200,000 scudos, each scudo 4s. 2d. sterling, £41,666 2s. 4d. Bergenroth, Calendar, vol. i, p. 23. Treaty.

‡ " Bearing in mind what happens every day to the Kings of England, it is surprising that Ferdinand and Isabella should dare to give their xxviii (daughter) at all. This was said with great courtesy in order that they might not feel displeasure or be enraged." Bergenroth, Calendar, vol. i, p. 7. Puebla to Ferdinand and Isabella. (Ed.)

of the House of Lancaster, who was reigning as Henry VII., thought he had extinguished all possible competition by espousing the Princess Elizabeth, daughter to Edward IV., and sister to the two young princes who had been murdered in the Tower of London by order of Richard III. He thus claimed to have united the white and red roses, and, according to him, no one could dream of disputing the crown with him, his marriage having united the claims of the House of York to his own.

The Spanish ambassadors did not think that the question of legitimacy had been so entirely disposed of, and did not share the security that King Henry VII. appeared to enjoy. They said so plainly to the English commissioners. However, if Puebla's testimony can be trusted, this objection was presented with a smile and so much courtesy that the matter was redeemed by the manner, and there was no offence to the British pride.

Then the pecuniary question was taken in hand, and the royal marriage was haggled over like a bargain in the London market. This was really acting like those who would then have been termed the meaner sort. At last, after prolonged debate, the English commissioners consented to a considerable abatement of their pretensions, reducing the amount of their original demand. They said they would be contented with a sum of two hundred thousand crowns as the princess's portion.

As to the second part of the treaty, that which bore on the hostile attitude that England was to assume towards France, in concert with Spain, there were a good many more difficulties. When Henry was directly addressed, he praised Isabella and Ferdinand in the most exaggerated language, and said he was completely devoted to them, but that he could not honourably conclude a treaty directly and absolutely adverse to Charles VIII., to whom he was under great obligations. The ambassadors declared themselves dissatisfied with this reply. They wanted something more precise.

At last the English commissioners concluded by taking "a mass-book, and swearing in the most solemn way, before a crucifix, that it is the will of the King of England, first to conclude the alliance and the marriage, and afterwards to make war upon the King of France, according to the bidding of Ferdinand and Isabella."*

Sepulveda, having to return to Spain, demanded a farewell audience of the king. Puebla went with him. Every time the names of Ferdinand and Isabella were mentioned, Henry VII. humbly "took his bonnet off his head," and showed the greatest respect towards those sovereigns.

He said he was aware of the oath taken by the commissioners who had been charged to conclude

* Bergenroth, Calendar, vol. i, p. 9. Puebla to Ferdinand and Isabella.

the alliance in his name, and he added "that we must accept it for plain truth unmingled with double dealing or falsehood."*

The real character of this covetous, obsequious, and undignified king may be recognized in these little details. In order entirely to gain over the Spanish ambassadors he wished them to be presented to his family. And therefore Sepulveda and Puebla went to visit the Queen and the Prince of Wales, who were then living in the country. The little prince had just attained the venerable age of twenty months. He was dressed to be shown to the ambassadors, and then undressed and put back into his cradle. He was probably a fairly handsome child, but the praises lavished upon him by Puebla were beyond measure. The utmost that flattery could invent within the bounds of possibility was poured upon the Prince of Wales by this skilful courtier. Henry accepted the flattery in all simplicity, believing that his son already possessed all possible perfections, and requested Sepulveda to take his portrait to Spain, to give Ferdinand and Isabella some notion of the charms of their future son-in-law.

He seemed on the point of attaining his object. The draft of the treaty of alliance and marriage, which was signed on July 7th, 1488, by his commissioners and the Spanish ambassadors, contained

* Bergenroth, Calendar, vol. i, p. 10. Puebla to Ferdinand and Isabella.

nothing that could compromise his interests. The mutual assistance to be given by the allied monarchs was restricted to the event of invasion of their respective countries by France. It was a purely defensive treaty.

But, before this treaty could take effect, it had to be ratified by the king and queen of Spain. On the return of Sepulveda, Ferdinand blamed him for over-haste, and for having yielded too much. The king wrote in the same strain to Puebla, who had been left in England, stating that he had never intended to exceed a sum of one hundred thousand crowns in Spanish money, as the portion of his daughter Catharine. As to the clause respecting France, he did not care to have it inserted in the principal treaty, saying that he would accept it as an additional clause, but that, in reality, he wanted an absolutely offensive alliance. That is to say, he required the King of France to restore to him Cerdana and Roussillon, and, if this restitution were not effected within a certain time, Henry VII. should be bound, on the first summons, to give Ferdinand his assistance against France.

Such a proposition, couched in such language, did not seem acceptable. Counter propositions from Henry were submitted to Ferdinand, and at last accepted. These were the new conditions, which gave some reciprocal advantages.

"In case the King of France voluntarily restores

Normandy and Acquitaine to England Henry shall be at liberty to conclude peace with him without the consent of Spain; or in case the King of France restore Roussillon and Cerdana to Spain, then Ferdinand and Isabella shall be at liberty to make peace with him without the consent of England, all other clauses of this treaty remaining in full force." *

On this basis was concluded the treaty of March 27th, 1589.

In fact, a war against France was carried on by England and Spain; the King of England having withdrawn his troops from Brittany, made an expedition against Boulogne, after which the King of France restored Cerdana and Roussillon to Spain. Henry VII. could therefore treat with France without violating his engagements. Only there was no immediate advantage to Spain from the matrimonial alliance of Cathariue of Aragon and the Prince of Wales from the moment when Henry VII. refused to make a second treaty with Spain, or enter into a fresh coalition against France.

A little later, in 1497, negotiations were re-opened, and reached what appeared to be a definite conclusion.

After the treaty of marriage had been ratified by both parties, it was determined that the religious ceremony should be conducted with great secrecy in

* Bergenroth, Calendar, vol. i, p. 22. Treaty between England and Spain. (Ed.)

the royal chapel of the Manor of Bewdley. The Bishop of Lincoln had scruples about assisting in this ceremony, because the dignitaries of the Church were forbidden to celebrate a clandestine marriage. Doctor Puebla at last succeeded in overcoming all his objections. The marriage therefore took place, though only by procuration, on May 19, 1499.

Meanwhile, there occurred the young Earl of Warwick's unfortunate attempt at escape, his trial, condemnation, and execution. The death of the last of the Plantagenets is alleged to have put an end to the indecision of Ferdinand and Isabella respecting their daughter's marriage, by removing their doubts of the stability of the Tudor dynasty. They must have mentioned it to Catharine herself, for in the next reign, after her divorce from Henry VIII., she allowed the expression to escape her that she had never expected much happiness from her union with the Tudor family, since that union had been purchased at the price of royal and innocent blood.*

However, the fresh delays to Catharine's departure for England, which were interposed by the Spanish Government, may be attributed to other reasons, certainly neither honourable nor lofty. It seems that, on closer examination of the treaty of marriage, Ferdinand thought that he had been tricked in the

* Hall, 51. Bacon, 112. Lingard ed., Lond. 1837, vol. v, p. 322. The execution of the young Earl of Warwick took place Nov. 28th, 1499.

value of the dowry assigned to his daughter. This difficulty, which would seem hardly worthy to create a hindrance in the case of private individuals, was the occasion of a somewhat sharp discussion between the two kings. The irritation on both sides became so great that the marriage was on the point of being broken off.

These epistolary disputes lasted a considerable time. In the year 1500, in consequence of an interview of Henry VII. with the Archduke Philip, a report arose that the three princes had discussed the marriage of the Prince of Wales with Margaret, Archduchess of Austria, whose first husband, the Infant of Spain, was just dead.

Then the matter seemed to be at an end. The bargaining over the marriage portion and dowry came to an end. A multitude of practical details were discussed, their object being to regulate the rank and private life of the Princess Catharine in England. Thus she had hitherto only drunk water, and it was requested that she might gradually accustom herself to mix wine with it, because almost all over England the water was bad and unwholesome. Again there was a promise that she should take advantage of the residence of Margaret of Austria in Spain to learn French. Then Ferdinand and Isabella desired that there should be a certain number of male and female attendants in her suite; and Henry, on the other side, wanted them to be as few as possible. But on one point the latter king insisted, and seemed to have very much at heart; and that is that all the matrons or maidens sent to England should be beautiful, or at least very agreeable, and that the ugly, or deformed, should be pitilessly excluded. In his eyes this was a most important matter. He saw in it a means of regenerating the lines of nobility in England by marriages with persons of pure blood and rare beauty.

Next the question was whether Catharine of Aragon should be sent at once to England. Don Pedro d'Ayala* was of opinion that the Court of Henry VII. was not a very desirable place for so young a princess. On the other hand he acknowleged that, if her coming to England were put off too long, she would find it very difficult to become accustomed to so very different a climate, and especially to rougher ways and customs, to a less luxurious life, without those surroundings of courteous politeness to which Spanish ladies were habituated. He laid these doubts and considerations before Queen Isabella of Castille.

Isabella thought it best to wait till the young Arthur, Prince, of Wales, should have reached his fourteenth year; at that time the period fixed for kings' attainment of their majority. Learning that vast sums were to be expended on the reception

* Spanish Ambassador to England.

and wedding of her daughter, this noble queen estimated and criticised beforehand the exaggerated pomp of these preparations in these forcible and dignified terms :—

"I am told that the king my brother has ordered great preparations to be made, and that much money will be spent upon her reception and her wedding. I am pleased to hear it, because it shows the magnificent grandeur of my brother, and because demonstrations of joy at the reception of my daughter are naturally agreeable to me. Nevertheless, it would be more in accordance with my feelings, and with the wishes of my lord (King Ferdinand), if the expenses were moderate. We do not wish that our daughter should be the cause of any loss to England, neither in money nor in any other respect. On the contrary we desire that she should be the source of all kinds of happiness, as we hope she will be, with the help of God. We therefore beg the king our brother to moderate the expenses. Rejoicings may be held, but we ardently implore him that the substantial part of the festival should be his love; that the princess should be treated by him and by the queen as their true daughter, and by the Prince of Wales as we feel sure he will treat her. Say this to the King of England.

"Dated March 23rd, 1501."*

* Bergenroth, Calendar, vol. i, p. 253. Queen Isabella to De Puebla.

Long before, in the year 1497, the time when the first promises of matrimonial alliance had been exchanged between the Sovereigns of Spain and England, Isabella had sanctioned a correspondence in the Latin language between the betrothed, with the double object of cultivating feelings of mutual affection and promoting their improvement in good Latinity. But, though this language still continued to be the tongue of diplomacy and science, it was not that of love. Besides, the letters of the young lovers were inspected by an army of tutors, preceptors, confessors, bishops, governors, and governesses, who superintended, and, when needful, revised these laborious compositions.* Thus there is no chance of finding anywhere a spontaneous expression of feeling. All the correspondence is hackneyed and artificial. As literary exercises, several of these letters are not devoid of merit. One letter may be mentioned from Prince Arthur, dated from Ludlow Castle in 1499, expressing with some eagerness his impatient desire to see and embrace his very dear wife. The reply from the Alhambra is colder and more strained. The traces of Spanish eti-

* Miss Strickland, Lives, &c. Catharine of Aragon. We regret that she does not give the Latin text of any of these letters. Bernaldes, in his memoir on the Catholic kings, mentions a last official English embassy of the King of England, reaching Grenada May 21st, 1501, that received the final consent of the Sovereigns of Spain to the union of Catharine and Arthur.

quette are perceptible. But, in Ciceronian elegance, Catharine is not inferior to her literary rival.

The whole bears the character of that period of revival of learning, when small regard was paid to the vulgar languages so newly formed, and there was an attempt to recall classic antiquity.

CHAPTER II.

Catharine's Arrival at Plymouth—Her Warm Welcome—
Difficulties of Spanish Etiquette removed by the Authority
of Henry VII.—Renewal of the Promise of Betrothal—
Baynard Castle and the Alhambra—Catharine's Marriage
celebrated at St. Paul's, London—Tournament and Symbolical Representations—Stage Appearance of Alphonso
the Wise—Arthur and his Court at Ludlow Castle in
Shropshire—His Death—What was the Cause of it?—
His Monument at Worcester—Cruel Situation of the
Young Widow.

IN the month of August, 1501, Catharine embarked at Corunna for England. Contrary winds drove her back to the coast of Old Castille, and she was seriously ill. As soon as her health was restored she embarked, on the 26th of September, in a better vessel, and, after a good passage, landed at Plymouth on the 2nd of October. Her arrival was a signal for public rejoicings. A number of the gentlemen of the neighbourhood collected to form an escort for their future queen. Henry VII. had sent Lord Brooke, grand seneschal, to meet the princess, and provide for all her wants; the Earl of Surrey and Duchess of Norfolk were to be especially attached to her

VOL. I.   E

person. The duchess was immediately admitted, and from that moment continually kept her company, and served as her guide and adviser.

Henry VII. himself left his Palace of Shene on the 4th of October, to meet his daughter-in-law. But the weather was so rainy, and the roads so abominable, that he was compelled by weariness and tempest to stop at Chertsey to rest for the night. Next morning the king and persons in attendance set forth again for Hampstead, where he found Prince Arthur. It seems that the arrival of the young queen was not yet known, for the king halted at this place, and only set forth again in a leisurely manner the next day. At last the king beheld the protonotary of Spain, followed by some horsemen in full splendour, coming to meet him and bring him an official message. This was to forbid, in the name of King Ferdinand, the Prince of Wales and his father from seeing the young bride until she appeared at the altar; for in Spain it was not thought proper to raise the princess's veil before the celebration of her marriage, nor might an English eye, not even that of her future spouse, behold her features.

" This truly Asiatic injunction of King Ferdinand threw the whole royal party into consternation, and brought them to a dead halt."[*]

King Henry was not an absolute foe to etiquette, and his Court observed a certain amount of ceremony,

[*] Miss Strickland, ed. i, 1842, vol. iv, p. 78.

but these truly Asiatic prohibitions could not but be highly repugnant to an English prince. So, after a minute's hesitation, he called the members of his privy council around him in the open field, and propounded to them this strange problem for solution. Although exposed to an icy autumnal rain, the members of the council gave their opinions in tolerably lengthy harangues. The result of their deliberations was that, as the Infanta of Spain was now in the heart of Great Britain, Henry was the sovereign master, and might do with her as might seem good to him.

Henry VII. took this advice to the very letter, and in consequence, making his son remain on the down, he rode without drawing bridle to Dogmersfield, the nearest village, where the infanta had only arrived two or three hours before. The king's demand to see Catharine put all her retinue into a terrible perplexity. She had with her the Archbishop of Santiago, the Bishops of Osma and Salamanca, the Commander of Cardenas, and Doña Elvira Manuel, first Lady of Honour. The Archbishop of Santiago and another prelate opposed the king's entrance into the princess's apartments, saying that she had retired to her chamber. This resistance only stimulated Henry's curiosity, and he cried out that " if she were even in her bed he meant to see and speak to her, for that was his mind and the whole intent of his coming" through all this bad weather. The Spaniards did not venture to carry their opposition further. Catharine dressed herself, and received tho king in a room close to her chamber. Neither understanding the language of the other, each could only catch a few of the polite expressions almost the same in both tongues.

After this short interview the king went to take off his riding dress and attire himself. Half an hour afterwards Arthur arrived, who had soon wearied of spending more of a November afternoon on the open downs. In a short time the king again desired to be admitted to the infanta's presence, and to introduce his son. This time the bishops were present, and, by the help of Latin, notwithstanding the difference of pronunciation, they served as interpreters for Henry VII., and the parties managed to understand one another. The king desired the betrothed to renew by word of mouth their promise of marriage, and this they immediately did.

The two companies then travelled together. When Catharine was tired, or the weather was bad, she was carried in a litter.* The Spanish mules ridden by the prelates and ladies in attendance were not inferior in their paces to the horses of the princes of the blood and English lords.

By several stages Richmond was reached, and then

---

* A litter placed between two horses or mules, carrying it one in front the other behind, as might be seen in Sicily a few years ago.

Baynard Castle. In the first of these residences, Catharine found her future mother-in-law, Queen Elizabeth, who received her most affectionately; in the second there were lakes, cascades, old centenary oaks, and a multitude of delightful spots.* But Elizabeth of York could not make the young Spanish infanta forget Isabella of Castille; and again there was no comparison between the damp and foggy residence on the banks of the Thames and the dazzling marvels of the Alhambra.

A few days afterwards, Catharine entered London with a great attendance of lords and ladies; on her right was the Duke of York, on her left the pope's legate. Her beautiful light chestnut hair hung down beneath the brim of a large hat, and flowed abundantly over her shoulders.

The men of the City had made great preparations for the reception of the infanta on the feast of her patron saint, St. Catharine. At the door of St. Paul's was a very fine triumphal arch, and the young princess was led through it to her destination, that is to say, the bishop's palace near the church where the marriage was to be solemnized. The interior of the sacred edifice was arranged and decorated with great skill and magnificence, and on November

---

* This seems to be an embellishment of "situated right pleasantly on Thames side, and full well garnished and arranged, and encompassed outside strongly with water." Miss Strickland, vol. iv, p. 80.

14th, 1501, the young Duke of York, afterwards Henry VIII., her future second husband, conducted the young princess from the bishop's palace to St. Paul's Cathedral. The English were much surprised at the strangeness of Spanish fashions; it was remarked that the bride wore a headdress of white silk wreathed with a scarf having a golden fringe, enriched with pearls and precious stones. This scarf hung down like a veil, concealing some portion of her face and person. This was the Spanish mantilla, said to be a legacy from the long veils of the Moorish women; only the mantilla bordered the face, and did not hide it entirely.

The Archbishop of Canterbury performed the nuptial ceremony, assisted by nineteen bishops and mitered abbots.

Festivities of all kinds followed the celebration of the marriage. There was a brilliant tournament held, and the prizes were given to the victors by the young bride. There were also pageants and allegorical representations. In one of these presentments Catharine was symbolised by the western star, Hesperus, and Arthur by Arcturus, the most brilliant of the stars at night. But attention was most excited by the appearance on the stage of Alphonso the Wise, one of the ancestors of the young princess, who came forward with all the insignia of astrology, a science that this learned monarch was said to have cultivated with success; and the royal astrologer did not fail to predict a brilliant fortune for Catharine and a long and glorious life for Arthur.*

Alas! this may well seem a double mockery of the fate that awaited the young couple! Arthur was fated to live only a few months, and, though his young consort was destined one day to wear the crown, this crown was woven with bitterly envenomed thorns.

A short return of fair weather and a few rays of the sun had favoured these nuptial feasts. But the thick fogs of November soon arose, spreading their dark mantle over London and all England.

Catharine was a little more than sixteen years old, and in all the bright freshness of her youth; Arthur, born September 20th, 1486, was only just fifteen. The young princess's appearance had given rise to most agreeable predispositions in her favour at the Court of Henry VII. Those who had been able to approach her were charmed with her beauty and graceful modesty. Her angelic piety had struck all the members of the royal family she had joined, and especially the Prince of Wales, who seemed equally to love and admire her.

Arthur himself was a handsome and engaging youth, but as yet far from manhood. His learning was very precocious, and, if his tutor's testimony may be trusted, he had read and annotated with his own hand the principal classics of the ancient

* Miss Strickland, vol. iv, p. 82.

heathens even before his marriage. This did not prevent his attention to all the physical training that was then an essential part of a royal education.

King Henry VII. had made a gift of Ludlow Castle, in Shropshire, to the Prince of Wales. Arthur held his Court there during the winter after his marriage. It was then that, in order to complete his political education, he obtained careful instruction from learned men and distinguished statesmen on the principles of administration and government, as well as on the constitution of Great Britain. His good qualities, and his ardent desire to make himself worthy of one day wearing the crown, were the delight and hope of all England. This hope was sadly disappointed; he died a few months after his marriage, on the 2nd of April, 1502.

Most authors say that the young prince's health was delicate, and gave way under the severity of the winter; but this is contradicted by the Spanish chroniclers, who derived their information from Catharine herself. They say he was strong and robust, but was carried off suddenly by the plague, which was then prevalent in part of England. This statement is indirectly confirmed by the *Herald's Journal*, which, after describing the magnificent funeral of the prince at Worcester, mentions that at the very time of the ceremony the principal inhabitants of the city had assembled in the cathedral to deliberate on the measures to be taken against the prevailing disease.*

Arthur was buried in the cathedral at Worcester. His body was placed on the right of the sanctuary. The tomb destined to enclose his mortal remains was enshrined upon the side wall of a charming little Gothic chapel. This exquisite jewel of sculpture was very much injured by the fanatical rage of the Puritans, when they had gained the famous battle of Worcester over Charles 1.,† and made the whole cathedral a stable for their horses; however, there is still left plenty to interest antiquaries in the numerous statuettes of kings and queens of England to be found there, and the quantity of coats-of-arms and carvings that cover the walls. On the monument of Prince Arthur his little prince's coronet and his shield, engraved with the royal arms of England, are supported by two angels, whose countenances are those of Henry VII. and his queen Elizabeth. The face of Catharine, the virgin widow, as Miss Strickland calls her, appears in several places on the bas-relief. On one side she wears the coronet of Princess of Wales, with a slight drapery and a veil; on another side she holds in her right hand the castle emblematic of Castille. Lastly, in another compartment, she is represented again with the attributes of

* Miss Strickland, vol. iv, p. 88.
† The author means the *first* battle of Worcester, between Prince Rupert and Essex. (Ed.)

Saint Catharine wearing a nun's veil, but bearing the pomegranate upon her breast as a distinctive mark.

The unfortunate princess found herself alone and desolate in a foreign land, of whose very language she was ignorant.* Absorbed in her grief, she would willingly have spent the most of her life in prayers over the grave. But diplomacy takes but little account of these conjugal feelings, and was fated to make this princess the plaything of political negotiations, in which her destiny was coldly discussed, being connected with the interests of two great states, Spain and England.

* Catharine only learnt English later, when she gave up all expectation of returning to Spain, and determined to accept the hand of the new Prince of Wales, who was afterwards Henry VIII. At the time she became a widow she was a little more than sixteen, being born at the end of the year 1485. Arthur, born September 20th, 1486, was nearly fifteen; he died April 2nd, 1502.

CHAPTER III.

Grief of Queen Elizabeth, Catharine's Mother-in-law—Isabella Wishes to recall her Daughter to Spain—Ferdinand desires to Marry her again in England to the new Prince of Wales—The Young Princess at first appears not to favour this Union—Henry VII. proposes to marry her Himself—Indignant Reply of Isabella—Renewal of Negotiations—Treaty of Marriage arranged between Catharine and her Brother-in-law, Henry, Prince of Wales—The Pope's Bull—The Betrothal—Death of Isabella of Castille—Pecuniary Wranglings between Ferdinand and Henry VII.—Catharine is held by the Latter as a Living Pledge—Protest of the Prince of Wales against his Betrothal to Catharine—Henry VII. wishes to Marry the Queen-Dowager of Naples—Remarkable Negotiations on this Matter.

IN the early days of Catharine's widowhood, Queen Elizabeth, overcoming her own intense grief at the death of her son, was much occupied herself with her daughter-in-law, procured her mourning garments, and made her return to her at Croydon Palace. She treated her with the most affectionate consideration. It seems that the two royal ladies wept together for the object of their common affection.

On the other side, Isabella's first thought is said

to have been to recall her daughter to Spain. A mother such as she was could not but understand the cruel desolation of her daughter's condition, and long to give her maternal consolations. But by her side was Ferdinand, who put forward political necessities, and was in no such haste for the return of his daughter; so as he had the chief influence, and kept the right of decision in the management of foreign affairs, he gave full scope to Isabella's wishes in the first part of the instructions given to the Duke of Estrada, whom he sent to England, but in the second part he furnished his ambassador with the means of doubling back according to circumstances.

So the noble duke was ordered:

1st, To reclaim from the King of England the one hundred thousand scudos which have been paid as the first instalment of the marriage portion of the said Princess of Wales.

2nd, To demand that the King of England should deliver to the Princess of Wales those towns, manors, lands, etc., which have been assigned to her as her dowry, which is to amount to one third of the revenues of Wales, Cornwall, and Chester.

3rd, To beg the King of England to send the Princess Catharine to Spain in the best manner, and in the shortest time possible, and, if necessary, himself to superintend the arrangements for her departure.*

* Bergenroth, Calendar, vol. i, p. 267.

This seemed categorical enough, but the postscript desired the plenipotentiary to endeavour to ascertain whether the marriage of Henry, the new Prince of Wales,* to his sister-in-law, the Princess Catharine, was desired in England; and, in that case, he was authorised to negotiate this union in the names of the Catholic Sovereigns.

Ferdinand had authorised the Duke of Estrada to make use of any means in his power to discover whether the first marriage of Catharine had really been consummated. Doña Elvira, the first of the ladies of honour to the princess, had written to Isabella that the young couple had never lived together. This letter of Doña Elvira's has not been preserved, but the queen makes an evident allusion to its contents in a dispatch to the Duke of Estrada.

"Our daughter remains such as she was here; for so Doña Elvira has written to us."†

Isabella says, in the same despatch, that, according to secret information which she had received, she has reason to believe that Henry VII. wishes the young widow to marry the Prince of Wales; but she adds that he must wait, and not let it be supposed that the Spanish sovereigns have the same views, for, if he suspected it, Henry VII. would make harder conditions.

---

* This title had been conferred by Henry VII. two months after Arthur's death.

† Bergenroth, Calendar, vol. i, p. 272.

However, Henry VII. did not hurry himself to declare his intentions; he neither said nor did anything that could commit him for the future.

In all these negotiations no one seems to have taken the slightest account of Catharine's personal wishes; but she showed great repugnance to this union that was to be forced upon her. She wrote to her mother that it was very repugnant to her to promise obedience to a prince considerably younger than herself, and hardly beyond boyhood.* As if to show her aversion to any project of marriage in England, and her desire to return to Spain, she obstinately refused to learn English.†

And so the correspondence of Queen Isabella at this time would almost lead to the belief that she neither hoped nor desired to succeed in her matrimonial negotiations. She displays in it some very fine sentiments, worthy of a tender mother and good Christian, and yet the woman of policy awakes at times most unexpectedly. The first impulse is all motherly, the second is due to the promptings of reasons of State. She says to the Duke of Estrada:—

"I command you, because it is very necessary, that you press much for the departure of the Princess of Wales, my daughter, so that she may

---

* Miss Strickland, vol. iv, p. 89. Lingard, vol. v, p. 333; note.
† There could not be anything more significant in the case of a clever and studious woman.

immediately come here. You must say that the greater her loss and affliction the more reason is there for her to be near her parents, as well for her consolation as on account of her age. Besides, the Princess of Wales can show the sense she entertains of her loss better here, and give freer vent to her grief, because the customs of this country better permit it than do those of England.

"You shall say to the King of England that we cannot endure that a daughter whom we love should be so far from us when she is in affliction, and that she should not have us at hand to console her; also it would be more suitable for a young girl of her age to be with us than to be in any other place."*

Isabella then asks that the King of England should appoint an honourable person to accompany the Princess Catharine, and to have a vessel freighted at once to receive her, and take her back to Spain.

So far the language is motherly, full of forethought, affection, and care. But there was in the Queen of Spain another person who speaks in her turn. It is the politician who dictates the following words. After desiring demand to be made for the one hundred thousand scudos, paid as part of the marriage portion, to be returned, and the dowry handed over, she says :

"If, whilst urging the abovesaid two things, they

* Bergenroth, Calendar, vol. 1, p. 278.

should speak to you about the betrothal of the Prince of Wales with the princess you shall hear what they have to say, and ask how it is to be done, and in what manner, and all the particulars; not showing any desire for it or any goodwill towards it. If they merely mention it, however, in order that you should talk about it, then, without going so far as to press it, say that, if it be not proposed only in order to delay the departure of the princess, you will consult us about it."

Events turned out as perhaps the mother had feared, and as the politicians had too cleverly calculated. Henry VII. at last made overtures to Doctor Puebla, the Spanish ambassador, for the marriage of the Princess Catharine to Henry, Prince of Wales. In order to bring about this fresh union he offered most advantageous terms to Spain; he promised that he would satisfy Catharine in every point as to the payment of her dower, and that it should be done within a year.

The negotiations at first were pursued on both sides with an equal desire for success. But an unexpected incident suddenly altered the state of affairs, namely, the death of Queen Elizabeth, wife of Henry VII.

It is said that the king greatly lamented her, as she well deserved; but, if his regrets were keen and sincere, it will soon be shown that they were not very lasting.

PROPOSAL OF HENRY VII. TO MARRY CATHARINE.

We here meet with an astonishing fact hitherto unknown to historians, but which is revealed by the unpublished letters collected and made public in the "Calendar of State Papers." When the learned editor, Bergenroth, had deciphered them, he could not believe his own eyes.

Henry VII., the very day after the death of Elizabeth, hardly waits to wipe away his tears; he is already contemplating a fresh marriage, and to whom?—is it credible? To the widow of his son Arthur—to the Princess Catharine herself!

Doctor Puebla was requested to sound the Catholic sovereigns. In a letter from Queen Isabella we find: "The Doctor (Puebla) has also written to us concerning the marriage of the King of England with the Princess of Wales, our daughter, saying that it is spoken of in England."*

The learned editor observes: "It is true De Puebla seems only to have written that the English said, 'a marriage between King Henry and the Princess of Wales might be contracted;' the words 'the English' might mean the Privy Council, according to the manner in which De Puebla was accustomed to express himself. But there is very little doubt that it here meant the king himself."†

This time Queen Isabella could not restrain herself, her indignation broke forth in bitter language; she

---

* Bergenroth, Calendar, vol. i, p. 294.
† Introduction, p. xcvi.

wrote to Puebla himself that she could not understand how he could have allowed King Henry to conceive such a notion :." We clearly cannot patiently suffer anything more to be said about a thing which is so devoid of truth and virtue, or right and reason, and which is so disrespectful to our own persons, and towards the Princess of Wales, our daughter. Therefore, if a remedy be not speedily found for these things, we shall consider that the principal responsibility of the failure rests upon you."*

As Isabella knew Puebla's intimacy with the King of England, she had some grounds for conjecturing that he was acting in concert with that prince, of whose full confidence he was recipient, especially on the affairs of Spain.

The same day, or the next, the queen wrote again to the Duke of Estrada a letter no less vigorous, and at much greater length.

" The Doctor has also written to us concerning the marriage of the King of England with the Princess of Wales, our daughter, saying that it is spoken of in England. But as this would be a very evil thing— one never before seen, and the mere mention of which offends the ears—we would not for anything

* Bergenroth, Calendar, vol. i, p. 294. Queen Elizabeth died February 11th. Isabella's letter from Spain to De Puebla is dated Alcala, April 11th. The letter to Estrada, also dated April 11th, is endorsed as received by him at Durham House, London, on May 14th, so that nearly six weeks were consumed in transit. (Ed.)

in the world that it should take place. Therefore, if anything be said to you about it, speak of it as a thing not to be endured."*

She had informed Puebla of the approaching departure of her daughter, and, in the further portion of the same despatch, addressed to the Duke of Estrada, she still more strenuously insists on her leaving England.

"However, should the King of England not be willing immediately to settle the betrothal of the Princess of Wales with the Prince of Wales, as aforesaid, in that case the Princess of Wales shall depart at once for Spain. She shall do so, moreover, without waiting to recover the one hundred thousand scudos of the portion of which the King of England has to make restitution, should he not immediately give them.

"For it would not be consonant either with reason or with right, human or divine, but would, on the contrary, be a most barbarous and dishonest proceeding, if the King of England (provided he could) were to keep by force that which the Princess of Wales took with her, and which belongs to her.

"If the King of England should not be inclined to give the money, it will be sufficient on our part that the affair should have received an explanation.

"We now deem it right they *(i.e. the King of England and his kingdom)* should know that if she remain

* Bergenroth, Calendar, vol. i, p. 295.

in England, it is by the wish of the King of England, and not by ours.

"Having made these two explanations, let the said Princess of Wales, our daughter, depart immediately without any delay, God willing, and without consulting us any more about the matter. Let her also come in the above-mentioned merchant fleet, or in some other ships belonging to our subjects, which you shall be assured by the navigation company now established are seaworthy."*

Considering this very decided language, and these formal commands, it would seem that all chance of matrimonial alliance between Catharine and the House of Tudor must be broken off. But it appears that, after the copious expression of her indignation, Isabella remembers that, though she is a mother, she is also Queen of Castille, and must not be too ready to sacrifice the interests of Spain, and that it may be not impossible to come to an arrangement. She thinks that if she gives scope to the matrimonial fancies of Henry VII., and offers him a marriage both flattering to his pride and satisfactory to his avarice, he will relinquish the senseless and culpable idea that he has allowed himself temporarily to entertain, and that, being thankful to the rulers of Spain for this advantage, he will resume his wishes in favour of the union of his son Henry to the Princess Catharine.

* Bergenroth, Calendar, vol. i, pp. 300, 301, 302.

In consequence, after having written or dictated the letter from which we have quoted, and signed it, Isabella caused to be appended a postscript, which made the ambassadors believe that she did not intend to press any decisive measure that might lead to a rupture, or her daughter's departure. She desired them to sound the King of England and find out whether it would suit him to marry the Queen Dowager of Naples, Ferdinand's niece. This queen was, at most, six and twenty years old. She had lately become a widow, and had inherited from her husband some very considerable estates in the kingdom of Naples. Ferdinand promised to add two hundred thousand ducats. Henry seemed to like this proposal, or, at least, to take it into very serious consideration, and thereupon renewed negotiations for the marriage of his son and the Princess Catharine, who, understanding her mother's postscript like the ambassadors, had not started for Spain. These negotiations were actively pursued; they terminated in a marriage contract, which was agreed upon, and signed at Richmond on the following 23rd of June, by Henry VII. on the one hand, and the Spanish ambassadors, representing Ferdinand and Isabella, on the other. We give the clauses and conditions of this treaty in full, as it is very important to study them in order to be able properly to follow the history of the future Queen of England.

"1. Ferdinand and Isabella, as well as Henry VII., promise to employ all their influence with the Court of Rome, in order to obtain the dispensation of the Pope, necessary for the marriage of the Princess Catharine with Henry, Prince of Wales. The Papal dispensation is required because the said Princess Catharine had, on a former occasion, contracted a marriage with the late Prince Arthur, brother of the present Prince of Wales, whereby she became related to Henry, Prince of Wales, in the first degree of affinity, and because her marriage with Prince Arthur was solemnized according to the rites of the Catholic church, and afterwards consummated.

"2. If the aforesaid dispensation be obtained, Ferdinand and Isabella on the one side, and Henry VII. on the other, promise that a marriage *per verba de præsenti* shall be contracted within two months after this treaty shall have been ratified by both the contracting parties.

"5. When the Princess Catharine contracted her marriage with Prince Arthur, Ferdinand and Isabella promised to give her a marriage portion of two hundred thousand scudos, each scudo being worth 4s. 2d. of English money. Of this sum one hundred thousand scudos were paid into the hands of King Henry VII. at the time when the said marriage was solemnized. Ferdinand and Isabella renounce, in their names, and in the name of the Princess

Catharine, all right to demand restitution of this payment.

"4. Ferdinand and Isabella promise Henry VII. to pay, on the marriage of their daughter to Henry, Prince of Wales, a marriage portion of two hundred thousand scudos, each scudo being worth 4s. 2d. of English money. Henry VII., on the other hand, confesses that he has already received one half of the said two hundred thousand scudos. The remaining one hundred thousand scudos are to be paid in the following manner, viz., sixty-five thousand scudos in coined gold; fifteen thousand scudos in plate and vessels of gold and silver, according to the valuation of silversmiths in London; twenty thousand scudos in jewels, pearls, ornaments, etc., of the Princess of Wales, according to their price in London, which is to be fixed by sworn valuers. All these payments are to be made in London within ten days before or after the solemnisation of the marriage. The marriage is to be solemnised as soon as Prince Henry shall have completed the fourteenth year of his age, and as soon as Ferdinand and Isabella, or their successor, can show that the whole marriage portion is in London, ready for delivery. Ferdinand and Isabella pledge their and their subjects' fortunes as security for the punctual execution of this clause of this treaty.

"5. Prince Arthur had settled on the Princess of Wales her dowry, consisting of lands, manors, etc., the revenues of which amount to the third part of the revenues of Wales, Cornwall, and Chester. She is to give back within ten days before or after the solemnisation of her new marriage all documents and title-deeds respecting this dowry; and Prince Henry will endow her on the day of the solemnisation of the marriage with a new dowry, as great and as well secured as her first dowry was. Henry VII. promises to ratify the constitution of the new dowry within one month after the solemnisation of the marriage. The Princess Catharine renounces all other claims on the revenues of Wales, Cornwall, and Chester, and promises to be content with her dowry.

"6. In case the Princess Catharine become Queen of England, she is to have, besides her dowry as Princess of Wales, a dowry as queen, consisting of the third part of all the revenues of the crown of England. She is to hold both dowries for life.

"7. The right of succession to the crown of Spain is reserved to the Princess Catharine.

"8. If the Princess Catharine become Queen of England, she is to enjoy, during the lifetime of her royal husband, all the privileges and revenues that other Queens of England have enjoyed before her. Henry VII. pledges the whole of his fortune and the fortunes of his subjects as security for the punctual fulfilment of his obligations.

"9. If Henry, Prince of Wales, should die before

his father, and leave a son or sons born of the Princess Catharine during her marriage with him, Henry VII. promises to create such sons, or the first-born son, Prince of Wales, and to do all in his power to secure to the said son the succession to the throne after his death.

"10. Both contracting parties promise to ratify this treaty within six months after the date of its conclusion.

"Richmond, 23rd of June, 1503."*

Precautions could not be carried further than they were by Henry VII. The various clauses of this contract display the distrustful, avaricious, and mean character of this politician, or rather this royal attorney. He will have the weight and quality of all the valuables sent by Ferdinand examined in London; thanks to his goldsmiths and sworn valuers, he hopes that he shall not be deceived in the jewels.

However, when the marriage contract had been signed by Prince Henry and Catharine, Henry VII. seemed at first no less anxious to conclude the business than the King and Queen of Spain. Even before the marriage contract, ratified first by the King of England, had been ratified in Spain, Ferdinand wrote to Rome to solicit a dispensation from the pope in favour of the projected marriage, in fulfilment of one

* Bergenroth, Calendar, vol. i, pp. 306, 307, 308.

of the first stipulations of the contract.* The following passage of his letter is important, and is therefore quoted:

"In the clause of the treaty which mentions the dispensation of the pope, it is stated that the Princess Catharine consummated her marriage with Prince Arthur. The fact, however, is that, although they were wedded, Prince Arthur and the princess never consummated the marriage. It is well known in England that the princess is still a virgin. But, as the English are much disposed to cavil, it has seemed to be more prudent to provide for the case as though the marriage had been consummated, and the dispensation of the pope must be in perfect keeping with the said clause of the treaty. The right of succession depends on the undoubted legitimacy of the marriage."†

This letter is very remarkable; it witnesses to the fact that Catharine never ceased to affirm.

On his side, Henry also displayed his anxious desire to obtain the pope's dispensation, as is proved by the following letter:—

"HENRY VII. TO PÔPE JULIUS II.

"Had written to Pope Alexander VI. and Pope Pius III., asking them to grant the dispensation

* The ratification took place in Spain by Ferdinand and Isabella at the end of the month of September, 1503.
† Bergenroth, Calendar, vol. i, p. 309.

necessary for the marriage of the Princess Catharine of Spain with Henry, Prince of Wales. Both these popes, his immediate predecessors, had received his demands so favourably that the dispensation would have been given long ago, if they had not so suddenly died.

"Had repeated his demands afterwards very often in his letters and by his ambassadors. The consequence was that he (Julius II.) promised in different letters, and by word of mouth, to send the desired dispensation by Robert Sherborne. Robert Sherborne, however, has returned to England without the dispensation, and it even seems as if nothing at all had been done at Rome in the matter. Repeats his former prayers that the dispensation may be granted as soon as possible, and that it may be delivered at once to the English ambassadors who are remaining at Rome.

"Westminster, November 28th, 1503."

This displays the great interest that Henry VII. then took in his endeavours to obtain the bull of dispensation.

In the month of January, 1504, Julius II. signed and published a bull of dispensation for the marriage of Henry and Catharine.

"Pope Julius II. has been informed that the Princess Catharine of Spain had contracted a marriage

* Bergenroth, Calendar, vol. i, p. 341.

with Arthur, late Prince of Wales, and that this marriage has, perhaps, been consummated.

"Notwithstanding this authorises, in his quality of the Head of the Church, Henry, Prince of Wales, and the Princess Catharine to contract a lawful marriage."*

The divorce that Henry VIII. afterwards caused to be pronounced makes these documents of capital importance.

Before the bull had been confirmed by the formalities that gave solemnity and authenticity, Julius II. secretly sent an abstract of its contents in the form of a brief to Isabella of Castille, who, already attacked by the sickness that brought her to the grave,† in her last moments, was cheered by this communication.

A little before the death of the great Queen Isabella, as the pope's dispensation had been granted, preparations were made for Catharine's betrothal to the Prince of Wales. The young princess had written to her father, Ferdinand, that she had no great inclination for a second marriage in England, but, at the same time, requested her parents not to take her individual tastes or comfort into account.‡

* Bergenroth, Calendar, vol. i, p. 322, dated in Latin in the first year of Julius's papacy.

† See the account of Isabella's death in the introduction; she was ill a long time, and did not die till the month of November, 1504.

‡ Lingard, vol. v, p. 333, from Mariana Hist., Introduction.

No account was taken of her respectful and timid opposition; she was betrothed to Henry, Prince of Wales, on June 25th, 1504, in the private chapel of the Bishop of Salisbury in Fleet Street.

Soon after this ceremony, the death of Isabella left Catharine at the mercy of two politicians, both of whom were disposed to speculate, each after his own fashion, on the unfortunate plight of the young princess, who was then almost entirely left alone.

As to Henry VII. in especial, he was still expecting the payment of one hundred thousand crowns* that were due to him, and, without deciding on Catharine's fate, he kept her in his hands as a kind of personal security, a living pledge for the balance due to him.

In order to render her fate still more uncertain, and to stimulate the fears as well as the hopes of Ferdinand, the day after the Prince of Wales, his son, attained his fifteenth year,† the king made him sign a protest that he had never done, or intended to do, anything to legalise the contract of marriage that had been made during his minority. In case Ferdinand should complain of this strange proceeding, the

---

* This sum was the balance of that two hundred thousand scudos promised to Catharine on her first marriage to Arthur; only one hundred thousand scudos of it had been paid, and the King of Aragon had contributed to this payment, but he intended that the balance should be paid by the new sovereigns of Castille, successors and representatives of Isabella.

† Lingard, vol. v, p. 329, says fourteenth. Which is right? Henry VIII. born June 28, 1491; so fourteen is right.

ambassadors of Henry VII. were commissioned to explain that the Prince of Wales would only be relieved by this protest from any constraint that might have been put upon him, that he had always been desirous of marrying Catharine, but that he was at liberty to marry another woman.*

* "Se tenia por libre para casarse con quien quisiese." Zurita, vi, p. 193., editor de Saragossa, 1610. The date of this document is June 28, 1505, it therefore was very little before the death of Philip the Handsome; but as the date of a secret document is not certain, and Miss Strickland thinks it may well have been ante-dated to avoid the inferences that might have been drawn from this strange act, unfavourable to the policy of Henry VII., if there had been a possibility of its being proved that he did not think of it till he had heard of the death of Juana's husband and had formed the idea of marrying her. It was the cautious Fox, Henry VII's chaplain, who presided over this act of protestation; he composed it with a secretary, in the presence of a very few of the household, in a ground-floor room standing quite apart at the palace of Shene. Then the young Prince of Wales was fetched, and his signature extracted from him without his knowing what he did, perhaps without having been completely informed of the bearing of the deed he signed. It is to be observed that he had an inclination for Catharine at this time. This protest was kept secret at first, and only published several years afterwards, much to the public surprise.

CHAPTER IV.

Opposition of a Divine to the Betrothal of Henry, Prince of Wales, and Catharine—Henry VII. seems to have Serious Thoughts of a Marriage with the Queen Dowager of Naples—Remarkable Negotiations entered upon Through the Medium of Catharine—Matrimonial Catechism—The Queen declares that she will not marry again—Destitution of Catharine—Dona Juana and the Archduke Joseph in England—Henry VII.'s Exercise of Constraint to keep them in England—He does not allow Freedom of Communication between Catharine and Juana—The Archduke's Departure—Urgent Letter from Catharine to her Father, Ferdinand—Catharine's Sufferings—Troubles connected with Royal Marriages.

WHEN the betrothal of Henry and Catharine took place in 1504, in the Bishop of Salisbury's palace, Henry VII. caused a divine to attend among the witnesses and present objections written in Latin, founded on the unlawfulness of unions between brothers and sisters-in-law; but Doctor Barnes replied also in Latin that the ensuing marriage would become legitimate, according to the laws of the Church, by means of the pope's dispensation, which had been demanded and was said to be granted.*

* See Hardwick's papers, 1-13., quoted by Hallam, Constitutional History of England, vol. i, p. 44.

The objection thus put forward was intended as a kind of touchstone, a sort of indication of a cause of nullity which might be advanced to alarm the Spanish Government and enhance the price of the final union of Catharine and the Prince of Wales.

Perhaps also Henry VII. kept in reserve this allegation of a voiding impediment, as a means of breaking off a matrimonial alliance that might cease to be agreeable to him.

His project had been to create a grand position for himself in European politics by this fresh connection with Spain. But he would attain this object much more directly if he himself married the Queen Dowager of Naples, the niece of King Ferdinand; that prince himself having, as is well known, suggested the idea.

While he got a footing in Spain by this marriage, he might marry his daughter Mary to some great prince on the Continent. His eldest daughter Margaret was the wife of the King of Scotland. So his project was thus to create for himself a grand position in Europe, and to be able to play the part of mediator between all the Christian princes.

Thus, a short time after the betrothal of the Prince of Wales, in the month of August, 1504, when the Duke of Estrada was returning to Spain, he begged that nobleman to speak seriously to the King of Aragon about the proposed marriage with his niece. Before an answer could be received to this application, in the month of October following, he told Puebla that he had not quite made up his mind to marry again, but that he wished to have the advice of the members of his council on this matter. This advice, as may well be supposed, was not unfavourable. However, before coming to a definite resolution, he desired to know something of the features of the Queen Dowager of Naples. He even desired, if it were not considered improper, to have her portrait painted upon canvas and sent to him. And he promised to keep this a most absolute secret. And the portrait to be "put in a case." Again, he desired what would be hard to manage, " without the Queen of Naples or Her Serene Highness the Queen her mother knowing or suspecting anything about it," and, in a letter a little later, " for your Highnesses must know that, if she were ugly and not beautiful, the King of England would not have her for all the treasures in the world, nor would he dare to take her, the English thinking so much as they do about personal appearance." *

Puebla did not fail to inform Ferdinand that the King of England was much taken up with this new matrimonial scheme, talked about it continually both in private and with the Privy Council whenever there was a chance. He extolled the goodness of Ferdinand and Isabella† in making this proposal to him. He

* Bergenroth. Calendar, vol. i, pp. xcix, 334, 344.
† " Lauded your Highnesses above the Cherribim." Bergenroth, Calendar, vol. i, p. 344. Puebla to Ferdinand and Isabella. (Ed.)

was delighted when he was told that it was the best possible marriage for him.

The Queen Dowager of Naples was living with her mother, Ferdinand's sister, vice-regent of the kingdom of Valencia, and residing at Valencia itself, the capital of that country. Henry VII. decided on sending three ambassadors to these two queens, Francis Marsin, James Braybrooke, and John Stile. They were the bearers of a list of queries in twenty-four sections.

These are King Henry VII.'s instructions and the ambassadors' replies :—

" 1. After delivering to the queens the letters from the Princess of Wales, to note well the estate that they keep.

"The ambassadors arrived at Valencia the 22nd of June. Next day had an audience of the queen. Delivered the Princess of Wales's letters ; the queens giving their thanks with a grave, steadfast countenance. The queens have their lodgings severally by themselves, though they keep their estates and households jointly in the king's palace, and they maintain a noble, sad rule and order among their household.

" 2. To mark the estates and households kept by the queens, and to note whom they have about them.

" The principal points are answered in the first article. Suits are made daily unto the said queens' court of lords, spiritual and temporal, respecting matters and causes such as might be brought to a king.

"3. To note the manner of ordering their estates, and the discretion and wisdom the queen may show in her answers to the ambassadors.

"Ever since the young queen came to Spain, she and her mother have kept their estates together. On the delivery of the letters, the old queen replied for herself as a noble, wise woman, and afterwards the young queen, with a sad, noble countenance, not speaking many words.

"4. Whether the young queen speak any other languages besides Spanish and Italian.

"She understands both Latin and French, but does not speak them.

"5. To note well her age, stature, and features of her body.

"Her age is twenty-seven, and not much more. Could not come to any perfect knowledge of her stature, by reason of her wearing slippers after the manner of her country. A man could not lightly perceive the features of her body, for that she wore a great mantle of cloth.

"6. To mark her visage, whether painted or not, fat or lean, sharp or round, cheerful, frowning, or melancholy, steadfast, light, or blushing.

"Is not painted; of a good compass, amiable, round, and fat; cheerful, not frowning; a demure, shame-faced countenance; of few words, but spoken with a womanly, laughing cheer and good gravity.

"7. Clearness of skin?

"Very fine and clear.

"8. Colour of hair?

"Seems to be of a brown colour.

"9. Eyes, brows, teeth, and lips?

"Eyes greyish brown; brows like a wire of brown hair; teeth fair, clean, and well set; lips somewhat round and full.

"10. Nose and forehead?

"Nose rising in the middle and bowed toward the end. Forehead not perfectly to be discerned, for that her kerchief came down to her brows.

"11. Complexion?

"Fair, sanguine, and clear.

"12. Arms?

"Round and not very small; in length a good proportion.

"13. Hands?

"Right fair; somewhat full and soft.

"14. Fingers?

"Right fair and small, and of a meety length and breadth.

"15. Neck?

"Full and comely, not mis-shapen.

"16. Breasts?

"Somewhat great and full, and trussed somewhat high.

"17. Whether any hair on her lips?

"As far as could be perceived none.

"18. To endeavour to speak with her fasting, and that she may tell them some matter at length, so that they may see whether her breath be sweet?

"Could never come near to her fasting, but at other times have approached her visage as near as they conveniently could, but never felt any savour of spice, and believe her to be of a sweet savour.

"19. To note her height?

"Seemed not to be of high stature; but by reason of her clothing, and being somewhat round and well-liking, she appeareth somewhat lesser.

"20. To inquire whether she hath any sickness of her nativity, blemish, or deformity?

"Having considered that such secret causes be to all persons unknown, save to her physician or apothecaries, had applied to Pastorell, who is in a manner physician to both queens, and who made answer that he had served her many years, and she had ever been in good health, of a noble nature and complexion.

"21. Whether she be in any singular favour with the King of Aragon, and whether she resemble him?

"He right well loveth and favoureth her. It is a common saying in all Spain that she is to be married to the King of England by means of the King of Aragon. Somewhat resembles him in the fashion of her nose and complexion.

"22. To inquire the manner of her diet?

"Is a good feeder, and eateth well her meat twice a day; drinketh not often; most commonly water, sometimes cinnamon water, and sometimes ipocras, but not often.

"23. To inquire for some cunning painter who may draw a picture of the queen, to agree as nearly as possible in every point and circumstance with her very semblance; and if at the first or second making thereof it be not made perfect, then the same or some other most cunning painter shall renew it till it be made agreeable in every behalf to her very image.

"No answer made to this article.

"24. To inquire what jointure she hath, or shall have, and to know the value thereof?

"Have been informed by one Martyn de Albystur that the value of her jointure is thirty thousand ducats of yearly rent, secured to her and her heirs by King Ferdinand of Naples, while the old queen has forty thousand, but the great Captain Gonsalvo Ferdinando having confiscated their property in Naples, the King of Castille pays them fifteen or sixteen thousand ducats yearly for their expenses."*

Catharine was supposed to be the person desirous of the portrait, as she is the one who made the move in this matter; the ambassadors carried letters from her to the two queens, and they seemed to

* Bergenroth, Calendar, vol. i, pp. 359, 360, 361.

be her messengers, and not those of King Henry VII.

But this mission failed completely. There was no need to put the talent of the Spanish painters to the proof; the young queen would not consent to have her portrait taken. She also declared that she was quite averse to such a marriage, and her mother shared her repugnance. Ferdinand was consulted by his sister and niece, but thought he ought not to oppose their wishes. He himself was already seeking the hand of Germaine de Foix, and seemed to draw towards King Louis XII. Now, every step that he took towards France removed England to a greater distance.

Catharine suffered from this recoil of policy against Henry VII. Perhaps even the prince owed her a grudge for the ill-success of his matrimonial negotiations. He first ordered Catharine's little Court to be broken up. Then she was deprived of any house of her own, and had to live with her father-in-law. On the pretext that her expenses were provided for, she was left absolutely destitute of everything. She often had no means of paying the salaries of her ladies of honour, nor even of defraying her personal expenses in dress and toilette.

A letter that she wrote to her father, King Ferdinand, in the month of September, 1505, shows the need of money to which she was reduced.

In this letter she speaks of a marriage proposal for one of her ladies of honour, Doña Maria de

Salazar,* a member of one of the most illustrious families in Spain.

"MOST HIGH AND MOST PUISSANT LORD,

"It is known to your highness how Doña Maria de Salazar was lady to the queen my lady, who is in blessed glory, and how her highness sent her to come with me; and, in addition to the service which she did to her highness, she has served me well, and in all this has done as a worthy woman. Wherefore I supplicate your highness that, as well on account of the one service as the other, you would command her to be paid, since I have nothing wherewith to pay her, and also because her sister, the wife of Monsieur d'Aymeria, has in view for her a marriage in Flanders; of which she cannot avail herself, nor hope that it can be accomplished without knowing what the said Doña Maria has for a marriage portion." †

But it was not the will of Providence that Maria de Salazar should be married in Flanders, and thus be separated from Catharine, whom she had consoled in the dreary, melancholy days of her youth, and

* Contemporary English writers are very apt to confuse Spanish names, and call this lady Marie de Salucces or de Saluzzi. Now she was the daughter of Don Salazar, captain of Ferdinand's guard, and by her mother was related or connected to Catharine of Aragon. Ferdinand, who was often involved himself, owed arrears of pay to Captain Salazar, and Catharine also pressed for the payment of this.

† Wood's Letters of Royal and Illustrious Ladies, vol. i, p. 126.

whom she was destined to attend upon even in her last agonies. She remained in England, and gained the affections of the rich heir of the ancient house of Willoughby d'Eresby. The noble lord married her without inquiring whether she had any marriage portion.

Towards the end of this same year Catharine, sinking under her heavy load of troubles and privations of every kind, fell seriously ill. While confined to her bed she wrote to her father, in the early part of December, the following letter, in which she attributes all the sufferings of her melancholy life to Doctor Puebla, who was a mean flatterer of Henry VII., and encouraged him in all his tyrannical measures.

"Your highness shall know, as I have often written to you, that since I came into England I have not had a single maravedi, except a certain sum which was given me for food, and this such a sum that it did not suffice without my having many debts in London; and that which troubles me more is to see my servants and maidens go at a loss, and that they have not wherewith to get clothes; and this, I believe, is all done by the hand of the doctor, who, notwithstanding your highness has written, sending him word that he should have money from the King of England, my lord, that their costs should be given them, yet, in order not to trouble him, will rather intrude upon and neglect the service of your highness. Now, my lord, a few days ago Dona Elvira de Manuel asked my leave to go to Flanders to get cured of a complaint which has come into her eyes, so that she lost the sight of one of them; and there is a physician in Flanders who cured the Infanta Dona Isabel of the same disease with which she is afflicted. She laboured to bring him here, so as not to leave me, but could never succeed with him; and I, since if she were blind she could not serve me, durst not hinder her journey. I begged the King of England, my lord, that until our Dona Elvira should return his highness would command that I should have, as companion, an old English lady, or that he would take me to his court." *

In this letter she afterwards accuses Doctor Puebla of having advised Henry to deprive her of her little court, and not to leave her a household of her own, such as seemed required by her title of Princess Dowager of Wales, and her rank as Infanta of Spain. She says that Puebla seems to belong rather to the service of Henry VII. than to that of the King of Spain, and she decidedly adds that he ought to be replaced by another ambassador.

Ferdinand knew that Puebla had the ear of the King of England, and thoroughly understood Continental politics, so he was deaf to Catharine's complaints, and retained his ambassador.

* Wood's Letters, vol. i, p. 131.

This prince is, not unreasonably, accused of great duplicity, but he behaved quite loyally at least towards his son-in-law Philip the Handsome and his daughter Juana.

When Queen Isabella was already dangerously ill he did all he could to prevent Philip from leaving Spain and going to Flanders. He represented to him that, if the queen should die, he and the archduchess could enter peaceably into possession of the kingdom of Castille, if they were on the spot, but that, if they were away from Spain, their claims to the succession might be contested. Philip would not attend to this wise counsel; he went to Flanders by land, and on his way negotiated a treaty with the King of France, in the name of the Sovereigns of Spain, though they had given him no directions to that effect.*

A short time after the young couple reached the Low Countries, Philip fell violently in love with one of the Spanish ladies who formed part of the suite. Juana, in the hall of the palace, in the presence of several persons of the Court, fell upon her too charming rival with her fists, and, in a desperate excess of jealousy, became so violent as to tear out the beautiful hair that had excited the admiration of the faithless archduke. Philip was greatly enraged by

---

* Letter of Ferdinand to De Puebla, June 22nd, 1505. Bergenroth, Calendar, vol. i, p. 155. The letter recapitulates matters that had occurred some time before.

this attack; he expressed his wrath against the princess in most unsuitable and unchivalrous language, and declared he would have nothing more to do with her. The news of this sad affair aggravated Isabella's illness, and perhaps hastened her end.

Her will expressly ordained that, in case of the absence or incapacity of Juana, Ferdinand should administer the affairs of Castille as regent.

But Ferdinand made a treaty with France, and married Germaine de Foix, niece to Louis XII., thus rendering himself so unpopular in Castille that he was obliged to give up the regency and hand over the government of that kingdom to the Archduke Philip.

Then Philip and his wife, who had become reconciled, left Zeeland, and embarked with a fleet of fifty sail. A fearful storm cast them upon the English coast, and they were obliged to take refuge at Melcombe, in Dorsetshire.* Some authors say that Philip was desirous of the alliance of Henry VII., and asked his permission to wait on him. According to another version, Henry invited Philip and Juana to his Court in terms that admitted of no refusal, kept them three months in a sort of brilliant captivity, and seized the opportunity of extorting some political concessions from them. This last version is Lingard's.†

Perhaps these two views may be reconciled, or, at least, brought pretty near together.

* And not at Falmouth, as several authors say. † Vol. v, p. 330.

In fact, we find that Philip at first went alone to Windsor Castle to see Henry VII., leaving his wife at the sea-side. So his intention seems to have been to obtain a short interview with the King of England, and to embark again soon after with Dona Juana. But he gave way to the very pressing requests, or perhaps to some actual pressure from his royal host, and prolonged his stay far beyond the period that had been fixed. Henry VII. began by sending the Earl of Arundel and Lord Mountjoy to Juana to conduct her to Windsor. Meanwhile Catharine took a great deal of trouble on Philip's account, hoping to conciliate his favour and protection. She danced a Spanish dance before him with a lady of her household, and asked her brother-in-law to join them. The prince testily answered her that he was a sailor, and not a dancer; then he returned to his conversation with Henry VII.*

Queen Juana, attended by her personal suite and the two English lords, arrived at Windsor the 10th of February, a little more than a week after her husband. In order to avoid a solemn, ceremonious reception, she entered by the back of the palace, but Henry VII. came to meet her as far as the foot of the staircase, and embraced her very tenderly.†

Then it was Catharine's turn to come and welcome the queen. She presented herself with her sister-in-

---

* Miss Strickland, from the *Herald's Journal*.
† The reason for these particulars being given will appear.

law, Mary,* expecting that, after this presentation, she should be left alone with Juana, and be permitted to give free scope to the confidences that seemed a real necessity for two sisters who had been parted for so many years. But Henry VII. insisted on the interposition of etiquette to stop the display of their mutual affection. Catharine waited a long time without a chance of a private interview with Juana, thanks to the distrust of the King of England. This distrust was on two accounts. First, he feared the complaints that Catharine might make of the ill-treatment she had experienced. Secondly, he feared her opposition to the secret treaty he had just extracted from Philip, and which was unfavourable to the interests of Castille. Besides, by this treaty Philip had with extreme reluctance engaged to give up to Henry an English lord—Suffolk—who had taken refuge in the Low Countries, and who had received from the archduke most formal promises of protection.† Finally, Henry VII., after his disappointment at the refusal of the Queen Dowager of Naples, had requested from Philip the hand of his sister, the Archduchess Margaret, who was twice a

* Daughter of Henry VII., and sister of Henry VIII., afterwards third wife of Louis XII., married in 1514.

† Henry VII. had promised to respect this nobleman's life, and so contented himself with shutting him up in the Tower. But when he died, he charged his son Henry to have his victim executed. Henry VIII. defrayed this legacy with exemplary exactitude. (This was Edmund, second son of the Duke of Suffolk. Lingard, vol. v, p. 331. Ed.)

widow, first of the Infant of Spain, and then of the Duke of Savoy, so that she had two dowries. What a captivating bait for such a selfish schemer as the King of England!*

Philip probably did all he could to effect this marriage, but the Princess Margaret declared that she did not choose to marry again.

On February 12th, Juana commenced her journey to Plymouth in a rich litter that had belonged to Queen Elizabeth; she was detained with her husband upon the English coast until the middle of April, either by contrary winds or by the policy of Henry VII. Catharine had only been able to have one short interview with her sister, in which she described her painful situation. No doubt she was encouraged to speak by her sister Juana having perceived and taken notice of her state of destitution.

She wrote to her father, Ferdinand, about the same time—that is to say, in the month of April—the following letter:—

"I cannot speak more particularly, because I know not what will become of this letter, or if it will arrive at the hands of your highness, but when Don Pedro d'Azala shall come, who is now with the king and queen in the harbour, your highness shall know all

---

* There was also at this time some suggestion of the marriage of the Princess Mary, Henry VII.'s daughter, and Prince Charles, afterwards Charles V. Philip had consented with pain to this proposal, only under the weight of moral pressure.

by ciphers. I have written many times to your highness, supplicating you to order a remedy for my extreme necessity, of which " (letters) " I have never had an answer. Now I supplicate your highness, for the love of our Lord, that you consider how I am your daughter, and that after Him" (God) "I have no other good remedy except in your highness; and how I am in debt in London, and this not for extravagant things, nor yet by relieving my own" (people), "who greatly need it, but only for food; and how the King of England, my lord, will not cause them" (the debts) "to be satisfied, although I myself spoke to him, and all those of his council, and that with tears; but he said that he is not obliged to give anything, and that even the food he gives me is of his own good will, because your highness has not kept promise with him in the money of my marriage portion. I told him that I believed that in time to come your highness would discharge it. He told me that that was yet to see, and that he did not know it, so that, my lord, I am in the greatest trouble and anguish in the world; on the one part, seeing all my people that they are ready to ask alms, on the other, the debts which I have in London; about my own person, I have nothing for chemises, wherefore, by your highness' leave, I have now sold some bracelets to get a dress of black velvet, for I was all but naked, for since I departed thence " (from Spain) "I have nothing except two new dresses, for till now those I brought thence have lasted me." *

Then Catharine begs her father to send her, as confessor, a Franciscan of the strict rule. She asks for a learned and discreet man, " because, as I have written at other times to your highness, I do not understand the English language, nor know how to speak it, and I have no confessor; and this should be, if your highness will so command it, very quickly, because you truly know the inconvenience of being without a confessor, especially now to me who, for six months, have been near death; but now, thanks to our Lord, I am somewhat better, although not entirely well." †

She finishes her letter by saying that she has entrusted it to one of her faithful servants, Calderon, going to Spain to be married, and that she has nothing she can give him in payment for his trouble and fidelity; she charged her father to do something for him. ‡

Thus sickness was added to all the moral tortures that Catharine had to undergo. It seems that the intermitting fever she complained of was very obstinate, for, in a letter of the 17th of

* Wood's Letters, vol. i, p. 138.
† Wood's Letters, vol. i, p. 140.
‡ This letter is dated April 22nd, 1506.

October following, she complains of its recurrence.* At this time she felt discouraged, melancholy, and hopeless. As at this time she had no inclination for Henry VIII., she saw no prospect of a future that could hold out any comfort or enjoyment. Her father seemed to wish that she should stay in England as long as she had any chance of becoming the wife of the new Prince of Wales, but she only lent herself to this alliance because her father wished it; if she desired success, it was in order to get out of the impoverished and wretched condition in which Henry VII. seemed desirous of keeping her indefinitely. Her heart had lately been wrung by the death of her mother, and she seemed to have fallen into a state of indifference and languor.

The deeper we can penetrate, with the assistance of the revelations of history, into the private life of royal families, the more we discover that kings' daughters find the trials of life increase in actual proportion to their elevation. In their matrimonial alliances in especial, difficulties of every kind arise and multiply. There are not merely private interests to be considered, there are dynastic or national considerations to which the first of human interests, domestic happiness, must be sacrificed. It seems in these kind of marriages as if personal suitability and inclina-

* Letter addressed to her sister Juana. Bergenroth, Calendar, vol. i, p. 400. Juana's husband had just died, but Catharine did not know this when she wrote.

tion go for nothing, or at least disappear in the midst of political combination. Reasons of state appear in all their harshness, the car, that nothing can stop in its progress, pitilessly crushing under its wheels the sweetest and most sacred feelings of nature.

CHAPTER V.

Why does not Ferdinand pay Catharine's Marriage Portion?—Puebla himself comes at last to pity this Princess—Death of the Archduke Philip the Fair—Henry VII. asks the Widow Juana in Marriage—Ferdinand makes Delays, but gives Hopes—Henry VII. is satisfied, and treats Catharine better—She serves him as a go-between in his Matrimonial Negotiations—Under Henry's Influence, she writes a very Strong Letter in favour of this Marriage—Subtlety and little Dissimulations of the Princess required by the Necessities of her Position—The Treaty of Marriage between Henry VII. and Juana absolutely comes to an End—This Check makes Catharine's Wretched Condition still worse—Ferdinand's Great Anger with Henry VII., for he neither will marry her to the Prince of Wales, nor let her go back to Spain—Ferdinand is on the point of declaring War against England, when he hears of the Death of Henry VII.

IT is a curious question why Ferdinand always deferred the sending of the hundred thousand crowns requisite to complete the marriage portion promised to Catharine. This was the principal excuse for the uncomfortable condition in which Henry VII. kept that princess, and the privations of all sorts that he made her undergo.

There is some sort of an explanation of the indefinite delay in the payment of this debt, in the state of things after the death of Isabella of Castille.

When the Archduke Philip returned to Spain with his wife Dona Juana, on whom the crown had devolved, considerable disagreement had broken out between the Archduke and Ferdinand. While making no difficulty about handing over the reins of the government of Castille to Philip the Handsome, the King of Aragon intended to relieve himself from paying the remainder of the marriage portion of the Princess of Wales by charging it upon him. He tried very hard to induce him as well as Dona Juana to keep Isabella's jewels as their part of the inheritance, and to send the value to England. Certainly the jewels were worth more than a hundred thousand crowns. Nevertheless, neither of the couple would consent to this arrangement.

When Henry VII. heard of these disputes, causing delay and coming to nothing, he fell into a violent rage, and poor Princess Catharine suffered greatly from it. The ill-treatment she had to endure was such that Doctor Puebla himself, who palliated everything, "sugared over"* everything, at last himself felt that the proceedings of the King of England towards Catharine were too harsh and too "unpleasant." Henry VII., who seemed determined to throw up the cards, went so far as impe-

* An expression of Catharine's own. Bergenroth, Calendar, vol. i, p. 412.

riously to express his desire that his son should become a suitor for a French princess. This may have been a diplomatic artifice. But the young Prince of Wales, who began to have a will of his own, would not give in to it; he was afraid that the game might at last be taken as earnest; he did not intend to elude the engagements resulting from his betrothal, notwithstanding the pretence of a protest he had been made to sign two years previously.

While this was going on, news came of the death of the Archduke Philip, and King Henry conceived the idea of marrying Doña Juana, that prince's widow.

This was on many accounts an extraordinary idea. If it had been carried out, and Catharine had at the same time married the Prince of Wales, the old king would have become the brother-in-law of his son and of his daughter-in-law. This would have produced a strange confusion in the family, especially if there had been children of both marriages. It might have been a source of troubles and civil wars. Certainly public opinion in England would have pronounced against such a project.

It is true that if Henry VII. had obtained the hand of the Queen of Castille, with the hundred thousand crowns due to him on Catharine's marriage portion, he would probably have broken off the marriage of that princess to the Prince of Wales, and have made her reside in England and live upon her dowry as widow.

But it was to Catharine herself that the old king applied, desiring her to sound Ferdinand on the proposal that he intended to make. The princess thought she ought to do as he desired, and wrote a very explicit and detailed letter to her father, informing him of the intentions of Henry VII.

·The reply to this letter was delayed a considerable time, because the King of Aragon was at Naples, and communications between England and the Two Sicilies were neither safe nor speedy at that time. Ferdinand wrote to his daughter that he would do all he could to induce Doña Juana to take a second husband, and that if she would do so that husband should be no other than Henry VII.* He also desired the most absolute secrecy, observing that nothing could really be done in this matter until his return to Castille, which was soon to take place..

This letter quieted the resentment of the King of England as if by enchantment, and caused Catharine to be better treated; she became a useful medium, and must be cultivated.

However, Ferdinand's reply was only a trick of diplomacy to appease Henry and gain time. He had already found out that it was impossible to live with a son-in-law married to a wife out of her senses, like Doña Juana. He might expect greater and

* Bergenroth, Calendar, vol. i, p. 405. (Ed.)

more numerous difficulties would arise from Henry VII. than he had already experienced with Philip the Handsome.

When Ferdinand's letter arrived, Henry VII. had been seriously ill, and still kept his bed, or at any rate his room. None of his privy-councillors were admitted to his presence. Nevertheless, when Catharine had sent him a communication of the information lately come from Spain, he sent for Puebla, and, though so weak that he could hardly speak, held a conversation lasting two hours.* On the morrow he had another Spanish ambassador with him nearly all day. Next he wrote two letters to Ferdinand in rapid succession, where we have the key-note of his character. In the first of these he asserts that he had received offers for the Prince of Wales of princesses with a much larger marriage-portion than that of Catharine. "Has, however, not accepted them, because he loves and esteems him so much, and is even willing that the payment should be postponed till the feast of St. Michael the Archangel." The letter is dated April 12th. So the delay was reasonable enough.

At the end of the letter he says with what great satisfaction he has received the favourable communications made to him, both by the Princess Catharine and by Puebla, concerning the bonds soon to unite

* The illness was a quinsy. Bergenroth, Calendar, vol. i, p. 408. (Ed.)

him with the Spanish royal family. In a subsequent letter he no longer expresses his satisfaction or pleasure, it is "rapturous joy" that he experiences at Ferdinand's proposal.* But all these transports did not prevent his again giving a reminder that he desired to be paid at Michaelmas at latest.

It is to be observed that from his side no one would suspect that there was any engagement or bond in honour due to Catharine, and that, if the King of England still reserved his son for her, it was out of entirely gratuitous kindness towards her, and disinterested affection towards her father.

As for the Princess Catharine, she became a veritable diplomatic agent when she consented to become a medium of communication between Henry VII. and Doña Juana. On this subject she had comprehended the first hint from Ferdinand, and quite understood that there was nothing serious in the business, and that it would never be carried out. But the sensual old king† had to be amused with this hope. Thus it appears that Catharine was not by any means a young innocent, nor, as some authors assert, a mere monastic devotee. The fact is, that, to a certain dexterity in the conduct of affairs, she added the habits of piety inculcated in her earliest childhood, and never given up. Under the bitter trials she had to endure, she sought consolation in her oratory

---

* Bergenroth, Calendar, vol. i, pp. 406, 407, written in Latin.
† Henry VII. was only fifty-two when he died. (Ed.)

from her Saviour. But she did not affect intermittent impulses of fervent devotion, she had a strict rule of life, and observed it exactly.

According to Saunders, during her widowhood she rose at midnight to recite her office, and then lay down again; then she dressed at five in the morning, and under her robes wore the scapulary of St. Francis. She confessed twice a week, and received the Communion every Sunday.*

Puebla indirectly confirms Saunders's description when he writes to Ferdinand: "And although she (the princess) has been a month at Westminster with the king, she is keeping the same rule and observance and seclusion which she did before in her own house."†

This was the woman whom Erasmus called *eleganter docta!*

Perhaps she might not have been much her mother's inferior in political ability. She probably only wanted a larger field and greater authority to have given proof of rare and eminent ability. Some years had passed, and she had seemed to go through them in passive and inert resignation. But her mind, after having been harshly restrained, at last, as will afterwards appear, forcibly underwent a strong reaction, and developed all its energy.

* Saunders quoted by Audin, Histoire de Henri VIII., vol. i, p. 74.
† Bergenroth, Calendar, vol. i, p. 345.

Henry VII. knew Catharine's intellectual power, and desired her, in concert with Puebla, to be the interpreter of his wishes and hopes for a marriage with Juana. As he had seen this princess in London, he did not, as in the case of the Queen Dowager of Naples, send a set of questions as to her eyes, mouth, complexion, the refinement of her hands, the smallness and shape of her feet, and so on; neither did he ask for Juana's portrait—her picture had remained graven on his memory; it might be said he fell in love with the recollection of her. Nothing stopped him in his passionate eagerness, not even the objection arising from the mental alienation of Juana. Henry asserted that popular feeling in England would take little account of the princess's mental debility, and would think about nothing but her chance of becoming a mother. Besides, if she had sometimes experienced moments of mental alienation, the cause was to be found in the reasons for jealousy that Philip had given her, and his unworthy behaviour towards her. Now Henry would treat her so well, and surround her with such care, that she should soon recover her reason and health in England. The most obsequious protestations cost him nothing. Philip had, it is true, been a bad son. As for himself, he would be a model of filial affection, and would be careful not to meddle in the affairs of Castille; he would leave the entire government of that kingdom to Ferdinand for all his life, but his own entire kingdom should be at the disposal of his father-in-law.* Ferdinand had a plan of going to fight the Moors in Africa, building castles there, and holding these ancient enemies of Spain in check. Henry offered his services in this war. The English archers seemed as if they must secure the success of such an expedition, and with their help in a few years all Africa might be subdued. Ferdinand would become the conqueror and father of this vast country, and Henry would accompany him thither as his ally and son. He added that he was but fifty-one years old, and thus several years younger than the King of Spain.

Were not these *hablerias* entirely in the Spanish taste, and were they not probably inspired by Puebla himself?

But Henry VII. did not confine himself to holding up these brilliant and fanciful prospects for the future; he added more real and more practical concessions, of immense value from his point of view, though perhaps not equally valuable in Ferdinand's eyes. First, a fresh delay in the payment of the marriage portion; then the acceptance of silver plate on account, at the value set upon it by experts; lastly, Henry announced that he had countermanded the departure of the ambassadors who had been

---

* *A la disposicion de usted* is a well-known form of Spanish courtesy, which is not very binding. No doubt the King of England uses this expression under Puebla's influence.

commissioned to arrange the Prince of Wales's marriage with a French princess.

He requested that the expense of the royal marriage should be defrayed either from the revenues of Castille, or from the personal property of Ferdinand, and that he should himself have a pension settled upon him of about equal value to that which had been assigned to Philip when he had gone to Spain.

When the proper time was come, Henry VII. would send ambassadors to conclude the marriage by procuration; but he would not admit the idea of the refusal of his hand by Juana; he declared that this would be dishonourable to his character. On this point the Princess of Wales, in her letters to Ferdinand, confidentially insinuated that she could not be of the same opinion.

Standing between two politicians, and obliged in some sort to deceive one or the other, she chose her father as the depository of her real thoughts, and reserved all her sincerity for him. Besides, it was notorious that the King of England's health was rapidly declining, and that he was hastening to the grave. He felt that so it was, yet pretended to play the young man. Thus, in the month of September, 1505, Henry writes to the Princess of Wales " that he enjoys perfect health, and leads a very agreeable life in the company of some nobles and a great number of gentlemen—spends his time in hunting and hawking."* A month afterwards, his good friend Puebla wrote to Ferdinand that Henry's late illness had produced a remarkable effect— "given him twice as good a constitution as he had formerly. He is growing stout."† Being resolved on doing all he possibly can to obtain the hand of Juana, he requires Catharine to write to her sister in favour of the marriage. This letter is so different both in style of expression and in matter from those written to her by Ferdinand on the same subject as to suggest that it may have been dictated by Henry VII. It must certainly have been submitted to him before being sent off; therefore, it cannot be expected to contain the true and independent thoughts of the Princess of Wales. Besides, the constrained and ceremonious tone pervading the passages we quote is clearly perceptible.

After expressing the personal regrets she had experienced when her sister, Doña Juana, left England with her husband, the Archduke Philip, Catharine continues: "My lord the king was also much disappointed in consequence of it, and if he had acted as he secretly wished, he would by every possible means have prevented your journey. But as he is a very passionate king, it was thought advisable by his council that they should tell him he ought not to

* Bergenroth, Calendar, vol. i, p. 432.
† Bergenroth, Calendar, vol. i, p. 439.

interfere between husband and wife,* on which account, and for the sake of other mysterious causes with which I was very well acquainted, he concealed the feelings occasioned by the departure of your highness, although he is very certain that it weighed much upon his heart. The great affection he has felt, and still feels, towards your royal highness from that time until now is well known. I could not, in truth, express, even though I were to use much paper, the pleasure which my lord the king and I felt on hearing that the king, our lord and father, had returned to Castille, and was abiding there with your highness, and that he was obeyed throughout all the kingdom, peace and concord prevailing everywhere."

Then she extols the advantages that might arise from the alliance with the King of England.

"He is a prince who is feared and esteemed at the present day by all Christendom, as being very wise, and possessed of immense treasures, and having at his command powerful bodies of excellent troops. Above all he is endowed with the greatest virtues, according to all that your highness will have heard respecting him.

* That is to say, because her husband treated her badly; but, as she had forgotten all the wrongs Philip had done as soon as he was dead, it was no means of pleasing her to recall them. This awkwardness must have been Henry's dictation, not Catharine's own language. If left to her own inspiration, she would have used much more discreet and delicate expressions.

"If what my lord, the king our father, shall say to you should please, as I think it will please your highness, I do not doubt but that your highness will become the most noble and most powerful queen in the world. Moreover, nothing will more conduce to your pleasure and satisfaction, and the security of the kingdom of your highness. In addition to all this it will double the affection subsisting between my lord, the king our father, and my lord, the King of England. It will also lead to the whole of Africa being conquered within a very short time, and in the hands of the Christian subjects of your highness, and of my lord, the king our father.

"I entreat your highness to pardon me for having written to you, and for having meddled in so great and high a matter. God knows what my wishes are, as I have already said; and I have not found it possible to resist the desire I felt to write to you. For it appears to me that, if this be not done, it will be committing a great sin against God, against the king, our lord and father, and against your highness, whose life and royal estate may our Lord guard and increase.*

"Oct. 25th, 1507."

No doubt Catharine ought to have wished for an alliance that would have brought her sister within

---

* Bergenroth, Calendar, vol. i, pp. 439, 440, 441.

reach, but she knew very well that it could not be hoped for. Besides, in the month of January, 1508, Ferdinand had seen and conversed with his daughter Juana. That princess continued to have her husband's coffin dragged after her. Every attempt to persuade her to have him buried had been unsuccessful.*

On the first day of the year she had demanded a royal salute for the body. Ferdinand made his royal correspondent say that it was impossible to speak to the princess of a second marriage until this strange ceremony had been accomplished. Afterwards he advised Henry VII. not to make any serious approaches towards Juana herself until her first husband was buried. The King of England at last saw that he must renounce the hope of obtaining Ferdinand's consent to the marriage of a woman suffering under such absolute insanity.

It has been shown that the Princess Catharine had accepted the post of negotiator in forwarding the marriage that Henry VII. desired to contract

* In the last universal great Exhibition in the Champ de Mars, 1878, was to be seen a picture of M. Pradilla representing "Juana la Loca" gazing, with bewildered eye, at the coffin of Philip the Handsome, which she is dragging after her for burial at Grenada. She is encamped at night in a desert plain in Andalusia. "On the right of the queen, near a fire grate, is a group of women seated on the ground, who, wearied by a long march, are half asleep; on the left a monk is saying prayers; in the background are the attendants."—*Revue des Deux-Mondes*, August 15th, 1878, by Victor Cherbuliez, p. 879.

with Doña Juana. She seemed to have entered into the ideas and feelings of this old monarch, and had assumed a great appearance of zeal in pleading his cause. But it must be confessed that, in acting thus, her especial aim had been to gain the favour of the King of England, and to prevent his breaking off the marriage that had been arranged between herself and the second Prince of Wales.

In judging of the concessions that she thought she ought to make under such circumstances, the extremities to which she was reduced must be remembered. Her poverty, indeed it may be called distress, increased every day. The King of England maintained that, as long as Ferdinand remained his debtor, he was not obliged to advance money to Catharine, even for her subsistence, and she bitterly felt the necessity that compelled her to live upon alms. In truth her father had once sent her two thousand ducats; but the creditors and purveyors had very soon laid hands upon that sum. In the month of September, 1507, on the complaint of Catharine herself, Henry sent an order for two thousand pounds to the princess, telling her that if she was in want it was the fault of her servants. Nothing could be more unjust; for she had been unable to pay them anything for a long time, and the less they received the more affectionate and devoted was their service. At this moment the only reason why Henry emitted this spark of generosity was because he wished to make the young princess favourable to him. It was less than a month afterwards that he asked her to write the matrimonial proposal he set such store by to her sister.*

What rendered the situation so precarious was that she could not hope for the conclusion of her marriage with Henry, Prince of Wales, till he had obtained his majority. Ferdinand himself acknowledged as much. But as the Prince of Wales began to lose patience, and his father feared a clandestine marriage, the young prince was closely watched, and he was not allowed to see his betrothed, or to converse with her, even for the three or four months while he was living in the same palace with her. Catharine, on her side, struck with the manly air and masculine beauty of Henry of Wales, who had become a grown man and accomplished cavalier, perhaps irritated by the harsh refusal to allow any communication with him, determined to take this means of escape from the cruel entanglement in which she was caught, and expressed to her father her desire of seeing the marriage accomplished. It is stated that she then proceeded to learn English diligently.

Her position at the Court of Henry VII. was becoming quite intolerable. When she complained to that prince of the miseries she had to endure, he

* The letter, in which he boasts of hunting every day, and sends the order is dated September 7th. Catharine's to Doña Juana on the 4th of October following.

coolly replied that it was necessary that she should
suffer a little, to induce her father the sooner to pay
the part of her marriage portion still owing. The
pressure was therefore made with full knowledge
and calculation. Doctor Puebla was quite as bad
and as harsh as the king, and also much more coarse,
mean, and base, as is usually the case with persons
of the lower orders. He always took Henry's part,
was always ready to betray Catharine, and lay all
the blame on her. He cared no more for defending
her cause than he did for supporting the interests of
Spain. Henry, like Puebla, his worthy confidant,
was in turn harsh or obsequious towards the unhappy
princess, according as he thought he could manage
to get anything out of her by either of these means.
As to her, she saw completely through the designs
and policy of the king and the ambassador, and despised them both equally. She says, "his words are
kind, but his deeds are as bad as ever."*

However, she suffered less severely from her
personal troubles than from the poverty of her
servants, and her own impotency to relieve them; it
was especially for that reason that she called herself
the most unhappy woman in England.

In such a state of affairs the princess was obliged
to avoid direct opposition to Henry VII., to humour
him, and even make use of some dissimulation.† If

* Bergenroth, Calendar, vol. i, p. 426.
† It is most curious that, in spite of all his assumption of Machia-

a little duplicity or cunning can be excusable, it is when there is no other weapon available against crushing violence, and that was the case with the unfortunate Catharine.

She tells her father that she would refuse if anything was asked of her that was contrary to her dignity. "Though submissive, cannot forget that she is the daughter of the King of Spain."* She would sooner die than do wrong. Sometimes, however, she seems almost exhausted, and losing her energy. She has her moments of profound depression, and plainly enough threatens Ferdinand that she will give up everything, "and spend the short remainder of her days in serving God, which would be the best thing that could happen to her."†

The Princess of Wales also felt that she was isolated, and without support. She begged to have an ambassador sent to London to whom she could fearlessly speak honest words, that is to say, to whom she could speak freely and openly. She could

---

velism, Henry was the dupe of Ferdinand's cleverness, as is well shown by M. Mignet in one of his late works. "Henri VII. ayant déclaré la guerre, Ferdinand lui avait persuadé de transporter ses troupes à Fontarabie et de les joindre aux siennes, afin de prendre la Guyenne. Le crédule Henri VII., sans rien acquérir pour lui, avait aidé son beau-père à s'emparer de la Navarre sur Jean d'Albert et à compléter ainsi vers les Pyrénées la frontière espagnole.—Rivalités de François I. et Charles Quint, par M. Mignet, vol i, p. 49. Paris, 1875.

* Bergenroth, Calendar, vol. i, p. 411.
† Bergenroth, Calendar, vol. i, p. 470.

not do this with Puebla, nor even with the Duke of Estrada. She would have liked to see Don Pedro de Ayala return to England; failing him, she mentioned and requested, as Spanish ambassador, Fuensalida, commander of Membrilla.

Don Pedro was obliged to refuse by ill-health. So Fuensalida was sent, and undertook the mission with eagerness. At the same time the banking house of Grimaldi in London engaged to advance the deficient amount of the Princess Catharine's marriage portion.

Unhappily the diplomatic correspondence of Fuensalida is not forthcoming. It would seem that if Puebla continued to act as the assiduous flatterer of Henry VII., and the Duke of Estrada showed such weakness that it came to the same thing, Fuensalida showed perhaps rather too much sharpness and stiffness. Henry VII. was not accustomed to be spoken to in the tone which the Spanish ambassador at first assumed towards him, and would not receive him a second time. Fuensalida had some very violent scenes with the members of the privy council.

Also about this time Ferdinand's opposition to the projected marriage between his grandson Charles and the Princess Mary of England seemed to arise; while, on the contrary, the Emperor Maximilian was favourable to it, and Henry VII. dwelt a great deal on the consent of the emperor, the paternal grandfather of the young prince.

But this persistence only augmented Ferdinand's distrust; he remembered that when the Archduke Philip the Handsome came to govern Castille in the name of his wife, Doña Juana, Henry VII. had favoured all his pretensions and approved his policy, though it was quite contrary to that adopted under the reign of Isabella. Anything that gave Henry a chance of depriving Ferdinand of the preponderating authority in Castille was becoming the aim of his policy. Besides, the King of Aragon was surprised at the kind of obstinacy with which the King of England had demanded, and seemed ready to demand again, the hand of Doña Juana. Such a prince, he said, could not be capable of sincere affection; his real passion was to obtain an opportunity or a pretext for meddling in the affairs of Castille.

The same reason made Ferdinand secretly hostile to the projected marriage between his grandson Charles and Mary of England.

Henry VII., being thus crossed in his matrimonial schemes, by way of reprisal placed fresh obstacles in the way of the completion of the marriage between his son and the Princess Catharine. He on his side manifested some alarm lest Ferdinand might, by means of his daughter, acquire a strong political influence over his son-in-law, and induce the young Prince of Wales to oppose his own father.

But it was very late to perceive this inconvenience, and raise serious objections on that account.

It was odious to hold the Princess Catharine under ward almost as strict as if she had been in prison, and to forbid the Prince of Wales from trying to see his betrothed. So Ferdinand, in the course of the year 1508, began to lose patience; he wrote to Fuensalida that at last he saw plainly that Henry VII. was a most detestable person, and a stranger to every feeling of honour and loyalty.

"In all these matters Henry has shown extreme covetousness, and but little love for him, the Queen of Castille, and the Princess of Wales. Would have felt much inclined to have no longer any brotherhood or amity with him, only that he trusts the Prince of Wales will show himself to be more amenable to reason. Does not know why Henry should exhibit so much ill-will towards him. Fears, from what Membrilla *(Fuensalida)* says, that the marriage of the Prince of Castille to the daughter of Henry, instead of augmenting their friendship, would produce quite contrary results. Everything seems to prove that it would be better for him to break entirely with Henry. Would do so at once, but for the affection he bears the Princess of Wales. For the sake of bringing her marriage to a conclusion, will not take umbrage at the ill-will shown to him by Henry. Membrilla must, therefore, use his best endeavours speedily to bring the marriage to a conclusion, and must take heed to say nothing which may afford an excuse for breaking it off. If, nevertheless, the marriage should not take place, will then feel that he is not responsible for anything that may happen in consequence."*

If Henry consents to the immediate performance of the marriage, the one hundred thousand crowns remaining are to be paid entirely in coin and bullion. Only the payment that the banker Grimaldi is to make must be kept a profound secret, for this speculating king would be capable of raising the rate of exchange to take advantage of it. The ambassador must take the greatest care not to let Henry get possession of the money without performing his promises. "And be able to carry the money off. All this I say, because in treating with people of no honour and indifferent character it is necessary to take care that we receive no injury, and that we are not cheated." The King of England's demand that, in case of the Princess Catharine's death, her marriage portion should never be required back ought not to be entertained, and this cautious man "be freed from the temptation of killing the Princess of Wales."†

Henry VII., who thought himself a profound politician, because there was no method he shrank from employing, had conceived great hopes from an expedition that Maximilian had attempted in Italy. His calculation was that, if that prince drove Ferdinand

---

* Bergenroth, Calendar, vol. i, p. 461.
† Bergenroth, Calendar, vol. i, p. 463.

out of Naples, the imperial troops, with English help, would find it easy to chase the same prince out of Castille; but the battle of Cadoro, where Maximilian and the imperialists were routed, ruined all his hopes in that quarter.

He afterwards asked the hand of the Princess Margaret of Austria, and wanted to become a member of the league of Cambrai, whence he would have excluded Ferdinand. But Margaret persisted in the refusal she had before given, while Ferdinand, who had gained himself great consideration on the continent by his dexterity and success, was admitted into the league, and Henry was not. Thus all Henry's plans successively failed, and the ground was giving way under his feet.

Ferdinand was driven to extremities by this hostile and cunning policy, and resolved to put an end to all communication with Henry VII. He made a formal demand for his daughter, the Princess of Wales, to be sent back to him in Spain, and declared he meant to break with the King of England. Henry at last threw off the mask, and declared that, even if the marriage of the princess to his son did not take place, he would not permit her to leave England. Thus he intended to keep the Princess of Wales as a sort of hostage. This was the conclusion of his policy; and thus he justified all the former suspicions of his duplicity and perfidy.

Thereupon Ferdinand broke out. He felt the

blow to his affections as a father; to his honour as a king.

"For the love I bear the Princess of Wales," he writes, "and the esteem in which I hold her are so great that, if such a thing were to happen, which God forbid, I would risk my person and my kingdom, and that of my daughter the queen, with the greatest readiness, in order to make a worse war on the King of England than on the Turks. The King of England must keep faith in this matter, or, if not, the world may perish. This I say in order that you may know my determination." *

However, the King of France, whose alliance Ferdinand claimed, contrived to restrain this indignation, very excusable, but most impolitic, especially at this moment. For Henry VII. was dying of consumption, and the prince, who was destined to become Henry VIII., had always shown himself very well disposed towards the Princess Catharine. All agreed in a favourable judgment of him. Puebla praised the strength and lofty stature of the young Prince of Wales. The Duke of Estrada spoke of his prudence, his dexterity, and the immense riches he was to inherit. Fuensalida himself said he had an excellent opinion of his morals and intelligence. In consequence of these various reports Ferdinand thought it his duty to assure the young prince of

* Bergenroth, Calendar, vol. i, p. 460.

his paternal affection, and make him the most kindly offers of service.

Upon these events came the death of Henry VII., putting an end to difficulties and complications that might have become dangerous. He was little regretted. Even among the English people his ill-treatment of Catharine had been the cause of much displeasure. His detestable foreign policy during the last years of his life had completely destroyed his popularity.

As for the Princess of Wales she was about to escape from poverty and oppression, and to share one of the first thrones in Europe with a lively and learned prince, reported to be of noble and chivalrous character, and who apparently felt real affection for her. Who could have told her that, after such painful trials in her youth, there were reserved for her, in ripe age and the decline of life, still greater miseries and more cruel misfortunes?

CHAPTER VI.

Clerical Education of Henry VIII.—A Stop to all Misunderstanding between Ferdinand and England—The New King's Council recognize the Validity of the Bull of Dispensation of Pope Julius II.—Marriage and Coronation of the Queen—Popularity of Henry VIII.—Restrictive Explanations given by Henry of his Coronation Oath—Affectionate Correspondence of Henry and Ferdinand—Dexterity and Diplomatic Artifices af Ferdinand—Henry VIII. goes to Fight in France—Catharine Regent—The Victory of Flodden—Coolness between Henry and Ferdinand—Marriage of Henry's Sister to Louis XII.—Presents of Ferdinand to Henry, and Reconciliation of the Two Kings—Charles V.'s Voyage to England—Work of Henry VIII. against Luther—He Receives the Title of Defender of The Faith—Portrait of Henry VIII., by a Venetian Ambassador.

HENRY VIII. was eighteen when he inherited the English crown, on the death of his father. The early education of this prince had been strict and peculiar. Henry VII., during the life-time of his eldest son, Arthur, had considered that the best way of securing to his family a considerable share of influence in the Church, would be to dedicate his youngest son to the priesthood, and rapidly push him up all the steps of the ladder of ecclesiustical dignities. Prince Henry, who was known before his brother's death under the style and title of Duke of York, would have been at an early age the Archbishop of Canterbury, the Primate of All England, and a cardinal. Why should he not, one day, become Pope?

It would not be surprising if this notion had crossed the brain of the first of the Tudors; it seems quite natural to that spirit, ever prone to the strangest ambition, to that enterprising and adventurous spirit!

This same Duke of York, who ended by becoming King Henry VIII.,* was not Pope of the Church of Rome, but he wished to be Pope of the Church of England. And that his father had neither desired nor foreseen.

At any rate the young Duke of York began to learn sacred music when he was seven years old, and soon made great progress, first as chorister, and then even as a composer.† At nine years old he talked Latin with wonderful ease. At ten he was learning the *Scholasticon*, and was reading the *Summa* of St. Thomas Aquinas. Thus early, perhaps too early, he had that half knowledge in theology that is so

---

* The date of his accession was April 22nd, 1509.

† At eleven or twelve years old he composed the music of the anthem in the vulgar tongue, "*O Lord, the maker*," written for four voices. M. Audin gives the words and the music at the end of the first volume of his history of Henry VIII. It is said that it is still sometimes sung at Christ Church, Oxford.

dangerous when not regulated by a spirit of submission and humility.

When he became Prince of Wales, upon the death of his brother Arthur, he was trained to bodily exercises and the management of weapons, in which he very soon excelled. He was considered an accomplished knight. He was, besides, very tall, and graceful in every action. When he rode on horseback, richly dressed, with his plume floating on the winds, he looked so magnificent that he had surprising influence over the people.

When he caused Catharine to be told that she might rely upon him, he was sincere, and entertained a real affection for her. The difficulties placed in the way of his marriage by Henry VII., and the trials she had to undergo, only excited his passion. As soon as he found himself master of his destiny, and legally of age, his first thought was to conclude the long-deferred marriage as quickly as possible.

These delays, as we have suggested, had arisen from two causes that were in some way connected; on one side they may be attributed to the distrustfulness of King Henry VII., who was afraid that Catharine's influence over the young Prince of Wales might add to the influence of the King of Spain in England.* It is probable that Ferdinand's opposi-

* He was also afraid that the Prince of Wales himself might become too considerable a personage, with too much power over England through his marriage. See a letter of Almazan. Bergenroth, Calendar, vol. ii, p. 15, dated May 18th, 1509.

tion to the marriage of the Princess Mary, Henry VII.'s daughter, to Charles V., then a child,* arose from a similar motive. But now there was no suspicious old king in England to vex himself over the influence obtained by Catharine of Aragon. And as to the marriage of the young emperor to the English princess, Ferdinand trusted to time to break the bonds formed by their premature betrothal. Besides, as soon as Henry VIII. had given him satisfaction, the King of Aragon had no longer any occasion to make use of those species of political reprisals against his family, as there would have been no reason for them.

There is also a letter of Ferdinand's attesting his real feelings at this time, written to his daughter.

"A courier, who has arrived in eight days from Flanders, has told him that the King of England is dead. Has written to the Knight Commander of Membrilla, his ambassador in England, and has told him what he must do in case this news be true, in order to bring her marriage to a speedy conclusion. Sends at the same time instructions to the ambassador respecting what he must do in case the king should still be alive. As the ambassador will communicate to her all his instructions, it is not necessary to repeat them here.

"Has her welfare, and especially the speedy conclusion of her marriage, more at heart than anything

* Charles was hardly nine years old.

else on earth. Hopes she will assist his ambassador in his negotiations, for he has always served her faithfully, and never written any letters in Spain which could prejudice her in any respect.

"Had intended to send a prelate as ambassador to England, in order to conduct the negotiations for her marriage. As, however, it is said that the King of England is dead, he has thought it advisable not to change his ambassador, since such change would cause delay."*

In the course of the next few days he wrote letter after letter to his ambassador, desiring him to take advantage of the great change in the Princess Catharine's position, owing to the death of Henry VII. Ferdinand is in haste to see his daughter at last receive the reward of her perseverance and the recompense of her protracted trials.

He tries every means of gaining, and, so to speak, of wheedling the young king. Thus Almazan, the first secretary, writes, by his orders, to the Princess of Wales:

"As soon, however, as the death of King Henry VII. was known, King Ferdinand granted to the present king all that he had refused to his father. He loves her most of all his children, and on her account looks on the present King of England as though he were his own son. King Ferdinand will henceforth communicate to King Henry all his secrets, and expects

* Letter of May 11th, 1509. Bergenroth, Calendar, vol. ii, p. 10.

in return that King Henry will conceal nothing from him."*

Ferdinand himself, in letters directly addressed by him to his daughter, showed the greatest affection for his son-in-law; he said he was ready to put himself at the head of an army, if necessary, and go to England to protect the interests of his children. He forwarded several presents to Henry VIII. as pledges of his friendship.†

But all this manœuvring to catch the young king was unnecessary. One of the first acts of Henry VIII. had been to call his council together for a consultation respecting his marriage to the Infanta of Spain. Warham, Archbishop of Canterbury, put forward an objection devised from the relationship of the parties. This objection was triumphantly refuted. In favour of the validity of the marriage of Henry VIII. and Catharine of Aragon was cited the princess's oath that her former marriage had not been consummated, the king's acceptance of this oath, and lastly the sovereign bull of dispensation of Pope Julius II.

The discussion that took place on this point in the king's council seemed only to be to show with what complete knowledge of the circumstances the council unanimously pronounced in favour of the legitimacy of the marriage between Henry VIII. and Catharine, Infanta of Spain and widow of Prince Arthur.

* Bergenroth, Calendar, vol. ii, p. 15.
† Bergenroth, Calendar, vol. ii, pp. 19, 20, 21, 22, &c.

THE MARRIAGE.

However, without ostensibly resting on anything but his own will, nor seeming to obey anything but his personal inspiration, Henry VIII. at Greenwich on June 11th, 1509, led to the altar the Princess Catharine of Aragon, who had long been betrothed to him. It was noticed that the bride wore her hair flowing and a robe, the virgin garment not permissible to widows.* This was significant.

After so many struggles and sufferings the marriage itself was, to the new queen, more than compensation or restitution, it was triumph; and to this well-deserved triumph were added inward satisfaction and pure heart's delight. She had loved Henry VIII., and at this moment was really loved by him.

After the gloomy and morose reign of Henry VII., there must have been great relief all over England when Henry VIII. mounted the throne. He seemed to realise the idea of a king. Everyone felt the charm of this very popular king, even those who were afterwards obliged to oppose him, such as Fisher and Sir Thomas More, and even they held to their deceptive illusion as a sort of monarchical creed; they only renounced it with great difficulty, and in the last extremity, because their duty as Catholics was bound to prevail in their consciences over their chivalrous attachment to their sovereign.

Some days after the marriage, a fresh ovation was

* Audin, Vie de Henri VIII., vol. i, p. 80.

prepared for Catharine and her husband, the ceremony of coronation.

On the 21st of June the king and queen had slept at the Tower ; on the 29th they left the old fortress and went to Westminster, going along the streets of the City, which were all hung with tapestry and richly adorned as for a grand festival. All along these narrow streets stood young girls clothed in white, with bunches of flowers in their hands ; the queen, in an open litter drawn by two white horses, was blazing with jewels. All eyes were attracted by her attire; she gained all hearts by her grace and beauty, and loud cheers resounded along her whole course.

There is still in existence in the Vatican an autograph letter from Henry VIII. to Cardinal Sixtus de la Rovère, giving that prince of the Church an account of the royal marriage and the subsequent coronation. We produce the text, where, beneath the official formalty of style, may be seen the deep content of the young king.

" Ut de imperio post Serenissimi regis ac patris nostri obitum successurus Vestra Reverentia Dominatio certior fiat significamus, illi qualiter paulo ante nos prospicientes ad ogregias virtutes illustrissimæ principis D. Catharinæ, Serenissimi regis Aragonorum filiæ illam nostri connubio dignam duximus. Quare eam desponsavimus et uxorem duximus, moxque una cum illa coronati sumus solemniter ut moris est, cum incredibili totius regni nostro gaudio, exultatione, et applausu. Quod vestræ Reverendissimæ Dominationi utpote amicissimum nostro scribendum duximus, non dubitantes quin his nostris secundis rebus sit gavisura. Ex palatio nostro Greenwici, Die VIII. Julii, 1509, et regni nostri prima.*

Thus the king himself is a witness to the immense enthusiasm with which his whole nation welcomed the coronation of the queen and himself.

In another point Henry VIII. showed at this time that he had in reality very few scruples, though, after the thing was done, he thought he had a right to add to his most solemn oaths, explanations more or less restrictive.

Thus he had sworn publicly on his knees before the Archbishop of Canterbury that he would maintain the liberties of the Church guaranteed by the former Kings of England, and in the minute of declaration of the oath that he signed in the sacristy, he secretly added, "Saving my jurisdiction and royal dignity."

He promised to keep the peace between the Church, the clergy, and people; he explains the meaning of this promise, thus correcting the form he had just made use of. "I swear to labour for the union of the people and clergy under my royal dominion." He swore to make the laws of the kingdom respect-

* Cod. Vaticanus, 6210. In a letter written to Ferdinand, of June 17th following, he says, "The multitude of the people who assisted was immense, and their joy and applause most enthusiastic." Bergenroth, Calendar, vol. ii, p. 20. In Latin.

ed, "saving the rights of the crown and imperial dignity."

These clandestine interpolations,* that cannot be justified, show Henry's absolute determination to maintain his prerogative, and, to speak plainly, his absolute authority, and that he was quite determined to uphold it, if need were, against the liberty of the kingdom and the Church.

Such ripeness in cool calculation and political foresight in a king of eighteen, are surprising, and we ask, almost startled, whence he had acquired the idea of such a Machiavellian performance before the works of Machiavelli had been published.

Certainly he was greatly in love with Catharine at this time, and even transferred to his father-in-law, Ferdinand, a large portion of the affection that he had for her. This may be perceived from the following letter to Ferdinand:

"Rejoices to learn how tenderly he loves him. Regards him as his new father. From an intimate alliance between England and Spain nothing but the greatest advantages to both kingdoms are to be expected. Prefers an alliance with him to any alliance with other princes, and would not hesitate, if necessary, to reject them all in order to preserve his friendship. Promises like a dutiful son to obey all

* Audin, in his "Histoire de Henri VIII.," has given a facsimile of this minute, with the interpolations that were mysteriously written by the king in a room close to the sacristy of the chapel at Westminster.

his behests as he would obey the behests of his late father, if he were still alive."

Then he proceeds to politics, and gives some good reasons against the destruction of the republic of Venice. That city is a bulwark against the Turks, and an obstacle to the ambitious hopes of certain Christian princes.

"The queen is pregnant, and the child in her womb is alive. As he and his kingdom rejoice at this good news, so it is to be expected that he and Queen Juana will also hear it with pleasure."

He ends with thanks for his affection and paternal solicitude, and again promises to obey him as a father.*

In this same letter he says that he is impatiently expecting the new Spanish ambassador, and that he will give the most full and frank answers to all his communications. We should be glad to believe that Henry was sincere at that time, and did not make a parade of his frankness.

While this was going on, Membrilla having been recalled to Spain, and his successor not yet arrived, Queen Catharine was to some extent the intermediary in diplomatic correspondence with Ferdinand. She informed her royal spouse of the contents of her father's letters. They seemed then to have had no concealments between them; they seemed most closely united, and no cloud appeared on the horizon.

* Bergenroth, Calendar, vol. ii, pp. 23, 24. Nov. 1st, 1510.

In the month of May, 1517, Catharine informed her father that she had given birth to a still-born child—a daughter. She says: "Some days before she was delivered of a daughter. That her child was still-born is considered to be a misfortune in England; has, therefore, not written sooner, or permitted any other person to send the news of her, confinement. Begs him not to be angry with her, for it has been the will of God. She and the king, her husband, are cheerful. Thanks God and him that he has given her such a husband as the King of England." *

Meanwhile the Spanish ambassador, Louis Carroz, had arrived. He was an able man, possessed Ferdinand's entire confidence, and fully deserved it. To a certain extent the ambassador took Henry at his word in the professions of devotion to his father-in-law. He asked for, and obtained, a treaty of alliance between the two kings, reduced to writing in proper form as a written manifestation of this devotion. But this defensive alliance was not enough for Ferdinand; he wanted Henry VIII. to enter into a league against France with the emperor and some Italian states.

The idea was to be suggested to the King of England so dexterously that he might fancy he had invented it, and taken the initiative. Henry VIII. must conscientiously look upon it as a duty to sup-

* Bergenroth, Calendar, vol. ii, p. 38.

port the Church, the pope, the emperor, and the little Christian princes of Italy.

In case of need Catharine's influence over her husband was to be made use of. Ferdinand says:

"Should, however, the queen refuse to persuade the king to break with France, and prefer to see him at peace, although all the world go to pieces, he is to make use of the friar, her confessor, and through him persuade her to use her influence with the king." *

Being now Queen of Great Britain † the princess might become too much of an Englishwoman. Ferdinand seemed to be afraid of this; so he provided for any difficulties, and took any means in his power to smooth them over. As it might possibly happen that the confessor himself might have scruples respecting this war with France, the Catholic king would, in that case, cause a request to be preferred to the Pope to deal with the confessor of the queen, and of the king himself.

This is a specimen of Ferdinand's remarkable political artifices; he already sees that his daughter does not blindly follow his advice, and that he must bring other influences to bear upon her.

He attained his object. He contrived that England should make war upon France in concert with Maximilian, Emperor-elect of Germany.

* Bergenroth, Calendar, vol. ii, p. 52.
† England. (Ed.)

Catharine could not regard this war unfavourably. First because it seemed to have a religious object; secondly because it was blindly desired by her husband and her father. She therefore made a pilgrimage to Our Lady of Walsingham to pray for a victory for this so-called Holy League against Louis XII., King of France. The people joined the queen in imploring divine protection for the arms of England. There was a ballad composed at this time, in which the poet begged the Saviour, Saint Mary, and Saint George to make the red rose bloom and flourish over all the coasts of France.* This ballad

> "The Rosse will into Fraunse spring,
> Almythy God hym thyther bring,
> And save this flowr, which is our king;
> Thys Rosse, thys Rosse, thys Royal Rosse,"

became popular, and was soon to be heard sung everywhere as a sort of national anthem.

On his departure for France, Henry appointed Catharine regent, and the choice was generally approved.

While Henry was winning the battle of Guinegatte, and taking the city of Tournay, James IV., King of Scotland, invaded the north of England with a powerful army. Queen Catharine had but few troops to oppose him, but they were well disciplined and admirably led. The Earl of Surrey

* See the text of this old ballad in a note to Audin's History of Henry VIII., vol. i, pp. 144, 145.

was commander-in-chief. James IV. suffered a bloody defeat at Flodden, and was himself left among the slain.

Catharine was on excellent terms with the members of the council present in London, and kept up a correspondence with Wolsey, who, after completing the preparations for the French campaign, had followed the king as almoner of his household. Some of Catharine's letters are affecting from the signs of tender solicitude she shows on her husband's account. She is anxious and sleepless; without Henry she can find nothing good or happy on earth.

In another of her letters she speaks enthusiastically of the victory of Flodden, and says, perhaps with justice, that the conquest of Scotland would be of more use to England than even that of France.*

At this time of her life she displays not only the virtues of a devoted wife, but also a real power of government and incontestable political capacity.

When the King of England was informed of the victory of Flodden he speedily left France, landed secretly at Dover, and returned incognito to Richmond, to surprise Catharine, and address to her the most ardent congratulations on the way in which she had exercised her power as regent.

While this was going on, Ferdinand I. had come

* Ellis's Letters, vol. i, p. 88. The victory of Flodden was gained in the month of August, 1513.

to an understanding with Leo X.,* who had relieved Louis XII. from excommunication, and proposed a treaty of peace with France in concert with the emperor. Henry VIII. was requested to join. But as one of the conditions of the treaty would have been the restoration of Tournay to Louis XII. the King of England could not consent.

On the other hand the emperor and King Ferdinand agreed to break off the marriage of their grandson, Prince Charles, with the Princess Mary of England, because they were negotiating a more advantageous match for him.

Enraged at being in this kind of way left in the lurch, even by his father-in-law, in whom he had hitherto had unshaken confidence, Henry threw himself into the arms of France. One of the prisoners of Guinegatte, Louis of Orleans, Duke de Longueville, consented, at the request of Wolsey, to propose a reconciliation between the two kings of France and England.

Louis XII. had just lost his wife, Anne of Brittany. He had no children.† If he married the Princess Mary he might be more fortunate. This marriage was to become the basis of a close and permanent alliance between the two kings.

It is true that it was necessary to persuade a young girl of scarcely sixteen that there was no dis-

* Successor to Julius II., the soul of the Holy League.
† No son. He had two daughters. (Ed.)

proportion in the ages of herself and of a king of fifty-three, exhausted by the fatigues of war and the worry of politics. The Princess Mary was asked whether she would give up Prince Charles; she answered that she had never loved him, but not a word was said of her having bestowed her heart upon anyone else, such as some great noble of the English Court.*

At any rate, on the 13th of August, 1513, she was married to Louis XII., his proxy at Greenwich being the Duke de Longueville. On the 5th of November following she was crowned Queen of France at St. Denis. Among the maids of honour she took with her, and who remained in her service, was Anne Boleyn.

It was contrary to English policy to run any risk of the transfer of the crown of England by inheritance to a foreigner. But, on the one hand, Queen Catharine was pregnant, and, on the other, Louis XII. had white hair, and was old before his time. Three months had hardly elapsed since his marriage when he died of atrophy.

Henry VIII. had been glad enough to become independent of Spain, but he was not long in finding out that he had only exchanged one yoke for another. Informed of this change of disposition, Ferdinand wrote a very flattering letter to his son-in-law, and

* Her attachment to the Duke of Suffolk is well known, and she married him when she became a widow.

tried to be reconciled to him. He sent splendid presents with it, Andalusian horses of great beauty, with rich and magnificent trappings. He sent also a jewelled collar for the king himself. The impression made by these presents exceeded all expectation. King Henry wrote a letter to his father-in-law, in which he poured out an effusion of childish joy and enthusiastic thankfulness. He says he "loves him as much and as sincerely as he ever did before, and even more. Has forgotten all the disagreeable things which have passed between them. Begs to be allowed to regard him as a brother or a son. Often looks at the presents, and, every time he sees them, his (King Ferdinand's) image is recalled to his mind's eye."*

And Queen Catharine herself wrote to Ferdinand a short time afterwards. "The King of England is very proud of the splendid presents he has sent for him.† All say that never did more magnificent presents come to England. It is due to his presents that the treaty with England is concluded, and the alliance renewed. This treaty will be much better observed than the preceding one. His ambassador will write to him more fully on this subject. The former treaty contained clauses which the King of

* Bergenroth, Calendar, vol. ii, p. 271. October 20th, 1515.
† . . . El quel esta el mas soberbio del mundo con la gran dativa que Vuestra Alteza lo embyo. Y todos in su Regno claramente conocen y confiesan che a sydo la major que nunca à Yngliterra vino.

England and his Council had never liked to consent to. These clauses were neither profitable to him (King Ferdinand) nor advantageous to the King of England."*

The treaty of alliance was purely defensive, but the great advantage that Spain obtained by it was that Henry VIII. was removed from French influence, and drawn nearer to his father-in-law.†

Amid the political disputes of her husband and father, Catharine's conduct was irreproachable. We give the testimony of Bergenroth, the editor of the Calendar, who is so very English and Protestant :—

" Queen Catharine behaved, during the whole of the quarrel between King Henry and King Ferdinand, as became a Queen of England. She loved and revered her father. It certainly made her unhappy to see that he and her husband had become enemies. But when King Ferdinand attempted to make use of her influence over her husband, she refused to serve any such purpose. Louis Carroz complained in the most bitter terms that neither he nor any other Spaniard could obtain the smallest advantage through her interference. Encouraged by her confessor, Fray Diego de Hernandez, she seemed,

---

* Bergenroth, Calendar, vol. i, p. 272.
† Joachim Legrand asserts, but does not give proof, that Henry VIII. chose to make Catharine responsible for her father's bad policy, and blamed her very much. None of our fresh documents confirm this assertion; it is at least rash. Histoire du Divorce, p. 39.

he said, to have forgotten that she was a Spaniard, and was desirous only to cultivate the good-will of the people which had become hers through her marriage. We congratulate the queen and her confessor that they so well understood what was befitting her position."*

This homage is pleasant to find. English authors in the time of Elizabeth would not have been so impartial.

The above mentioned letter of Louis Carroz shows how great the anger of Henry VIII. had been against Spain. "I am treated by the English not as an ambassador, but like a bull at whom everyone throws darts."†

Ferdinand appeased his son-in-law with presents, as children's tears are stopped with toys. Wolsey's intervention afterwards was more effectual than even that of the queen in the completion of the reconciliation that she so keenly desired, but to which she could only contribute with timid discretion. The English people were very grateful to her for this behaviour. It was a supreme injustice to nickname Marie Antoinette *l'Autrichienne*, but no one ever thought of calling Catharine the Spaniard.

The reconciliation with Ferdinand very speedily

---

* Bergenroth, Calendar. Intro., vol. ii, p. xcii.
† Bergenroth, Calendar, vol. ii, p. 248. The same letter in which he complains of the anti-Spanish influence of the queen's confessor.

brought forth fruit, for, during the course of the year, Henry VIII., together with the emperor, joined a fresh league against France; but these results were not of long duration. Just at the moment when everything seemed smiling upon the old King of Aragon, he died during the month of January, 1516.

Catharine had only officially announced to Ferdinand the birth of her daughter Mary on February 18th, 1515, in the letter of the month of October following, in which she thanked him for his splendid presents, and informed him of the excellent effect they had produced.* This shows that communication between her and her father had been very completely broken off during this period. She afterwards had two more children, but lost them both— they were sons—at a very early age. Shortly afterwards her star began to wane.

It may be observed that Ferdinand's death deprived her of a support that might have been very useful, as he had regained his influence over the mind of Henry VIII.

Her nephew, Charles V., had been elected emperor in 1519, and united the sovereignty of Germany to

---

* The laconic manner of her announcement to Ferdinand is surprising. "Gave birth to a child after Candlemas" (last sentence in letter). In the same letter she warmly recommends to her father the lady of honour whom she loved most, Maria de Salinas, and her confessor Diego Hernandez, who, she says, has served her "much better than certain persons pretend; both are going to Spain."

that of Spain, with a large portion of Italy, and had a more widely extended power than Ferdinand, but he never acquired the same influence over the mind of Henry VIII. Still he felt that it was an hereditary duty and kind of family charge always to patronise his aunt Catharine; and this was the more meritorious because in earlier times the Queen of England took but little pains to gain the affection of the young emperor. When he came to England, he spoke to her three times at Greenwich; she hardly answered him, and not graciously, says a Spanish ambassador present at their interview.*

Clearly she was afraid of seeming too Spanish in the eyes of the English. At Henry VIII.'s request, a few days afterwards, she had some long conversation with the emperor at Windsor. Henry VIII.'s reception of Charles V. ought certainly to be mentioned in this history, for it was not only cordial and magnificent, but had also a religious colouring. The day after the emperor's arrival, Henry took him on pilgrimage to Canterbury; the two princes received the holy communion together at high mass,† then they laid their pious offerings on the shrine of Saint

---

* The author seems to have misapprehended this. The ambassador speaks of himself, not of Charles V. "Said to the emperor that he had spoken three times with the Queen of England, but had not found her at all gracious."—Letter of Martin de Salinas, Bergenroth, Calendar, vol. ii, p. 448. (Ed.)

† At this period of his life, Henry was still very pious. Authors say that he told his beads every day.

Thomas à Becket. Did they really consider the meaning of the homage they thus paid to the bold champion of the liberties of the Church martyred by Henry II.'s tyranny? Alas! the ashes of this great saint were destined to be afterwards scattered to the winds and the mire of the highway by the same king who had worshipped them with such idolatry.

If Catharine was to be touched by Henry VIII.'s piety, his faith seemed to provide her with no less firm assurances, and perhaps of greater stability.

We mean the publication of the book entitled "Assertio septem Sacramentorum adversus Martinum Lutherum," composed by the King of England himself; in it he exalted the authority of the Holy See. Sir Thomas More considered that the august theologian had perhaps gone too far, and in jest threatened him with the statute of *præmunire*,* which seemed to be violated by this ultramontane exaggeration. Henry vigorously upheld his doctrine, and wound up his work thus:

"What is the use of a duel with Luther, who does

* Audin, Histoire de Henri VIII., vol. i, p. 261. The first statute of *præmunire* had been passed by Parliament under Edward I. to restrain the abuse of the papal power, to keep in bounds what were called *gratiæ* and *provisiones*. Persistence in these abuses, and the profits to be got from them, were punished with heavy, but not capital penalties. This statute was afterwards extended to fresh cases by Henry VIII. himself and his successors. The writ issued by the chancellor to prosecute this offence began with the words *Præmoniri facias*, and this was mispronounced *præmunire*.

not understand himself, who denies what he has just affirmed, and affirms what he has just denied? If you take weapons of faith to attack him, he opposes reason; if you call reason to your aid, he throws himself upon faith; if you cite the philosophers, he appeals to Scripture; if you invoke Holy Writ, he enfolds himself in the sophisms of the schools. Insolent author! he puts himself above laws, despises our doctors, and from the heights of his greatness divides the living lights of our Church, who assails with insult the majesty of our pontiffs, who outrages tradition, dogma, morals, canons, faith, and the Church herself!"

As soon as the work was finished, Henry VIII. had two splendid copies prepared, both with a dedication to Pope Leo, with this couplet, written by the hand of the king himself,

"Anglorum rex Henricus, Leo decime mittit
Hoc opus, et fidei testem et amicitiæ."

The two copies were presented to Leo X. with great solemnity by the two ambassadors of the King of England, Clerk and Pace. At the same time they presented an autograph letter from the king to the Sovereign Pontiff, containing assurances of the most absolute submission, and the most perfect devotion of the English monarch to His Holiness.

Leo X. replied to this royal homage by a bull couched in most flattering language. After consultation with the sacred college, he gave to the author

of the Assertio the title of Defender of the Faith.
The pope meant that this powerful king could defend the Church with the sword as well as with
the pen. It was a direct appeal to him to fill the
post of mediator between the pope and the Christian
powers, and, in case of a conflict, himself to descend
into the plains of Italy to throw his weight into the
scale on the side of the Sovereign Pontiff.

The emperor's ambassador, Juan Manuel, seems
to have suspected some political afterthought in all
this. With a somewhat dry laconicism, with a trace
of secret malevolence, he gives an account of these
novel communications between the King of England
and the Vatican.

"The King of England has sent a book against
Martin Luther to the pope. It is said that all the
learned men of England have taken part in its
composition. I hear that it is a good book. The
pope has given the King of England the title of
'Defender of the Christian Faith.' This title prejudices no one, as all Christian princes are, or ought
to be, defenders of the Faith." *

If all the learned men in England really had taken
part in the composition of the work against Martin
Luther, it might not have had any more effect. The
truth is that it was written by one single author,
Henry VIII. himself. Many of his contemporaries
did not know that this prince had spent some of his

* Bergenroth, Calendar, vol. ii, p. 381. Oct. 17th, 1521.

youth in the study of the *Summa* of Saint Thomas and of Latin literature under Skelton's direction. Quite lately he had extricated himself from business and pleasure, and shut himself up for several months at Greenwich, surrounded with manuscripts and folios, which he filled with marginal notes in his own writing, and which have been preserved to the present day as living witnesses of his personal labours and real learning.

Daughter of Catholic sovereigns, Catharine was proud of being the wife of a king who had been officially styled, "Defender of the Christian Faith." She had sometimes received offerings of the prizes gained by Henry for feats of arms at tournaments. He had just fought in very different lists, and had again come forth a victor, according to the decision of a competent judge, the Sovereign Pontiff. She was delighted at this fresh success.

Catharine's enthusiasm for the king will be better understood on reading the portrait left of him by an impartial witness, the Venetian ambassador, Giustiniani. It is true that this portrait relates to a somewhat later period,* but it describes the appearance of Henry in his youth, with his fresh and engaging attractions.

"And first of all his majesty is twenty-nine years old, and extremely handsome ; nature could not have done more for him. He is much handsomer

* Written about 1519 or 1520.

than any other sovereign in Christendom, a great deal handsomer than the King of France; very fair, and his whole frame admirably proportioned. On hearing that Francis I. wore a beard he allowed his own to grow, and, as it is reddish, has now got a beard which looks like gold. He is very accomplished; a good musician; composes well; is a most capital horseman; a firm jouster; speaks good French, Latin, and Spanish; is very religious; hears three masses daily when he hunts, and sometimes five on other days; he hears the office every day in the queen's chamber, that is to say, vespers and compline. He is very fond indeed of hunting, and never takes this diversion without tiring eight or ten horses, which he causes to be stationed beforehand along the line of country he may mean to take, and when one is tired he mounts another, and before he gets home they are all exhausted. He is extremely fond of tennis, at which game it is the prettiest thing in the world to see him play; his fair skin glowing through a shirt of the finest texture.

"He gambled with the French hostages to the amount occasionally, it is said, of from six to eight thousand ducats in a day.

"He is affable, gracious, harms no one, does not covet his neighbours' goods, and is satisfied with his own dominions, having often said to the ambassador, '*Domine orator*, we want all potentates to content themselves with their own territories; we are satisfied with this island of ours.'

"He seems extremely desirous of peace.

"He is very rich indeed; according to report, his father left him ten millions of ready money in gold, of which he is supposed to have spent one half in the war against France, when he took Tournay; and he certainly expended a considerable sum at that period, for he had three armies on foot: one crossed the Channel with him, another was in the field against Scotland, and the third remained with the queen as a reserve, in case the other two encountered any disaster.

"His revenues amount to about three hundred and fifty thousand ducats annually, and are derived from estates, forests, and meres; from the customs, or duties; from hereditary and confiscated property; from the Duchies of Lancaster, York, Cornwall, and Suffolk; from the County Palatine of Chester, and others; from the principality of Wales; from export duties; from the wool staple; from the Great Seal; from the annats yielded by church benefices; from the Court of Wards, and from New Year's gifts; for on the first of the year it is customary for His Majesty to make presents to everybody, but the value of those he receives in return greatly exceeds his own outlay.

"His Majesty's expenses may be estimated at one hundred thousand ducats, those in ordinary having been reduced from one hundred thousand to fifty-six thousand, to which must be added sixteen thousand for salaries, five thousand for the stable, five thousand for the halberdiers, who have been reduced from five hundred to one hundred and fifty; and sixteen thousand for the wardrobe, for he is the best-dressed sovereign in the world; his robes are the richest and most superb that can be imagined, and he puts on new clothes every holiday." *

If Henry VIII. had been carried off by death at the age of thirty or thirty-five years, England would have been pitied for the loss of such a good king, and the hope of a glorious reign. Such is the vanity of human judgment; we often deplore as a dreadful misfortune what is really a signal mercy of Providence. *

* "Ten Years at the Court of Henry VIII." Report of Sebastian Giustiniani, vol. ii, p. 312.

PART II.

DIVORCE OF HENRY VIII. AND CATHARINE OF ARAGON. SUFFERINGS AND DEATH OF THAT PRINCESS.

IN the second part of this work we have undertaken to write the history of the divorce of Henry VIII. and Catharine of Aragon. The claims of the truth and of the Church make us consider it a duty to describe the most private and most delicate incidents of the life of Catharine and Henry with the utmost minuteness. We address a grave and enlightened public, and trust our intention will not be mistaken.

It is necessary to. be pitiless towards vice and crime, and they must be displayed in all their horror that they may be branded and made detestable.

Heaven forbid that we should ever allow ourselves to heighten the colour of our pictures! That would be to exceed the rights of the historian. But we shall be careful not to conceal or diminish anything.

The impure origin of the English revolt against the papacy must be thoroughly made known.

We know that it contains a great historical scandal, but the scandal must recoil upon the heads of the actors.

CHAPTER I.

How was the First Idea of the Divorce conceived by Henry VIII.?—Fears of Fresh Civil Wars, if the King had no heir, by the Lords and Grandees of the Realm—Cooling of King Henry VIII.'s Affection for the Queen after Fifteen or Sixteen Years of Marriage and United Life—Excuses given for Henry VIII.'s Conduct by his Apologists—Falseness of these Excuses—Tardy Scruples of Henry VIII.—Theology and Policy furnish him with Pretexts after the Deed.

WE have seen that doubts were raised in the king's council by the Archbishop of Canterbury on the question of the validity of the marriage that Henry VIII. was about to contract with Catharine of Aragon. But the opposition temporarily led by that prelate was reduced to silence by the good fortune that this union appeared to have secured during its earlier years.

Thus, as the modern applauders of Henry VIII., and even Mr. Froude himself,* point out, if Catha-

* Vol. i, p. 117, et seq. However, the life or death of the children could make no change in the legal validity of Catharine's marriage. It was only a question of political importance.

rine's sons had lived, and had gathered around the throne, it is probable that conjugal peace would have continued almost unclouded between the married pair, or at least Henry, fearing to excite public censure, would not have allowed the discontents and troubles of his private life to have become public. But death struck down his sons in their premature births or in their feeble early infancy.*

The nobles and principal gentry of the country really seem to have felt some uneasiness. They had endured much suffering from the sanguinary wars of the red and white roses, and they dreaded their renewal. No doubt females were not excluded from succession to the throne, but Henry VII., who had married the heiress of the House of York, had never chosen to recognize any personal claim of his queen to the crown, because he chose to reign in virtue of his own right.

In a nation essentially military as the English were at that time, everyone must have preferred a male heir to one incapable of herself bearing arms

* Catharine was married June 3rd, 1509. Early in the spring of 1510 she miscarried—Four Years at the Court, vol. i, p. 83. January 1st, 1511, a prince was born who died February 22nd—Hall. November 9th, 1513, another prince was born who died immediately—Lingard. December, 1514, a still-born male child—Badoer, the Venetian ambassador. May 3rd, 1515, it seems there was a miscarriage—Four years, vol. i, p. 81. February 18th, 1516, the Princess Mary was born. July 3rd, 1518, again miscarriage—State Papers, vol. i, p. 2. Note to Froude, vol. i, p. 117.

and taking command. The opinion of the most distinguished lawyers* was that Parliament had the right to verify or confirm the legitimacy of the sovereign. Lastly, the papal authority itself had to be often consulted, when doubtful questions arose on the validity of a marriage having claims on the crown at issue.

Certainly Henry VIII. had only one daughter, in delicate health, and an insurrection against her would have had a fair chance of success; she might also die before reaching the age of royal majority. Forebodings and fears arising from this state of things gave birth to thoughts on the question of divorce that, though they were vague, were an excellent preparation of the ground for Henry VIII., if he should raise the point himself. This question, so to speak, was floating in the air until the king chose to give it consistency and determinate form.

But would Henry have determined to commence this dangerous proceeding, if he had only been swayed by considerations of public interest? Would he have ever had a notion of it, if his relations with the queen had continued to be as cordial and affectionate as in the earlier period of his marriage?

With unfortunate precocity, Catharine had soon

* Sir Thomas More was of this opinion; he even maintained that the Parliament had, in certain cases, the right of deposing the king. Appendix 2, to Third Report of the Deputy-keeper of the Public Records, p. 241. See also Froude, vol. i, p. 108; 2nd ed., 1858.

reached the period of maturity and decay. After she had been married fifteen or sixteen years, it became certain even to herself that she could never have another child. The disparity of age between herself and Henry,* scarcely perceptible at the time of the marriage, became more and more evident in consequence of the decline of her health, in consequence of her sufferings and domestic sorrows.

But was all this any justification for the coolness and even aversion that Henry at this time displayed for the companion of his life? Justice should be done to Catharine's unalterable good-humour, to her angelic amiability, to the serene resignation with which she bore the sorrows of her position, and pardoned conjugal infidelities that she must have known.

But her Castillian austerity is imputed as a crime to her, and her exacting habits in private life, and comparisons are made between her so-called cold and reserved obstinacy with the fiery obstinacy of Henry VIII.; it is stated that these two characters, at once like and unlike, must needs have clashed on the very sides where their resemblance lay.† But it is not taken into account that, when an oppressed woman keeps herself purely on the defensive, her pretended obstinacy ought to be called by another name and

* She was at least seven years older than the king. About 1524 or 1525, the time when Henry began to grow cool, she was hardly forty years old, but she had already aged much.

† Froude, vol. i, p. 119.

styled firmness, and when an imperious husband continues in a position of unjust aggression against a blameless woman, his obstinacy becomes inveterate tyranny.

It is said that Henry VIII. would have very well endured the vexations of his married life, and would never have revealed his passion for Anne Boleyn, if the interests of State and consideration of public order had not been in correspondence with his secret feelings; that he must have thought he saw a real moral obligation to do what he desired; also that a French ambassador, on coming to ask the hand of Mary, expressed, in the name of his master, doubts as to the legitimacy of that young princess, and that, when once these doubts were raised, they must of necessity be publicly and legally silenced.*

We shall have explanations to make on the alleged opening of this business by the ambassador, the Bishop of Tarbes. But that reasons of State were the first and predominant motive for the hostile attitude assumed by Henry towards Catharine, we cannot admit.

Even before the embassy of the Bishop of Tarbes, Henry had for two or three years been enamoured of Anne Boleyn, had consulted the doctors of canon law on the validity of his marriage, and he then only sought theological reasons drawn from divine law, in order to justify his desire that it should be annulled.

* Froude, vol. i, p. 114.

We can only say, with Bossuet, that he called his conscience to the aid of his passion.*

One excuse made for Henry VIII. is that he was misled by a delusion, and acted honestly; but in truth a person professing to act from disinterested motives, when only obeying personal feeling, soon deceives himself.

Such considerations would seem to justify a great many criminals who manage to seduce themselves by ingenious sophisms. Henry VIII. thought himself great in theology. Could he have spent eighteen years without opening his eyes to the "state of sin" in which he would have lived with his sister-in-law as his wife? Had he not been informed by the opposition of the Archbishop of Canterbury that there was a theological question to be examined? Why did he not proceed to this examination till he fell in love with Anne Boleyn? Then no doubt he worked hard to deceive himself; but, though he may have succeeded in creating a delusion at a later period, this first operation was not undertaken in good faith; and his want of openness and sincerity will often be displayed during the course of this affair.

Thus it is necessary to begin with inquiring as closely as possible into the irregularities of the private life of Henry VIII., to show how any serious thought of divorce was first conceived by him. Then we must show what Anne Boleyn was, how she was

* Histoire des variations.

brought up, and how she naturally found powerful supporters in her father and relations raised to high position in the State. The King of England yielded to influences of his own creating when he allowed himself to be led by the flatterers and courtiers around him. In this respect the surroundings of his life were no excuse for him. Besides, he consulted neither theology nor policy in setting forth upon the course he was determined to choose, he had no aim but the satisfaction of his passion; but he recruited theology and policy to assist his cause. This will be clearly seen in the latter part of this work.

CHAPTER II.

Was Henry VIII.'s Conduct Exemplary during the First Years of his Marriage?—Did the Real Piety that he professed preserve him from all Moral Failings?—What is to be thought of the Business of Compton, lately made Public in the Diplomatic Correspondence of Louis Carroz?—Was not this Strange and Mysterious Adventure the real Origin of Henry VIII.'s Hatred for Buckingham?—The King's Connection with Elizabeth Blount—Recognition of his Natural Son the Duke of Richmond—Honours heaped upon the Young Duke even before he was out of his Childhood.

HISTORY has heretofore thought fit to assert that Henry VIII.'s conduct continued to be quite exemplary during the earlier years of his married life. No doubt there was at first an amount of mystery enveloping his conjugal infidelities. But besides the absence of any document, or even any injurious report about him in this respect, during this privileged period of conjugal life, the strongest presumptions seem to concur in leading to the belief in his exclusive affection for Catharine.

At the time of her marriage and coronation, the queen was in the full prime of her beauty, and, according to contemporaries, she was admired for a considerably longer time.

The best known of her portraits was painted by Holbein when she was about forty-eight. He has represented her countenance marked by suffering, and too early wrinkled, and eyes swelled by tears. But Sir John Russell, who had seen her when she was only thirty-two or thirty-three years old, a member of the privy council of Henry VIII., speaks with admiration of Catharine. He praises the charm of her eyes as large and expressive; he says that she was then not inferior in respect of beauty to what Anne Boleyn and Jane Seymour afterwards were, and indeed surpassed them.*

Thus Catharine certainly seems to have preserved, seven or eight years after marriage, attraction enough to secure a husband such as Henry VIII. And we must not forget that this prince was then not only in the practice of religious habits, but of real devotion.†

It is true that, in the fifteenth and sixteenth centuries, princes, and even religious ones, paid a scandalous deference to their passions. Ferdinand the Catholic and Charles V. had natural children. It would not, therefore, be surprising to find in the King of England another example of that

* Miss Strickland, vol. iv, p. 116.
† See above the portrait of Henry VIII., by a Venetian ambassador, at the end of the first part.

monstrous mixture of religion and moral failure.

As to the young king, who had shown his skill in divinity by his contest with Luther, and had deserved and obtained the title of Defender of the Faith, it would be reasonable to admit that the habit of logic in reasoning was not likely to have deserted him in the actions of private life; besides, it is certain that Catharine had not yet ceased to be attractive to him.

And yet the recently published diplomatic correspondence reveals to us an obscure intrigue that occurred in 1510 in the king's palace, and the name of Henry VIII. occurs as connected with it, and perhaps seriously compromised. Particulars are given in the Spanish ambassador's letter, written to his master. This adventure took place only a year after the marriage of Henry VIII. and Catharine.

"Two sisters of the Duke of Buckingham, both of them married women, live in the palace; one of them being a pet of the queen's, while the other, it is said, finds grace in Henry's sight. The king is often in this lady's room. Some people say this love affair is not the king's, but Compton's. Compton, it is whispered, carries on the thing for Henry; which is likely, as the king has shown much anger at the whole affair. The lady whom her highness likes, being anxious for her sister's sake, took counsel with the duke her brother, with her husband, and her sister's husband, as to what they ought to do. After some talk the duke stole privily to his sister's room to see her, and, while they were engaged in talking, Compton dropt in to see her. Buckingham was hot. High words and even threats were used; on hearing of which the king, incensed at this unseemly quarrel in his palace, rated the duke so fiercely that his blood was roused. 'I will not sleep beneath this roof another night,' cried Buckingham, bouncing from the room. The lady's husband then rushed in, and carried her to a convent sixty miles away. Next morning Henry, suspecting the sister near the queen of stirring up this mischief, turned her out of doors. Thus all the Staffords have been driven from court. Nor is the king content with emptying Catharine's closet. In his anger he declares that he is watched by spies, who lurk about his palace waiting on his steps, and seeking in his unguarded moments for a cause of tattle with the queen. He says the queen's favourite sets them on. But that he fears to raise so great a scandal, he would clear the house. Everyone can see that he is vexed with Catharine, and that Catharine is vexed with him. No one knows how it will end. This storm is at the height." *

The ambassador afterwards mentions that he had

---

* Dixon's Two Queens, 2nd ed., pp. 85, 86. From letter of Carroz to Almazan, May 29th, 1510. Carroz to Ferdinand, same date.

questioned the queen's confessor. He rather boasts of having made an offer to the priest that in such delicate circumstances he would gladly put his experience, as a man of the world, at the queen's service. Such a curious offer was very coolly received by Don Diego Hernandez. He answered that he knew nothing of the matter; never meddled in such intrigues, and had every reason to believe the whole was a tissue of stories and lies. Louis was both disconcerted and irritated by such an answer.

The Spanish ambassador also complained of the queen's want of confidence and her excessive reserve with him. It seems to us that she only did her duty in keeping to herself the secret of the storms of her married life.

We, however, believe in the truth of Louis Carroz's story, as it is an explanation of the commencement of Henry VIII.'s displeasure with the Duke of Buckingham. A few years after the scene with Compton, Buckingham was called before the star chamber for having defamed the king; this was in the month of May, 1519. In May, 1521, he was accused of high treason, and on the 17th of the same month condemned to death, and beheaded.

It is true that the king was not the only person whom he had displeased; he is said to have also incurred the enmity of Cardinal Wolsey, upon whom, according to public opinion, rested the blame of this criminal prosecution and sentence of death. We ourselves think it was chiefly due to Henry VIII. himself brooding secretly over his hatred, and becoming the more implacable.*

It would be difficult to believe that a hasty and rude joke of Buckingham's with the cardinal could have stirred up that statesman to murderous hatred.†

Especial pains must be taken to display the character of Wolsey, because he plays an important part in the matter of the divorce. Some say he was the son of a butcher at Ipswich, others of a small tradesman of that place.

He began by being almoner to Henry VIII., and then Dean of Lincoln. Henry VIII. was so charmed with his good manner, won over by the elegance and superiority of his mind, that in the short space of three or four years he appointed him in succession a member of the Privy Council, Archbishop of York, and Lord Chancellor of England. The pope also

* Henry VIII. had other grudges against Buckingham for taking away one of his servants, and willingly giving ear to prophecies promising the crown of England.

† One day the Duke of Buckingham was holding the basin for the king to wash, when it pleased the cardinal to put in his hands. The royal blood of the duke rose in indignation, and he flung the water in Wolsey's shoes, who, with a revengeful scowl, promised Buckingham 'that he would sit on his skirts.' The duke treated the threat as a joke, for he came to Court in a jerkin; and, being asked by the king the reason of this odd costume, replied that 'it was to prevent the cardinal from executing his threat, for if he wore no skirts they could not be sat upon.'"—Miss Strickland, vol. iv, p. 119.

loaded Wolsey with favours, gave him a cardinal's hat, and raised him to the dignity of legate of the Holy See.*

King Henry, taken up with pleasure, and putting entire confidence in Wolsey, not only left him the entire administration of justice, but the management of the foreign and domestic affairs of the realm. As a statesman, Wolsey showed he was quite equal to the task laid on him. Very industrious, he was soon master of the state of Europe and inner history of the Continental courts. There was no better calculator of political chances. He was ready for any event, to find a remedy if it were unfavourable, to take advantage if it were fortunate. He was enthusiastic for the greatness and glory of his country.

Wolsey's despatches are real models of style and composition; Richelieu and Mazarin were not his superiors in the sagacity and ability of their diplomatic instructions.

We are able to give a portrait of this great minister in the words of a contemporary; these are remarks of wonderful truth; it would be excellent if it was more complete.

"This cardinal is the person who rules both the king and the entire kingdom. On the ambassador's first arrival in England, he used to say to him, ' *His Majesty will do so and so.*' Subsequently, by degrees

* Legatine powers granted by the pope were renewed every two years.

he went on forgetting himself, and commenced saying, ' *We shall do so and so.*' At this present he has reached such a pitch that he says, ' *I shall do so and so.*'

" He is about forty-six years old, very handsome, learned, extremely eloquent, of vast ability, and indefatigable. He alone transacts the same business as that which occupies all the magistracies' offices and councils of Venice, both civil and criminal; and all state affairs, likewise, are managed by him, let their nature be what it may.

" He is pensive, and has the reputation of being extremely just; he favours the people exceedingly, and especially the poor, hearing their suits and seeking to dispatch them instantly; he also makes the lawyers plead gratis for all paupers.

" He is in very great repute—seven times more so than if he were pope. He has a very fine palace, where one traverses eight rooms before reaching his audience-chamber, and they are all hung with tapestry, which is changed once a week. He always has a sideboard of plate worth twenty-five thousand ducats, wherever he may be; and his silver is estimated at a hundred and fifty thousand ducats. In his own chamber there is always a cupboard with vessels to the amount of thirty thousand ducats, this being customary with the English nobility.

" He is supposed to be very rich indeed in money, plate, and household stuff.

"The Archbishopric of York yields him about fourteen thousand ducats; the Bishopric of Bath eight thousand. One third of the fees derived from the great seal are his; the other two are divided between the king and the chancellor. The cardinal's share amounts to about five thousand ducats. By the new year's gifts which he receives in like manner as the king he makes some fifteen thousand ducats.

"Bath is that see which belonged to Cardinal Adrian, for whom, when the signory desired the ambassador to intercede, Cardinal Wolsey was so incensed that he would not hear of any terms, but became pacified at last, through the exertions of the ambassador; and whereas at the commencement he used to lavish all possible abuse on Venice, he now extols her to the skies, lauding the extreme justice of the signory, and says that thereby, and from merely observing the good order maintained in her towns, a wayfarer arriving in them would at once become aware that he must be in the Venetian territories, even if he knew not exactly where he was."*

The descriptions of the Venetian ambassadors are quite free from disparaging expressions—indeed, an excess of good-will may often be observed in them. They omit to mention the faults of statesmen, after having displayed their great qualities.

Thus there would be great gaps in the portrait of Wolsey. There was no mention of his venality,

* Four Years at the Court of Henry VIII., p. 314.

moral failings, and the boundless ambition which made him even aspire to the pope's triple crown. It is well known that Charles V. had promised to use his influence with the cardinals, but that he broke his promise, and that afterwards the policy of England became hostile to the emperor.

This partly explains the share which Wolsey consented to take in the matter of the divorce, and the slight interest he showed in Catharine of Aragon.

CHAPTER III.

Henry VIII.'s Love-affair with Elizabeth Blount—Almost Royal Homage paid to her Son, the Young Duke of Richmond—Increasing Coolness of the King to Catharine.

IF there is some doubt about the intrigue just described, there can be none on the nature of the relations of Henry VIII. and Elizabeth Blount. He had a son by her, recognised him, and loaded him with favours.

The king met this young person at Calais in the year 1513, and immediately conceived a great inclination for her. It seems he soon afterwards caused her to be named maid-of-honour to the queen.*

In the Christmas festivities of 1514, Elizabeth Blount is found to be present at Court, in a masked quadrille, in company with Mistress Carey, the king, the Duke of Suffolk, Sir Thomas Boleyn, and his son George. Mistress Blount danced and sang beauti-

* She is found borne on the Court account-books for a pension of one hundred pounds in the middle of the year 1513. Doctor Brewer therefore draws the inference that she then became one of the queen's household.—Introduction, vol. iv, p. cxliv, et seq.

fully; she had every talent for insuring success in the world, and made use of them to gain the king's heart.

Henry VIII. afterwards gave her a house in the county of Sussex; he often visited her when she lived in that retired spot. She there became the mother, in 1519, of a son, who was created Duke of Richmond six years afterwards. In 1522 or 1523 she married one of Wolsey's principal officers, named Gilbert Talboys, who was attached to the king's household.

By Act of Parliament, in the fourteenth year of his reign, Henry assigned to Elizabeth Talboys, shortly after the marriage, either in consideration of the son she had borne to him, or in recompense of the military services of her father, considerable sums of money, with the enjoyment for life of several manors situated in the counties of Lincoln and York.* In the autumn of 1524 Gilbert was knighted, and next year became sheriff of Lincolnshire.

The king's connection with Elizabeth Blount was long enveloped in mystery, and during the earlier years, if the queen knew it, she probably did not suspect that it might have serious consequences. But matters looked different when Henry thought he ought to recognise Elizabeth Blount's son as his own. About this time Tunstal wrote to the king: "The emperor himself told us that his highness

* See chapter xxiv of the Statute 14th of Henry VIII.

had only one living child by Catharine, the Princess Mary, and had no hope of any more posterity."

This is the explanation of the importance that Henry thought fit to give to the recognition of the little Duke of Richmond. The ceremony was performed on the 16th of June, 1525, with splendour absolutely royal. Cardinal Wolsey, and the principal lords of the kingdom, both spiritual and temporal, led the procession. The central figure was the fair young child, seemingly intended for an exalted and mysterious destiny.

He was conducted from the long gallery of the Bridewell to the king's chamber, where Henry VIII. received him in great state. "The young lord kneeled to the king in the dress of an earl; his majesty ordered him to rise; the king then received the patent from Garter, and gave it to Sir Thomas More, who read it aloud. On coming to the words, '*Gladii cincturum*,' the young lord kneeled down, and the king put the girdle about his neck, the sword hanging bendwise over his breast."* A month afterwards, the king added to all these dignities that of Lord Admiral of England, and afterwards made him large grants of land to support his dignity. His household was placed on a grand footing, and the magnificence of his establishment was the more evident by contrast with the parsimonious treatment of the Princess Mary, Henry VIII.'s

* Brewer, Calendar, vol. iv, part i, p. 639.

legitimate daughter, the recognised princess, and three years older than her little brother. The same deed that created the boy Duke of Richmond gave him precedence over all the English nobility, and over the princess, his sister, herself.

This last favour was too significant; it must have been a severe wound to a mother like Catharine, jealous for the preservation of her daughter's rights to the crown. But it is said that the queen only mentioned her resentment to three Spanish ladies of her household. These ladies had sympathised with her grief, they were accused of having aroused and kept up her resentment, and the king instantly dismissed them from the Court. It was a harsh and cruel proceeding, says the Venetian ambassador, who mentions the fact, but the queen was obliged to submit patiently.

From this day forwards, indeed, the unfortunate queen was obliged to exert a great deal of patience in bearing with such public insult. She had to expect espionage and tyranny in all the actions of her private life. She found herself isolated, and without either refuge or help. Henry VIII. was separating from her with ill-concealed aversion; her most innocent affections were suspected; all her power of love was concentrated on her daughter Mary, who certainly gave her every reason for maternal affection that she could desire, and all the satisfaction that her pride could wish. But she found, with undefined apprehension, that the future lot of this cherished daughter, destined to be Queen of England, was secretly threatened, and that she had everything to fear from the king.

It was then, in her state of desertion, that she remembered her nephew, Charles V., and wrote to him a short but affecting letter, to commend herself to his favour. This is the text of the letter that has come down to us:—

"MOST HIGH AND POWERFUL LORD,

"I cannot imagine what may be the cause of your highness having been so angry, and having so forgotten me, that for upwards of two years I have had no letters (from Spain), and yet I am sure I deserve not this treatment, for such are my affection and readiness for your highness's service, that I deserve a better reward."*

In 1510, when Catharine thought she perceived the first infidelity of her spouse, she was still energetic enough and had sufficient vigour to make a domestic scene; now she seems to sink under the weight of infirmities and mental suffering. She has not strength enough left to complain to her husband, nor to disclose her griefs. Her attitude is quite passive. When she can no longer possibly avoid a

* Gayangos, Spanish Calendar, vol. iii, pt. i, pp. 1018, 1019. Perhaps Charles V. had sent a message through his ambassador that he was annoyed at having no news of her for a long time.

knowledge of the scandalous conduct of Henry VIII. her prostration is so great that she can only groan in silence. Threats of a divorce alone were sufficient to rouse her, and make her show herself grand, dignified, and haughty.

CHAPTER IV.

Picture of the Court of England by Erasmus during the Youth of Henry VIII.—Origin and Social Position of the Boleyns—Their Morality and that of their Society—Anne Boleyn at the Court of France—Her Sister Mary Mistress of Henry VIII.—Anne recalled to England—Her Portrait—Her Success at Henry's Court—Plots contrived against Catharine by Anne Boleyn and her Family.

AT the beginning of the reign of Henry VIII., Erasmus wrote to his friend Ulrich von Hutten, describing the Court of that prince, saying that nowhere could be found so pure and modest a Court; the king choosing his intimate friends among men of learning and strict morality; preferring their society to that of younger men immersed in luxury, and like women, or to that of collared Midases,* or of proud and hypocritical officers, some suggesting foolish pleasures, others stirring up tyranny, others again inciting to the imposition of entirely new charges upon the people.†

* Is this in allusion to Dudley and Empson? (Ed.)
† Vix autem reperies ullam aulam tam modestam, et seq. See Far-

Some years afterwards the men of learning and strict morality were no longer in favour, but exactly the young men wrapped in luxury and inclined to give evil counsel. Erasmus' flattering picture seemed to have turned into the bitterest irony.

However, even at the time when this unhappy change was taking place, there was nothing to lead to the supposition that the new influences which prevailed at Court could induce Henry VIII. to dismiss Catharine from the throne, and replace her by another woman. This unworthy action was destined to be accomplished by the ascendancy of a fresh rival, taken from the ranks of the English gentry, but not from the highest nobility. This rival has a mournful notoriety, and was, as is well known, the young and attractive Anne Boleyn.

The Boleyns, without having been illustrious, belonged to a noble and ancient family. The first member who had been at all distinguished was Godfrey Boleyn, great-grandfather of the too famous Lady Anne and her sister Mary; he was a merchant, and Mayor of London in 1457.* His son, William Boleyn, gave up trade, went to court, and was made

rago Nova Epistolarum Erasmi, Bâle, 1519, p. 334. There is no date to the letter, it may be of 1510, or two or three years afterwards.

*Dreux du Radier tells us that this family goes back to the fourteenth century, and was originally French. He mentions a deed of 1344, in which a certain Walter Boleyn is styled a vassal of Baldwin, Duke of Avesnes, near Péronne. Memoires historiques et critiques et anecdotes sur les reines et régentes de France, vol. iv, p. 219; ed. de 1776.

a Knight of the Bath (?) by Richard III.; he married Margaret Butler, daughter of the last Irish Earl of Ormond, and joint heiress of a portion of his property. Lastly Sir Thomas Boleyn, son of William, attended Henry VII. in his expedition against the rebels in Cornwall, and made a marriage that connected him with the highest nobility of Great Britain; he married Elizabeth, daughter of the Earl of Surrey, afterwards Duke of Norfolk. Sir Thomas Boleyn and his son George were in good odour at the court of Henry VIII., and belonged to the constellation of his favourites, brilliant stars, but not very respectable. An idea may be formed of the morals of these intimate friends of the king by the following portraits drawn by Doctor Brewer from documents he has himself brought to light. The chief of these favourites were Sir William Compton, Sir Francis Bryant,* Sir Henry Norris, Sir Thomas Boleyn, and George Boleyn. To these should be added the Duke of Suffolk, who was only remarkable for his strength and stature, and the Duke of Norfolk, a small, spare man of dark complexion, cruel lips, and a temper more cruel than his smile.

Sir Thomas Boleyn had been raised to the peerage in 1525 by the title of Lord Rochford. He was the father of Anne Boleyn; the Duke of Norfolk was her uncle, George Boleyn was her brother, Norris her relative and admirer, Compton an intimate friend;

* Brewer, Sir Gilbert Pickering.

with them Henry passed the day in hunting and gambling, often losing great sums of money.

There was not one of these young noblemen who professed the smallest respect for the sanctity of marriage. Thus Suffolk had been betrothed to a young lady of good family, and had married another, but had dismissed her under the plea of the previous contract, and returned to the lady he had before rejected. Norfolk lived on most scandalous terms with his duchess.

Sir William Compton had been cited in the ecclesiastical court for living openly with a married woman. The conduct and ultimate fate of Norris and George Boleyn are too well known for it to be necessary to give the particulars.

Sir Francis Bryant was the chief of these gay companions; his business it was to provide for the king's amusement, he was the minister of his pleasures, and reputed to be the most dissolute of all the party of courtiers.*

It is evident that, under the influence of such companions, Henry VIII. would be little inclined to a serious life of business. His weariness and disgust were excessive when he saw a long file of despatches and papers laid out on his desk for signature. If he had ever seemed for a moment to desire to reign by

---

* Letters and Despatches, Brewer. Intro., vol. iv, p. ccxviii, ccxx. Norris and Boleyn perished on the scaffold. Bryant talked with revolting coarseness of the king's amours.

himself, he had very soon become weary of all kinds of work, and had discharged the cares of royalty upon Cardinal Wolsey, leaving him all the cares of Government.

Sir Thomas Boleyn's favour at court certainly cannot be explained by personal merit, and he was said to have been a husband wilfully blind; he was said to have made good use of his own interest and of the cleverness of a wife who shrank from no means of aggrandizing her family.* When the low morality of this pair is made known, there will be the less surprise that Sir Thomas Boleyn, in attendance upon the Princess Mary of England when she went to France, took with him his daughter Anne, still a child, and left her, after the death of Louis XII., at the court of Francis I., where there was great liberty in manners and morals. The young lady was attached to the service of Queen Claude, and brought up, as it were, on the knees of Francis' sister, the Duchess of Alençon,† who was afterwards

* It is said that Henry VIII., before he became king, was the favoured lover of Lady Boleyn, but that seems to us very unlikely. The Prince of Wales was then very young and strictly pious. Harpsfield believes in this criminal intimacy, and quotes Sir Thomas More's opinion in this matter. But Sir Thomas More's allusion expresses rather doubt than actual certainty. Harpsfield, pp. 236, 237. (This is probably Roman Catholic scandal.) (Ed.)

† There have been great disputes among the learned on the date of Anne Boleyn's birth, and what her age must have been when taken to France. Some say she was born in 1500 or 1501, others not till 1507, and therefore she was only seven when her father

Queen of Navarre, and held the sceptre of elegance and gallantry* in the court of Francis I.†

It is likely enough that Thomas Boleyn thought less of preserving his daughter's innocence and virtue than of enhancing her naturally brilliant qualities,

took her to France in 1514. This last opinion, which is that of the learned herald and antiquary Camden, seems of most weight. Miss Strickland, vol. iv, p. 159. (Lord Herbert says expressly that Anne Boleyn was twenty years old when she returned from France in 1521, so that she must have been born about 1501.) (Ed.)

* M. Armand Baschet says of this princess: "Homme d'Etat plutôt que femme, sans avoir rien perdu de ce privilége de grâce et de charme attaché à la condition de son sexe; tous les ambassadeurs l'ont admirée, tous l'ont montrée sage conseillère, esprit délicat et sûr, cœur dévoué, plus sérieusement lettrée encore que le roi François I., son glorieux frère. Lorsque Dandolo la vit, elle avait cinquante ans.

"Elle est de complexion délicate, dit-il, de sorte qu'elle ne promet pas d'avoir une longue existence: cependant, comme elle est fort réservée dans son mode de vivre, et, d'un naturel tres arrêté, il pourrait se faire qu'elle vécût longtemps. Je crois qu'elle est la personne la plus sage, non pas seulement de toutes les femmes de France, mais aussi de tous les hommes. Je n'en dirai pas davantage à cet égard. Je dois toutefois certifier que dans les affaires et les intérêts d'Etat, on ne peut écouter des discours plus sûrs que les siens. Dans la doctrine du christianisme, elle est si versée et si instruite, que bien peu de gens sauraient mieux en traiter. Je puis affirmer enfin qu'elle est très affectionnée à notre république."
—"La diplomatie vénitienne," par Armand Baschet, p. 412.

It is evident that if, when she was Duchess of Alençon, there was reason to regret the levities of youth, as Queen of Navarre, in riper years, more serious qualities resumed their sway. Confirmation of this may be found in a recent work: Marguerite d'Angoulême (sœur de François I.), Etude sur ses dernières années d'après son livre de dépenses, par M. le Comte H. de Laferrière-Percy. Paris, Aubry, 1862.

† Margaret was irreproachable in conduct. (Ed.)

and teaching her the art of pleasing kings and princes.

Mary Boleyn was a little older than her sister Anne, and, like her, had received a very careful education, but she had not gone to France to learn the science of refined coquetry and dexterous resistance.

So, before Anne Boleyn's return from France, Henry VIII. had paid his homage to her sister Mary, and succeeded in leading her astray.*

As for Anne, in 1521 Cardinal Wolsey wished to have her recalled to England, but for a very good motive, quite consonant with sound policy. Since the alliance of William Boleyn with the Irish Butlers, the two families had been at variance. The Boleyns had to obtain their share in the inheritance of the Earl of Ormond. The Butlers had upheld the cause of the Kings of England against the Irish with unshaken loyalty. Wolsey thought their old quarrels might be made up by the marriage of Anne Boleyn to Sir Piers Butler. And so, after receiving the king's permission, he wrote to Lord Surrey, the young lady's uncle, to sound the Earl of Ormond,

* Some deny this connection of the king with Anne Boleyn's sister. But, in two passages of his writings, Cardinal Pole blames Henry VIII. for his desire to marry the sister of his concubine. These are his words: "Anna didicerat, opinor, si nulla alia ex re, vel sororis suæ exemplo, quam cito te concubinarum tuarum satietas caperet. Soror ejus est, quam concubinæ loco apud te habuisti." Poli Epist. lvi et lvii.—"Ab eodem Pontifice magnâ vi contendebas, ut tibi liceret ducere uxorem ejus, quæ tua concubina fuisset." On the unity of the Church, by the same, imp. 1535.

Sir Piers' father, and see whether he would consent to the marriage. The earl seemed inclined to welcome this overture. The matter languished without any conclusion till near the end of 1521. Anne herself returned to England in 1522, before the end of the winter, no doubt because Wolsey had desired that her return should be hastened.*

After the sensation caused by her appearance at Court, she conceived a more ambitious project than had been devised for her.†

Everything concurred to securing young Lady Anne an excellent reception and brilliant position at the Court of Henry VIII. Her sister was the king's favourite. Her father and near relations stood on the steps of the throne. Her personal attraction was a still greater recommendation.

Holbein has painted several portraits of Lady Anne which are not exactly alike; the best known, which represents her in early youth, gives her an oval and regular face, fresh-looking, and with a kind of innocent ingenuousness. But those painted by this great master at later dates display more decided features. Her face is fuller, her look more languishing and tender. Her jet black hair is remarkable, contrasting so well with the diamonds placed in it

* State Papers, pp. 369, 372, 744. Letters and Papers, Brewer. Introduction, vol. iv, p. ccxxxviii.

† Some say that, though still very young, Anne Boleyn had been already the subject of scandal. But Sanders repeats from some pamphlets of the time that are not trustworthy.

on solemn feast days.* Her beautiful and expressive eyes are wanting in softness, and denote more cunning than great ability, more passion than real feeling. Her mouth and upper lip, thicker than the lower, bear an impress of sensuality that cannot be misunderstood.†

It is generally admitted that her features were less perfect than those of her sister Mary, but she was more attractive. She was especially pleasing in the graceful vivacity of her repartees, and the sweetness of her voice, that seemed to have some penetrating quality both in speaking and singing to the accompaniment of the lute. In dancing, as well as music, she was unrivalled at the court of Henry VIII. Besides, she spoke French admirably,‡ and that was an accomplishment much valued in England at that time. She had, however, some physical blemishes, such as a double nail on one of the fingers of her left hand, seeming like a sixth finger; and a rather large mole, shaped like a strawberry, on one side of her neck. The double nail seemed to her admirers to be a grace the more; and as for the strawberry, which might have been regarded as a slight de-

* Cranmer noticed this contrast on the day of Anne Boleyn's coronation.

† Froude, vol. i, p. 181, 2nd edition. This author cannot be suspected of prejudice against Anne Boleyn, so his opinion is valuable. We have very closely followed his words, with slight modification after other writers.

‡ But she wrote it very badly, and spelled detestably.

formity, she dexterously concealed it by wearing high collars, which were soon imitated in fashionable society in London. For, long before she ascended the throne, she had become the queen of fashion, and everybody dressed after her model.

Shortly after her return to England she was met in her father's garden, at Hever, by Henry VIII., who entered into conversation with her, and was delighted with her grace and beauty. When he returned to Westminster he told Wolsey that he had been conversing with a young lady who had the very soul of an angel, and seemed to him worthy to wear the matrimonial crown. Wolsey said it ought to be enough for her to be considered worthy of the king's admiration. And when Henry expressed his fear that this would not be sufficient for her, and that she would not be induced to accede to his wishes in that way, Wolsey replied that, when great princes choose to show their passion for a woman, and desire to induce her to share it, they have it in their power to use means that would soften hearts of steel.

It is to be supposed that the able and ambitious minister, having the government of the state in his hands, was not sorry to deter the king more and more from attention to public business by engaging him in another love affair; and it is said that he was the person who suggested that Anne should be attached to the Court as maid of honour to the queen.*

* Dixon's Two Queens, 2nd edition, vol. iv, p. 2. Doubts have

On the other side, what Wolsey did not know was that Anne Boleyn had brought back, from France, tendencies to Lutheranism, and what was called the "Reformed Religion." But she especially belonged to those Protestants who had principally sought in the new belief a pretext for the relaxation of morals, and a means of escape from the severe precepts of the Catholic religion.*

Among the noblemen who became her suitors, after her reception at Court, she specially distinguished Sir Thomas Wyatt and Henry, Earl of Surrey. These two poets celebrated her enthusiastically in their verses; their gallantry using the language of passion. Anne's free and bold tone, contrasting with the reserve and coldness then usual with the English, had a tendency to encourage any pretensions, and to multiply adorers. This worldly and intoxicating life would have been a difficult trial for a person more strictly brought up. But the education she had received, the examples and the lessons of her parents, were more likely to advance than retard

---

been raised as to whether Anne Boleyn was really a maid of honour, because her name is included in a list of persons employed about the Court, 1525, 1526. But this negative proof cannot overcome contemporary evidence. (Editor's Note.—Thus it stands in the French. Either it is a misprint, omitting "not," or she is not included among the maids of honour, but only among those persons employed at Court.)

* One-sided. The French Reformers were not Lutherans, and their morals were far stricter than those of the Court. (Ed.)

her course upon the dangerous slope to which she had been brought.

There is an anecdote related by George Wyatt, grandson of Thomas Wyatt, and a passionate apologist of Anne Boleyn. No doubt can be thrown upon it, as his grandfather must have told him. It displays the manœuvres and coquetries of which this young lady was capable when she first appeared at the English Court. No doubt such particulars seem unworthy of the gravity of history, but they throw a great light upon the manners of the time, and we may be excused for fully repeating so curious and characteristic a story.

"Among these (choice spirits) two were observed to be of principal mark; the one was Sir Thomas Wiat the elder, the other was the king himself. The knight, in the beginning, coming to behold the sudden appearance of this new beauty, came to be holden and surprised somewhat with the sight thereof. After much more with her witty and graceful speech, his ear also had him chained unto her; so as finally his heart seemed to say, *I could gladly yield to be tied for ever with the knot of her love*, as somewhere in his verses hath been thought his meaning was to express. She, on the other part, finding him to be then married, and in the knot to have been tied these ten years, rejected all his speech of love; but yet in such sort as whatsoever tended to regard of her honour she showed not to scorn, for the general favour and good-will she perceived all men to bear him." He then proceeds to tell how Sir Thomas on one occasion snatched from her a small jewel, "hanging by a lace out of her pocket," which he thrust into his bosom and refused to return; and that the king at the same time, after less honourable solicitations, fell to win her by treaty of marriage, "and in his talk took from her a ring, and that wore upon his little finger. . . . . Within a few days it happened that the king, sporting himself at bowls, had in his company . . . . the Duke of Suffolk, Sir F. Bryan, and Sir T. Wiat, himself being more than ordinarily pleasantly disposed, and in his game taking an occasion to affirm a cast to be his that plainly appeared to be otherwise. Those on the other side said, with his Grace's leave, they thought not; and yet still he, pointing with his finger, whereon he wore her ring, replied often it was his; and specially to the knight he said, 'Wiat, I tell thee it is mine,' smiling upon him withal. Sir Thomas, at length casting his eye upon the king's finger, perceived that the king meant the lady whose ring that was, which he well knew, and pausing a little, and finding the king bent to pleasure, after the words repeated again by the king, the knight replied, 'And, if it may like your Majesty to give me leave to measure it, I hope it will be mine,' and withal took from his neck the lace, whereat hung the tablet (miniature), and therewith stooped to measure the cast, which the king, espying, knew, and had seen her wear, and therewithal spurned away the bowl, and said, 'It may be so, but then I am deceived,' and so broke up the game."[*]

In consquence of the revelation Wyatt had made, Henry had a violent scene with Anne Boleyn; but she asserted that the gentleman had taken her trinket almost by force, that he had abused some old childish intimacies in order to put himself on a footing of familiarity with her, that she herself disapproved, and would find a remedy. At last she managed to appease the king in this matter, and made him more in love with her than ever. Only Wyatt was for some time banished from the Court.

About this time—that is to say, in 1523 or 1524— the young Lord Percy, son of the Earl of Northumberland, fell seriously in love with Anne Boleyn. It seems that he asked her hand, and, if there was not a regular betrothal, there was at least a mutual promise of marriage.[†] Wolsey was desired to inform the presumptuous lover that the king forbade this union, because he had other designs for the young

---

[*] Letters and Despatches, Brewer. Introduction, vol. iv, p. ccxli, quoted from Wyatt, Singer's edition, p. 426.

[†] That would be in 1524 or 1525, for Anne Boleyn, according to Cavendish, only returned to Court in 1524, after an absence of some length; but that could only be in 1525, for the marriage of Percy to Mary Talbot, arranged some time beforehand, took place in 1526, before the death of Percy's father, and the date of that has been discovered to be in the early part of 1527. See Cavendish, History of Wolsey, p. 180.

lady. As Percy showed himself resolved not to submit, Wolsey addressed himself to the earl, and he sent his son to live on his estates, and soon after made him marry Mary Talbot, daughter of the Earl of Salisbury.*

From this moment Henry VIII.'s passion was revealed to Wolsey by the commission that had been given him, which he so well performed. As for Anne Boleyn, she must have been able to perceive that the love manifested for her by the king was in earnest, and that she must avoid the example of her sister; for that if she made a dexterous and determined defence she might hope for a legitimate position and a share of the English throne.

Then, no doubt, the too clever young lady, in concert with her worthy father, set to work to win over divines to suggest scruples to Henry VIII. re-

* In Cromwell's papers there was found a mysterious letter, addressed by some unknown person to a Mr. Melton, also unknown, supposed to furnish proof that Lady Anne had been more seriously engaged with some other person than Lord Percy. It seems that Cromwell, who no doubt had the key of the puzzle, made use of this letter to invalidate the marriage of Anne and Henry VIII. This is the beginning, and it is very significant :—
" Mr. Melton,—This shall be to advertise you that Mistress Anne is changed from that she was at when we three were last together. Wherefore I pray you that ye be no devil's sakke, but, according to the truth, ever justify, as ye shall make answer before God, and do not suffer her in my absence to be married to any other man." If she could not honestly marry another man, that would give grounds for believing anything. Ellis, 3rd series, vol. ii, p. 131, and Froude, vol. i, p. 183, 2nd ed.

VOL. I. O

specting the validity of his marriage with Catharine of Aragon.* This was the first act in a real conspiracy in which Anne Boleyn herself played the principal part, and her accomplices were those unworthy courtiers, almost all related to her, whose manners we have described and remarked their pernicious influence.

Anne's ambition was not for the glory and greatness of power; she only saw the brilliant and frivolous side of the royal crown, without the power of conceiving the lofty aspirations that a higher though still culpable ambition might have proposed as its aim.

As to her relations, "it was not merely the cardinal whom they wished to pull down," says the Protestant Doctor Brewer, " but the whole hierarchy, of whose wealth and influence many were envious, and whose employment as statesmen and diplomatists they regarded with jealousy and partly disliked, from a better motive, as detrimental to the morals of the clergy, and destructive of their spiritual character and functions. The whole party who now gathered round Anne Boleyn were anti-clerical." †

Now we can understand the origin of the doubts of Henry VIII. on the possibility of conscientiously continuing to live with Catharine.

* This is attested by several contemporaries.
† Letters and Despatches, Brewer. Introduction, vol. iv, p. ccxlv.

CHAPTER V.

Wolsey and Longlands were the Originators of the King's Doubts and Scruples as to the Validity of his Marriage—Judicial Farce contrived between Wolsey and Henry VIII. concerning the Pretended Nullity of Marriage with Catharine of Aragon—This Farce remains a Secret and without Result—Capture and Sack of Rome by the Imperial Army—Henry VIII. and Francis I. try to renew and strengthen their Alliance against the Emperor—The first Notion of Divorce falsely attributed to the Bishop of Tarbes—Matrimonial and other Negotiations between France and England—Proposed Marriage of the Princess Mary to Francis I., or his Second Son, the Duke of Orleans—Difficulties are raised in the Clauses of the Treaty between Wolsey and the French Ambassador—Conclusions of the Treaty—Solemn Reception and Festivities at Greenwich Palace.

ACCORDING to Harpsfield, Archdeacon of Canterbury in Queen Mary's time, the two persons who were the first to excite serious doubts in Henry VIII.'s mind as to the validity of his marriage with Catharine, were his confessor Longlands,* afterwards

* Longlands, being only present at the second interview, could afterwards say, with some reason, that he had not been the first suggestor of divorce.

o 2

Bishop of Lincoln, and, before Longlands, Cardinal Wolsey himself.

Harpsfield, living while these historical events were in progress, asserts that the king was quite astonished the first time that Wolsey mentioned the matter from the theological point of view, and seemed assured of the success of the suit of nullity, if it were regularly commenced and prosecuted. Having at first remained silent, Henry VIII. at last answered him, "Take heed, I beseech you, reverend father, and well consider what a great and weighty enterprise you now take in hand,"* and then spoke of his wife in terms of the highest respect. He said that his marriage had been approved by the most learned doctors and most strict bishops of the kingdom of England and France, and, lastly, confirmed by the pope's authority, and that she had never consummated her marriage with Prince Arthur.

Some days afterwards Wolsey returned to the charge, this time bringing Doctor Longlands to help him, and he managed to make a great impression on the king's mind, and to persuade him that the question of the validity of his marriage ought to be legally examined, both at common law and equity.

These facts are attested by two other contemporaries, Polydore Virgil † and Tyndal;‡ their version agrees perfectly with that of Harpsfield. We are

---
* Harpsfield, p. 176. † See his Ecclesiastical History.
‡ Tyndal's Practice of Prelates, p. 320; published in 1530.

much inclined to accept this account as true,* though we do not believe that Henry VIII. was sincere with his own ministers; he affected a surprise that he did not feel, and made objections which were no doubt very weighty, but which he quite expected to see refuted by the complaisant and dexterous cardinal. However that may be, it is impossible to doubt that Wolsey at first showed himself favourable to the notion of a divorce, in the hope of seeing Henry VIII. marry a French princess. As a statesman, he saw a double gain in such a marriage, both as cementing a close alliance with Francis I., and as embroiling England with the emperor, Charles V., on whom he wished to be revenged. As a divine, he asserted that Catharine could not contract a valid marriage with her brother-in-law, Henry VIII., whether or not the first marriage had been consummated, and that there had been a voiding impediment to this marriage, wrongfully accepted as complete, by public opinion. That is what he called *impedimentum publicæ honestatis*.† But

* The work quoted is entitled "Treatise on the Pretended Divorce between Henry VIII. and Catharine of Aragon," by Nicholas Harpsfield, LL.D., Archdeacon of Canterbury. It was printed early in 1878 in London, at the cost of the Camden Society, by a learned member of the University of Oxford named Nicholas Pocock, and taken from a very small number of copies. Professor Pocock collated four manuscripts of the time preserved in the British Museum, and notes and an index to Harpsfield's work. The book is 344 pages.

† See a letter of Wolsey, July 27, 1527, no doubt only repeating an opinion already expressed. See also Letters and Despatches, Brewer. Introduction, vol. iv, pp. ccxlvii, viii. The

he did not believe that the king's passion for Anne Boleyn could end in marriage; he would not admit the possibility of such a mésalliance. He well knew the hostility of the Boleyn family, and that he would have everything to fear from the influence of Anne if ever she became Queen of England. And, while he admitted the possibility of the divorce, he did not believe that success would be so easily obtained as did the proud and imperious Henry VIII. No doubt he thought with the king—and in that he was mistaken—that Catharine, a lady so gentle, resigned, and pious, would make no great opposition to the divorce, if the ecclesiastical authority seemed inclined to pronounce it. But from that side—namely, from the English bishops and clergy—he foresaw much opposition, and expected still greater difficulty at the Court of Rome. No doubt very learned divines began to maintain, according to the Hebrew text of Deuteronomy, that divine law agreeing with natural law forbade any marriage between brother and sister-

learned author appears to have scarcely given the exact meaning of the letter, the words being, "by reason whereof there was no affinity contracted" (*i.e.*, the marriage being incomplete) "yet in that she was married *in facie ecclesiæ*, and contracted *per verba de præsenti*, there did arise *impedimentum publicæ honestatis* which is no less *impedimentum ad dirimendum matrimonium* than affinity." We take the meaning to be that the previously alleged defect of marriage with Arthur was not sufficient, because the marriage having taken place in the face of the church with both parties present, there did arise against the marriage to Henry an impediment of social propriety as effectual to make that second marriage void as affinity would have been. (Ed.)

in-law.* But these were isolated consultations that

* In the Latin letter of Doctor Richard Pace to Wakefield, professor of Hebrew at Oxford, quoted at the beginning of the third volume of L'Histoire du Divorce de Henri VIII., par Joachim Legrand. This letter was written at the beginning of the year 1526. According to the Abbé Legrand, Wakefield at first informed Pace that he appreciated his views, but afterwards went to see him, and told him that he desired that his highness himself should write what he wanted him to do, which side he was to advocate, and that, as the king might order, he, as professor of Hebrew, would give reasons that the English people could not contest. Joachim Legrand says he obtained this fact from the History of the University of Oxford, by Wood. See page 47, vol. i, of the Histoire du Divorce.

It is somewhat curious that in 1531, according to Chapuys, Charles V.'s ambassador, the opinion of a Jew was obtained. "The Jew sent for by the king arrived six days ago, notwithstanding all the efforts made by Mai to prevent his passage. I am told his opinion is not to impugn the queen's marriage, but that the king might take another wife, which advice is not to the king's taste, as it would be too infamous to attempt such a course. I believe his ground is that, though the king's marriage with the queen is legitimate, the issue must be reputed those of his brother, and it would be unreasonable that he should be precluded from having issue for himself. The Jewish law also permits him to take another wife, so that the said Jew, who says he has been some time ago baptized, under colour of charity, 'vouldroit semer telle dragee indaignee.'" Gairdner, Letters and Despatches, vol. v, p. 32. A month later, p. 59, he writes: "The Jew called hither, finding his first opinion not accepted, has forged another equally ill-founded, and says it is indeed lawful to marry a brother's widow, provided it is done with the will and intention to raise issue for the deceased brother; but without such intention the marriage is unlawful, and that God has reproved such unions by the mouth of Moses, so that issue shall not proceed of them, or shall not live long; and that it has been seen that the male children the king had of the queen scarcely lived at all, from which he inferred that the king had not the said intention, and consequently that the marriage is unlawful." (Ed.)

had no great influence on the opinion of the learned world.

According to Cavendish, Wolsey's secretary, when the king revealed to the cardinal his intention of obtaining a declaration of nullity of marriage at any cost, and of afterwards marrying Anne Boleyn, the great minister threw himself on his knees before his master, and remained there more than an hour, entreating him to do nothing hastily, to make up his mind to endure the delays of ecclesiastical forms, and to gain Catharine's consent gradually by gentle means.* In short, he did not conceal his strong opposition to any system of violence by which the king desired to carry the decision of the invalidity of his marriage.

Perhaps Henry VIII. thought he was making a half concession to Wolsey's ideas when he asked him to make essay of his high ecclesiastical jurisdiction by raising an inquiry into the validity of Catharine of Aragon's second marriage. This, then, is what took place, and has become known through fresh documents.

Early in the month of May, 1527, Wolsey made an appointment with the King of England that he might answer a complaint preferred against him in the Ecclesiastical Court in matter of divorce for his

* According to Cavendish, this took place towards the end of 1525. Life of Wolsey, p. 388. Some others place it after Wolsey's return from his mission to France.

cohabitation with his brother Arthur's wife for more than eighteen years. The cardinal, sitting on his right hand, explained the reason of the summons. "As legate of the Holy See, it was his duty to correct offences against the marriage law, and therefore, out of consideration for his office, and regard for his majesty's spiritual welfare, he had, in conjunction with the Archbishop of Canterbury, visited his majesty at Greenwich, and requested the king to appear on a certain day before him, that he might take cognisance of the cause. But as it was not fit that a subject should cite his sovereign to appear before him, he begged to hear from the king's own lips whether he consented to these proceedings, and was content that the archbishop should act as assessor. On receiving an answer in the affirmative, Wolsey proceeded to inform his majesty of the complaint made against him on account of his marriage with Catharine, since, though a dispensation had been granted him, yet, as the validity of it was questioned, the king ought to feel some scruples of conscience on the subject, and dread the vengeance of the Almighty, which, sooner or later, overtakes those who disobey him."*

The king made a short reply to Wolsey's address, recognizing the jurisdiction of the legate, and asking permission to be represented at future hearings by John Bell, his advocate or proctor. This was

* Letters and Despatches, Brewer. Introduction, vol. iv, p. cclvi.

allowed. After some formalities had been complied with, Wolsey adjourned the court for a fortnight. On the appointed day, Doctor Bell appeared before him, with a written plea of justification for the king, but admitting that the marriage might have been contracted, notwithstanding an impediment, voiding or not.

After several adjournments Wolman, the official promoter of the suit, produced his objections. Bell demanded a copy, and, as the case was very difficult of decision, the cardinal determined that the most learned theologians and civilians should be summoned—among others, the Bishops of Rochester, Lincoln, and London—to give their opinions on the matter. There were no more writings, and the proceedings were never wound up. No doubt their inconsistency was observed, and absurdity recognized. Evidently, if it had been established that Wolsey, sitting in an inferior court, had entertained the matter of the divorce, he could not have been selected to determine it again in the legatine court.*

Hence the secrecy observed in these pretences of proceedings not hitherto mentioned in history. It has never been permitted anywhere that the judge of first instance should ever be judge of appeal.

Information had just been received of the capture of Rome by the Constable de Bourbon, and the disgraceful sack of that city by an army chiefly

* Letters and Despatches, Brewer. Introduction, vol. iv, p. cclvii.

composed of Lutheran lansquenets. Such ravages, profanations, and ruin had not been seen at Rome since the time of Alaric and Genseric.* The pope had, with great difficulty, taken refuge in the Castle of Saint Angelo, and escaped the first massacre there. He was besieged, blockaded, and kept in close confinement. It must be allowed that Charles V. lost no time in disavowing the capture and sack of Rome, and blamed the excesses that he was unable to foresee, but might have prevented. He had immediately sent a commission to Lannoy, viceroy of Naples, to turn the undisciplined soldiery out of Rome, and stop their bloody orgies, and De Lannoy had been unable to accomplish this difficult task, only performed afterwards by the Marquis of Monçada,† with the help of the Prince of Orange.

The pope's captivity seemed to keep all church

* It is said that Clement might have prevented the horrors of this siege, if he had given Charles V. a sum of money he wanted to pay the arrears due to the lansquenets, and that his refusal was by the advice of the English ambassadors. M. Audin says the English envoys were commissioned to stir up Clement to try an unequal contest, and, if he was worsted, to buy his favour in the divorce suit with the offer of an armed intervention in favour of the Holy See. This supposition of M. Audin's appears to us to be very rash. No doubt Henry VIII. would not have recoiled from any means to obtain success, but this means would have been very ill-chosen. It ran a risk of throwing the pope into the hands and under the influence of the emperor; there was a close and certain danger. As to the delivery of the Sovereign Pontiff by England, there would have been immense difficulties in the way of it. Histoire de Henri VIII., vol. i, p. 414.

† Lannoy had died, having provisionally appointed him viceroy.

business in suspense. A pope who is not free cannot make valid decrees in matters of faith. But perhaps he might have been able to delegate his juridical authority to Wolsey, or the English bishops, and this calamity, while it struck all Christians with dismay, might have been taken advantage of for the business of the divorce. Certainly Henry VIII. caused offers of assistance to be made to Clement VII., and even sent him some pecuniary aid, hoping thus to dispose the pope in his favour.

The Kings of France and England also proposed to make an alliance against Charles V., and cement their union by family connection. Before the end of the winter, 1527, Henry VIII. offered Francis I. the hand of Princess Mary, then aged at most eleven years. No doubt he was not ignorant that the King of France was, by the treaty of Madrid, engaged to marry Eleanor of Austria, the emperor's sister; but it was consonant with his aims to multiply the causes of rupture between France and Spain. At the beginning of the spring of this same year Francis I. sent, as ambassadors to London, M. de Grammont, Bishop of Tarbes, and the Vicomte de Turenne, to request that the marriage with the Princess Mary should be celebrated immediately, though she was so young. Henry VIII. absolutely refused. Then it was arranged that, if not the king himself, the Princess Mary should at least marry the Duke of Orleans, his second son.

On the authority of Lord Herbert* it is alleged that the Bishop of Tarbes had conceived some doubts as to the legitimacy of the Princess Mary; that he had communicated to Henry VIII. his religious scruples as to the validity of his marriage to Catharine of Aragon, insinuating to that prince that, if he were free, he might himself very well marry a princess of France; that this would create as strong a bond of union between the two crowns as the marriage already projected. Some say that Henry had, previously, not put forward his scruples about the continuance of married life with a woman whom he was forbidden to marry by divine law.

Now we have given proofs that, in the spring of 1527, the question of divorce was not a novelty to the King of England. In London the Bishop of Tarbes must have learnt that this question had already been mooted and discussed. But it is quite inadmissible to suppose that a real ambassador could have substituted his own ideas for the formal instructions he had received; and certainly, if he had supposed that Mary of England could be considered as the illegitimate daughter of Henry VIII., he would not have signed the treaty of April 20th, 1527, without reference to his Court, with the stipulation that the princess should marry the King of France, or Louis, Duke of Orleans.

* Sanders relied on Lord Herbert for this. See L'Histoire du Divorce, par Joachim Legrand, vol. i, pp. 14, 15.

It is to be observed that in the diplomatic correspondence preserved in the archives of France there is not the slightest trace to be found of any hesitation concerning the legitimacy of the Princess Mary. Nor can there be found any vestige of the opinion said to be expressed by the Bishop of Tarbes on the invalidity of the marriage of Catharine of Aragon.*

If the king himself had opened the question in a private interview, and confided his doubts upon the point of his marriage, the ambassador's reply would not have had the authority of a theological consultation. When the King of England afterwards appealed to the authority of the Bishop of Tarbes, he must have made a wrong use of the kind of conversation that only grazes a question of the greatest importance, when a kind of assent, given for the sake of politeness or diplomatic acquiescence, to a powerful person not lightly to be offended or crossed, ought not to be considered of great weight.†

After a secret interview with the king, the Bishop of Tarbes and the Vicomte de Turenne were invited to dine at Greenwich. After dinner Henry VIII.

* See the evidence of Joachim Legrand, who was a diplomatist himself, and searched the archives of the Court of France with great care. Histoire du Divorce, vol. i, p. 49 and seq.

† The proof that there was no serious conversation on this matter between the bishop and the king, arises from what passed afterwards. The bishop and his colleague in the embassy, M. de Turenne, continued their request for the hand of Mary, either for King Francis or his second son, the Duke of Orleans, without any appearance of doubt as to the legitimacy of the princess.

himself led the two ambassadors to the queen's chamber; the Bishop of Tarbes talked a great deal to him of the intimate relations that he hoped to see established between the King of England and the King of France. The queen answered,

"You talk to me of the peace to be so firmly cemented between the two kings. It is no doubt very desirable. But why do you say nothing of the general peace that ought to prevail all over Europe?"

The prelate clearly understood that the queen thought of a peace that would include Charles V. But fearing to say something indiscreet, that might be displeasing to Henry VIII., he contented himself with answering that it was not the object of their visit; then he turned to the king, who smiled, and said to her that they were referring to the marriage of her daughter, the princess. Then the ambassadors asked the queen whether she approved of this marriage. She said that she gave her consent, and added that the interests of the two kings no doubt would not be found to be in opposition to the peace and well-being of the rest of Christendom. She even went so far as to insinuate that this alliance ought not to disturb the good understanding existing between the king and his nephew, when the ambassadors explained, perhaps somewhat abruptly, that the two powerful monarchs who had just made an alliance would be able to dictate their own terms. Henry VIII. added that he would do all he could for

France, and exhort the emperor to treat his two young captives with generosity, meaning the two sons of Francis I., kept as hostages in Spain by Charles V.

When alone with the ambassadors, Henry told them he would not give the Princess Mary in marriage till she was of age; and that, if she married the young Duke of Orleans, he should also wait till this young prince attained his majority, because it was necessary that both parties should be able to make a valid contract, so that a separation could not be demanded in their name, nor a divorce, founded on their being at the time of their union below the age of liberty and reason, according to legal presumption.*

This was strange language in Henry VIII.'s mouth.

Wolsey had some long conferences with two French diplomatic agents of inferior rank, and had obtained from them, with much difficulty, that a contribution of salt, and fifty thousand crowns annually, should be paid to the King and Queen of England during their lives. But Wolsey made it understood that, in case they desired an earlier date for a matrimonial alliance, without giving up the marriage of Mary Tudor to the Duke of Orleans at some future time, the hand of a French princess might be asked for the young Duke of Richmond. Since Margaret, the

* Letters and Despatches, Brewer. Introduction, vol. iv, p. cxci. and seq.

widow of D'Alençon had just married the King of Navarre, the only person who could be meant was Renée of France, sister-in-law of Francis I.

According to English authors, this unexpected request, this sort of change of front, considerably embarrassed the French diplomatists. But, according to the despatches of the French ambassadors, this proposal was not taken seriously, and they did not even appear to have heard it.* Lastly, the cardinal returned to his demand that, if Francis I. did not think he could himself marry the Princess Mary, she should become the wife of Louis of Orleans, who was still a prisoner in Spain, and that he should come and live with her at the English Court; Henry VIII. engaging that he would not give his daughter to any other person till the young prince was able to accept or refuse. Clearly no one thought of raising objections to the legitimacy of the Princess Mary. The matter was not even alluded to.

On the contrary, Henry was to pledge himself to do all in his power to procure the release of the children of France by pacific means, and not to declare war against the emperor unless all these efforts should fail. At all events, a perpetual alliance was made between the Kings of France and England and their successors on the above-mentioned terms.

* On ne fit pas seulement mine de l'écouter. See L'Histoire du Divorce de Henri VIII., by J. Legrand, vol. i, p. 46, and the third volume of authorities referred to.

As to Wolsey, who knew the pretended scruples of Henry VIII., he was not without fears for the future. However, he thought that, even if the Court of Rome should annul the marriage of the king and Catharine of Aragon, it would reserve the legitimacy of the children, issue of the marriage, as had often been done on the like occasions. Besides, he hoped the pope would feel himself under obligation to Henry VIII. for the efforts he made with Charles V., either for his deliverance from captivity in the castle of St. Angelo, or for some considerable relaxation.

Yet various obstacles arose to the conclusion of the treaty. There was the secret influence of the emperor's friends, who were numerous and powerful at the English Court, and opposed any closer alliance with France. Also the French ambassadors, when explaining or modifying the conditions that had been apparently accepted, insisted that the proposed marriage should take place with Francis I., and not with his son, and that, in consequence, the princess should be sent off sooner. To their great surprise, Wolsey told them that the king and his council had just learnt that Francis I. had made up his mind to marry Eleanor of Austria. Wolsey added that if this marriage took place Henry VIII. would refuse to make any engagement to go to war with the emperor.

These difficulties threatened to break off the negotiations. The Vicomte de Turenne wrote to the French Court: "We have to do in Wolsey with the most rascally beggar* in the world, and one who is wholly devoted to his master's interest." He was always on the alert, always ready to take an advantage. However, Wolsey consented to omit any clause relative to proposals of the marriage with Eleanor, and the project of alliance was resumed and eagerly pursued. Only, in addition to the previous conditions, it was stipulated that France should pay two million crowns to the Princess Mary on her marriage, to defray the cost of her enthronement.

Wolsey said he could not persuade the English to accept the French alliance, instead of that of the emperor, without a large pecuniary indemnity. And he also wished to procure money for his master, who, through his mother, had inherited the taste of the princes of the House of York for prodigality and display.

The treaty of peace having been settled between the 15th and 20th of April on the basis arranged by Wolsey, on the 23rd, Saint George's Day, Henry VIII. invited the ambassadors to a splendid banquet. After dinner he took them into the great hall of Greenwich Palace, where they found the Queen of England, the ex-Queen of France, widow of Louis XII., and the young Princess Mary, and the king desired them to talk to her in French, Latin, and

* Paillart.

Italian. She answered all the questions the ambassadors put to her with marvellous facility. She also played on the spinnet with great perfection. They were surprised at the young lady's great accomplishments when she was hardly twelve years old. But on this same occasion, when Henry VIII. at first only seemed taken up with showing off his daughter, he entered on a delicate matter with the ambassadors, namely, a journey to France, which he desired to make in person, in order to see Francis I., and finally ratify their treaties. The ambassadors answered that he might well leave that charge to the cardinal, whose zeal and ability he rightly estimated. The king sharply replied, "I have some things to communicate to your master of which Wolsey knows nothing." That confidence could have had nothing to do with peace or war, but the secret matter he had so much at heart.*

On the 30th of April, the treaty having been signed and sealed with the great seal, it was arranged that the heralds-of-arms of the two kings, Poyntz and Clarencieux, should be sent to Spain a little later, together with the Bishop of Tarbes, to carry the emperor a declaration of war and a challenge.

On the 4th of May there was a solemn audience at Greenwich, when the king appeared seated on his throne, beside him Cardinal Wolsey and his chief

* Correspondance de Dodieu. Letters and Despatches, Brewer. Introduction, vol. iv, pp. cciv, ccv.

ministers, the pope's ambassadors, and those of Venice. Behind the throne were ranged the Knights of the Garter, in their robes. The French ambassadors were introduced, and the Bishop of Tarbes, standing uncovered at the foot of the throne, addressed a Latin speech to the king, and he replied, complimenting the ambassadors and thanking God for the happy issue of the negotiations. Next day mass was said by the Bishop of London. At last it was all wound up with a splendid feast, when Wyatt and Rastall*figured as poets, and Hans Holbein was the painter. The day before "there was a joust, the challengers being four and the competitors sixteen, each of whom ran six courses." After a magnificent repast, at which the queen and princesses were present, there were dances in character that lasted all the evening. Towards midnight the king and the Vicomte de Turenne disappeared for a time, and returned with six other gentlemen disguised as Venetian noblemen, each having a lady for his partner. The king's was Anne Boleyn.

The Bishop of Tarbes did not fail to mention this fact in his diplomatic correspondence.†

* The poet Rastall had married the sister of Sir Thomas More. This feast cost Henry £8,000.

† See the third volume of L'Histoire du Divorce, par Joachim Legrand.

CHAPTER VI.

Perfidious plans of Cranmer—Catharine claims her Defence —Arrival in London of Mendoza, the Spanish Ambassador—He is long prevented from seeing the Queen in private—Wolsey goes to France—Mendoza takes advantage of it to communicate more easily with Catharine— Unpopularity of Wolsey, Popularity of the Queen— Catharine's Letter to Charles V.—Mendoza discovers and announces the preparations for the Divorce Suit—Consultation of Divines and their Evasive Answer—Cruel Conversation of the King with Catharine—Mendoza informs the Emperor of this Domestic Scene—Charles V. takes his Aunt's Side with Henry VIII., and at the same time uses influence with the Pope in her favour—Insidious Advice of Gardiner to Mendoza—Affectionate Letter of Charles V. to his aunt—Catharine endeavours to prepare her defence.

WE have seen that Catharine and her daughter continued to hold their proper position at Court, and that Henry VIII., in his external conduct, seemed to pay them great attention. But his hidden and ostensible policy did not correspond, and he was always working in darkness at what he called the secret business. His plan was to create a desert around Catharine and prevent her from having communication, first with her nephew, Charles V., then with all the churchmen, or any other persons who would be declared enemies of the divorce. By means of alternate threats and cajoleries, the silence and inertia of the unhappy queen might be protracted, and her submission obtained to the decision of the pope or his delegates, if she could first be persuaded to recognize the nullity of the bull of dispensation. The priest and theologian Cranmer,* who was the creature of the Boleyns, always more bold and hasty than Wolsey, advised that the suit against Catharine should be suddenly and quietly commenced, and she should be officially cited to appear before the ecclesiastical tribunal; at the same time, he wished that she should be induced to think that appearance or reply to this citation was a vain and useless formality. Then she would have been condemned by contumacy. After a certain delay, any judgment might have been given against her and her appeal not received.†

Thus Cranmer wished to carry the position by a judicial surprise and unjustifiable stratagem.

But all on a sudden Catharine, who had been thought to be intimidated, discouraged, and quite submissive, broke forth to the astonishment of all, and chiefly of the king and his accomplices. It is

* He was already chaplain to the Earl of Wiltshire.
† Cranmer's works, ii., p. 242. Letters and Despatches, Brewer Introduction, p. cclix.

not known how she had been informed of their machinations. She loudly demanded council, lay or ecclesiastic, who could teach her the judicial means of defending her cause and maintaining her rights.

This new incident disconcerted Henry's plans; he did not dare to take a step without making sure of the assistance of his new ally, the King of France, and therefore formed the design of sending Cardinal Wolsey to Francis I., as he already knew the five points of the business; besides, there was no cleverer diplomatist or more dexterous negotiator to be found. The excuse for this embassy would be the giving the finishing touch to the treaties of peace and war with France. Only neither Wolsey nor Henry VIII. suspected that the presence of one man in London would have been enough to enlighten Catharine and raise her courage. This man was Inigo de Mendoza, the new ambassador of Charles V. to the King of England.

It is true that Catharine had already turned her eyes towards Charles V. After two years of silence she had written an affecting letter to bring herself to his remembrance; she also had a little later the opportunity of sending information of her position to the emperor by a gentleman of her household,* named Philipp, a Spaniard, who had asked permis-

* Mendoza only mentions him in his letters of the month of August; perhaps he did not know that Philipp had started at the beginning of July.

sion to visit his sick father. The queen herself had not ventured to give this permission, but she had referred the decision to Henry VIII. The king thought perhaps that it was inexpedient to separate this faithful servant from Catharine, but when Wolsey was asked about it he wrote to the king that, as soon as Philipp had landed at Calais, he must, notwithstanding the safe conduct, be arrested in France on some alleged pretext, and be kept there indefinitely while his papers were searched. But, as soon as Philipp was provided with his permission and safe conduct, he proceeded to Spain by sea. Meanwhile Wolsey wrote to Ghinucci and Lee, the ambassadors at the imperial court, to inform them that reports of a divorce between the king and queen had prevailed in England, but that they should be attributed to Henry VIII.'s care to remove every kind of doubt as to the legitimacy of the Princess Mary from the minds of the French ambassadors, since her hand had been asked for Francis I. or his son. He insisted on their taking pains to forewarn the emperor of the odious calumnies that were in circulation on this matter.

The ambassadors themselves were well informed of the real intentions of the King of England, but they understood that they must deceive Charles V. and his Court, and no doubt they faithfully performed their mission.

But all these precautions failed. While the king,

Wolsey, and their agents multiplied artifices and tricks in order to thicken, both within and without the kingdom of England, the veils that concealed the true situation of the queen, Charles V. knew it perfectly, and was kept informed of all that passed by his new ambassador, Inigo de Mendoza.

This gentleman had been sent to England by the emperor in the middle of the year 1526, but, being detained in France by various obstacles, he was not able to land in England till towards the end of December of the same year. Soon after his arrival, he suspected, from the state of isolation in which the queen was kept, and the difficulties he encountered in approaching her, that she was fettered in all her movements, and even in the expression of her intentions and thoughts. He had secretly placed himself in communication with her, but she caused information to be sent him through his confessor that it was absolutely necessary to apply to Wolsey in order to see her, only Mendoza would have to give security that the only aim of his visit was to give the queen news of her friends in Spain. Wolsey, as an explanation of the reason of the continued refusal of this audience, alleged apprehension that the queen would speak of the marriage proposed between her daughter and a French prince, and send word to Charles V. to oppose it.

However, Mendoza went to see Wolsey, who had not yet gone to France; he told him that he had

been brought up by the care of Queen Isabella of
Castille ; that, while he was still very young, he had
been attached to the household, and even to the
person of the Princess Catharine, and so he had
many recollections to recall to that lady—could talk
with her of her parents and friends whom she had
left in her native land. The cardinal promised that
he should have an audience of her on the next Sunday. Mendoza was really admitted to see her and
converse with her at the time appointed, but the
cardinal was present at the interview, and there was
no chance of touching, however lightly, on the questions that were most interesting to the unhappy
queen. Besides, at the end of a few minutes, the
visit was abruptly terminated by the cardinal's saying
to the ambassador, "The king has many things to
tell you. Her highness will, perhaps, excuse us if
we take our leave. You shall have an audience at
another time."* His intention clearly was to prevent any confidential communication between Mendoza and the queen.

Being a Spaniard, as Mendoza observes in his
correspondence with Charles V., she keenly desired
the continuance of peace between her native and her
adopted country, and she might also have had some
vague suspicions that the proposed war against her
nephew had some connection with the meditated
attack upon herself. In this matter she was suffer-

* Letters and Despatches, Brewer. Introduction, vol. iv, p. cclxv.

ing under a twofold anxiety. Naturally, therefore, she must have been impatient to know the emperor's real feelings, both towards herself and King Henry VIII.

Wolsey left the English Court late in the spring to go to France. He was to go through Canterbury on his way to embark. Both the queen and Anne Boleyn viewed his departure with pleasure. The latter hoped that, when separated from this troublesome witness, Henry would be less guarded, and would not be so careful in the growing intimacy of his relations with her. The first plainly saw that she would be able to communicate more freely with Charles V.'s agents and Charles V. himself. Mendoza, on his side, perceived that he should not be closely watched by a king fully occupied with his pleasures and his attachment, whereas he had been very strictly observed by a careful and vigilant statesman, as perseveringly attentive to little things as he was used to be to important business. Even before Wolsey's departure, while the cardinal was engaged with the French envoys, Mendoza had obtained a private audience of the queen, and given her a letter from the emperor. She seemed to feel a pleasant surprise and great excitement on seeing his affectionate expressions, and could see that the insinuations made to her against the emperor were unfounded; she had been made to believe that he had forgotten her, and only looked upon her with cold indifference. No doubt these insinuations were due to Wolsey and to Henry himself.*

The queen seemed very much hurt at the way in which she was treated. Not only was she kept away from public business, but she was even left in ignorance of everything that could interest her personally. Mendoza told the queen that, to his great regret, he could not appeal to the name and authority of Charles V. in this matter, as it would be more injurious than useful to her; but he would endeavour to keep her informed of anything he knew, and not be sparing of his advice and assistance.

About the same time Mendoza wrote again to Charles V., to ask his instructions as to the conduct to be observed towards the queen. As to the question of peace or war the legate Wolsey was going so soon to France that he said he should not have time to receive proposals of alliance. He then laments that the queen's desire for peace with the empire is no longer an element in the councils of Henry VIII. Mendoza's correspondence attests that there was much irritation against the king, or rather his minister Wolsey, among the merchants of England, and especially the City of London. Men in trade desired to remain at peace with Flanders, as their chief mart; they, therefore, did not desire a breach between Henry VIII. and the emperor.

* Mendoza's letters of March 2nd and 18th, 1527. See Gayangos, Calendar, vol. iii, part ii, also pp. 185, 186.

A little later Mendoza goes so far as to say that there might be six or seven thousand men who would rise in the county of Cornwall, and at least forty thousand in the heart of England; but added that they must be led, and had no chief. Besides, there was no dependence to be placed upon the people. Nothing is more fickle than their favour or hatred. He says, elsewhere, that the Flemish workmen had been sent away, but the English workmen were not a bit more contented.

Thus the alliance with France was thoroughly unpopular, and Wolsey was execrated because he was ardently labouring to engage the King of England in it. There was also a grudge against him for being of the party against the queen, who was much beloved, and because he endeavoured to prejudice the mind of Henry VIII. against her.

The queen herself, when informed by Mendoza how favourable these popular sentiments were to her cause, and encouraged by him to renew her friendly intercourse with Charles V., wrote a letter to that prince almost the very day after the banquet given to the French ambassadors. She does not venture upon the question of the divorce; but her deep mental grief may be perceived.

"MOST HIGH AND POWERFUL LORD,—I hardly know how to confess the many obligations in which I stand towards your highness for the many favours conferred upon me. I hold it to be that your highness has chosen to show sorrow for my death, perceiving that neither my existence nor my services are such as to deserve being recalled to your memory. And yet, trusting in your highness's innate kindness and virtue, I will, with the help of God, employ my life in the furtherance of those objects which may be for your highness's service, though my abilities be scanty, and my powers small.

"As Francisco Poynes, gentleman, and esquire of the household of the king my lord, bearer of this letter, will inform your highness, I take this opportunity to write and request that he may be credited in whatever he may say in my name; the said Poynes being a person whom I entirely trust, and to whom I bear much goodwill, and am, besides, under great obligations on account of his many virtues.

"As I fear that my letter may be tedious to your highness, as written by one unexperienced *(lega.)* in these matters, I shall say no more here than beg and entreat your highness to have pity on so much bloodshed and perdition of souls, so costly, and redeemed at such a price; bearing in mind that this world is perishable and of short duration, and the next one eternal. There is urgent need that peace between Christian princes be concluded before God sends down his scourge, which cannot tarry if these quarrels and disagreements *(disconciertos)* continue between Christian princes.

"If, in the expression of these my sentiments, I have given the least offence, I beg your highness to pardon me; my ignorance alone is the cause. God, etc.

"Your good aunt,
"CATHARINE.*

"Grannuche (Greenwich), 10th of May."

It seems that Mendoza had advised her to send Poyntz to the emperor, and entrust to him by word of mouth what she did not venture to write. The queen alludes to an absurd and odious rumour current about her, namely, that she had plotted against the king's life.

In a letter written to the emperor a few days later Mendoza tells him that he has at last found out something about the proposed divorce. His letter contains most curious particulars.

"He hears, on reliable authority, that the legate, as the finishing stroke to all his iniquities† has been scheming to bring about the queen's divorce. She is so full of apprehension on this account that she

---

* Gayangos, Calendar, vol. iii, part ii, pp. 185, 186.

† He sabido por ciesto que este bueno del Legado por hechar el sello a todas sus maldades travaja por decasar á la Reyna, y ella esta tan medrosa que no ha osado hablar comigo. Han me certificado que está el Rey tan adelante en ello que a juntado alqunos obispos y letrados secretamenté, etc.

has not ventured to speak with him (Mendoza). It is added the king is so bent on this divorce that he has secretly assembled certain bishops and lawyers that they may sign a declaration to the effect that his marriage is null and void, on account of her having been his brother's wife. It is therefore to be feared that, either the pope will be induced by some false statement to side against the queen, or that the cardinal, in virtue of his legatine powers, may take some steps fatal to the said marriage. He (Mendoza) is perfectly aware, though the queen herself has not ventured, and does not venture, to speak to him on the subject, that all her hope rests, after God, on the emperor. Is convinced that the principal cause of all that she is made to suffer is that she identifies herself entirely with the emperor's interests. The cause is in itself so just that, independently even of the near relationship existing, the emperor might well espouse it. It would be very advisable if, with all possible secrecy, the pope were to be put on his guard in case any application should be made to Rome against this marriage; also that His Holiness should tie the legate's hands, and, by having the case referred entirely to himself, should prevent him from taking part in it, or appointing judges in this kingdom. Cannot learn what answer these bishops and lawyers have given the king on the subject of the divorce; and therefore thinks it advisable that, before the result of these consultations and meetings becomes public, the emperor should secretly inform his ambassador at Rome of the whole affair, that he may be on his guard. Believes that, if the affair should be proceeded with, it will soon be made public. Should the king see that he cannot succeed, he will not run the risk of any of the preliminary steps being known; but, should he insist on pursuing the course he has begun, some great popular disturbance must ensue, for the queen is much beloved in this kingdom, and the people are also greatly excited at the rumours of war. The queen desires perfect secrecy to be kept in this matter, at least for the present, so much so that the above wish of hers has been communicated by a third person, who pretended not to come from her, though he (Mendoza) suspects that he came with her consent."*

No doubt this letter was considerably earlier in date than the instructions which Wolsey had sent to the English ambassadors in Spain, desiring them to present the matter under an entirely false aspect. It must have been confirmed by Philipp's verbal account to the emperor, who thenceforth knew what to believe. There was no chance now of his being deceived by the cautious policy of Wolsey and Henry VIII.

In another letter, of a little later date,† Mendoza announces the immediate return of the Bishop of

* Gayangos, Calendar, vol. iii, part ii, pp. 193, 194.
† May 25th. Gayangos, Calendar, vol. iii, part ii, pp. 208, 209.

Tarbes to France, and also Wolsey's departure, and adds:—

"The suit against the Queen of England goes on secretly, but he (Mendoza) has been told that, if the legal terms are to be kept, the queen will neither be notified of it nor indicted for two or more months. Thinks there will be many more voices in her favour than against her, both because she is beloved here, as because the legate, who is suspected to be at the bottom of all this, is universally hated."

A contemporary writer[*] gives an account of what passed at the meeting mentioned by Mendoza, when he could not find out the conclusion, from the profound secrecy enjoined on all those present.

"My lord, being compelled to declare to his majesty this opinion and wisdom in the advancement of the king's desires, thought it not safe for him to wade too far alone, or to give rash judgment in so weighty a matter, but desired of the king to ask counsel of ancient and famous learning, both in the divine and civil laws. Now this being obtained, he, by his legation authority, lent out his commissions for the bishops of this realm, who not long after assembled all at Westminster, before my Lord Cardinal. And not only these prelates, but also the most learned men of both universities, and some from divers cathedral colleges in this realm, who were

[*] Cavendish, Life of Wolsey, chapter xv, p. 57.

thought sufficiently able to resolve this doubtful question.

"At this learned assembly was the king's case consulted of, debated, argued, and judged from day to day. But, in conclusion, when these ancient fathers of law and divinity parted, they were all of one judgment, and that contrary to the expectation of most men. And I heard some of the most famous and learned amongst them say the king's case was too obscure for any man, and the points were doubtful to have any resolution therein, and so at that time with a general consent departed, without any resolution or judgment.

"In this assembly of bishops and divers other learned men, it was thought very expedient that the king should send out his commissioners into all universities in Christendom, as well here in England as foreign regions, there to have this case argued substantially, and to bring with them from thence every definition of the same, under the scale of every university, and thus for this time were their determinations."*

It is evident that the bishops and members of the

---

* This shows that it was Wolsey who assembled the English bishops to give their advice on the divorce, that they declined to give an opinion on the king's marriage to Catharine, that they desired that other universities should be consulted, and that it was Wolsey, and not Warham, who convoked the bishops. Certainly, according to Lord Herbert, the latter assembled some divines at Lambeth, but not bishops. Legrand, vol. ii. Défense de Sandérus.

meeting were afraid of Henry's displeasure, in case they should express an opinion in favour of the validity of his marriage; therefore they had recourse to Pilate's expedient, and referred the case to judges of less authority than themselves. They only wanted to gain time in order to escape the responsibility which burdened their consciences.

It will afterwards be shown how the universities were consulted, what was the process, and what their replies.

A second meeting of doctors of theology alone, without bishops, took place afterwards, summoned by Warham, Archbishop of Canterbury. This has been wrongly confused with the former, and it seems to have been a little more favourable to the views of Henry VIII.* However, this conclusion still was that the case was sufficiently doubtful to be referred

Réfutation des deux premiers livres de L'Histoire de la Réformation, par Burnet, pp. 60, 61.

See the letters of the Bishop of Bayonne, of August 20th, 1528, and those of the months of October and May, when this prelate accuses himself of having been the author of most pernicious advice concerning the divorce. In the letter of August 20th, addressed to the Grand Master du Bellay, he says: "Pour vous en dire ma fantaisie, le roy en est si avant, qu'aultre que Dieu ne l'en saurait ôter." Anne had returned to Court; Wolsey complains to De Bellay that *terrible terms* have been used against him; the legate does not quite know how he stands. If this marriage takes place he will have difficulty in maintaining his credit. Legrand, vol. iii, p. 164. Preuves, p. 168.

* It was Lord Herbert who made this confusion, and after him Burnet. It is exposed by J. Legrand, Histoire du Divorce. Sanders' Defence, vol. ii, p. 61.

to the Court of Rome. However insufficient were the resolutions and decisions of the bishops and divines in their deliberations on the marriage of Henry VIII., they were thought to be weapons that could be used against the queen. Though Wolsey was always advising when at a distance, as well as near, to do nothing hastily, that all forms should be observed, and gentle means used rather than force, Henry VIII., perhaps pressed by Anne Boleyn, and unable to restrain his impatience, chose to come to an unreserved and open explanation with his unhappy wife. It is curious that this explanation took place almost the day after Wolsey's departure—that is to say, about the end of the month of June, 1527.

The king, having virtually separated from the queen from the date of the 20th or 22nd of June, gave her his reasons for this determination by revealing to her for the first time that they had both been in a state of mortal sin all the long years they had lived together. This was, he said, the opinion of many prelates and men learned in the canon law whom he had consulted; and therefore, as the continuance of such a life troubled, and even tortured, his conscience, he had taken the unalterable resolution of obtaining a separation from her *à mensâ et à thoro*, so she had only to name the place where she would take refuge.

We give Mendoza's account of this domestic scene in a letter written to the emperor July 13th, 1527.

"The queen, bursting into tears, and being too much agitated to reply, the king said to her, by way of consolation, that all should be done for the best (*todo se haria por mejor*), and begged her to keep secrecy upon what he had told her. This the king must have said, as it is generally believed, to inspire her with confidence, and prevent her seeking the redress she is entitled to; for so great is the attachment that the English bear to the queen that some demonstration (*escandulo*) would probably take place in her household (*apartamentos*). Not that the people of England are ignorant of the king's intentions, for the affair is as notorious as if it had been proclaimed by the public crier, but they cannot believe that he will ever carry so wicked a purpose into effect. However this may be, though people say that such an iniquity cannot be tolerated, he (Mendoza) attaches no faith to such popular asseverations, especially as they have no leader to guide them, and therefore, should this king carry out his design, and the suit now commenced go on, the people will most probably content themselves with grumbling *(con murmurar)*. The queen, having no one but the emperor to come to her aid, would, if she could, despatch a special messenger (to Spain), but these English are so suspicious at this time that no servant of hers would be allowed to sail. Besides, as at this point of the negotiations, and until the matters now pending between his majesty and this king be settled one way or another, such a step would by no means be advisable, he (Mendoza) has dissuaded the queen from sending a special messenger, giving her to understand that it was far better for her case that she should write a letter than despatch one of her own household." *

The queen had informed Mendoza that she wished that the pope would deprive Wolsey of his commission as legate. Mendoza vigorously supported this desire, and advised Charles V. to do all he could to procure the cardinal's disgrace at the Court of Rome. He wished to carry on open war against that statesman, detesting him cordially, and saying that it would be much better to have him for a declared enemy than a false friend, as he is now; and that, if the emperor could compass the fall of the minister, it would be a patent of popularity for his majesty in England.

Nevertheless, he strongly insists on the inconveniences that might arise if Charles V. and his ambassador seemed to interfere between Henry VIII. and his wife; he was afraid the king might be irritated to no advantage.

His language changes on this point, and his attitude is altered on the receipt of precise instructions from the emperor on the necessity of acting openly for the protection of his aunt. Charles V. thought the honour of his blood and of his race was concern-

* Gayangos, Calendar, vol. iii, part ii, p. 276.

ed, so he wrote a letter to the king, both moderate and firm, to claim for the queen the continuance of the respect due to her. Mendoza was to carry this letter to King Henry VIII., and proposed to make the communication with great circumspection and diplomatic precaution. "The morsel, however, shall be given to him in such disguise as to be as little repugnant as possible to his palate, though his conscience is so perverted that whatever is most for his good meets with the least favour."

Mendoza is quite afraid of the effect of Charles V.'s message to Henry VIII.

"But in truth the king is so swayed by his passions, and so determined to persevere in his error, that he is rather seeking the means of accomplishing his purpose than advice for abandoning it. Owing to which reason those who counsel him best he considers as his worst friends. But his majesty will act in this case as befits his rank and parentage, and, disregarding the inconvenience that may arise therefrom, will help with his authority and power wherever most wanted."*

It seems that, the ice having been broken between Catharine and Henry VIII. at their interview about the end of the month of June, her situation could not be made much worse. But it was the political good

* Letter of August 16th, 1527. Gayangos, Calendar, vol. iii, part ii, p. 326. The remonstrance must have been made, but there is no evidence to describe its effect upon Henry VIII.

understanding of the two monarchs that was very much threatened, and indeed the maintenance of peace. It was especially through this motive that Mendoza hoped to prevail over the King of England.

Charles V. also informed his ambassador that, as soon as he had got wind of the notion of divorce, he had sent a hint to the pope at Rome to put him on his guard against the intrigues of Henry VIII. Mendoza forwarded this information to the queen, deploring that she had not agents of her own at the Court of Rome, and that she could not correspond directly with a safe person, who could act in her favour with the pope. He recognized that the dangerous state of the roads in Italy greatly interrupted the regularity of communication in that country.

As to the business of the divorce in itself, Mendoza thought he had discovered that the persons who directed it were embarrassed, and were changing their plan of campaign; they did not confine themselves to maintaining that divine law absolutely forbids a marriage between brother and sister-in-law, but asserted that the dispensation granted by Julius II. was obtained upon false premises.

Upon this Dr. Gardiner,[*] who said he was greatly opposed to the divorce, and a strong partisan of the queen, came to see Mendoza, and tried to suggest to him that the existing pope could effectually remedy any defect in regularity of the original dis-

[*] He was Wolsey's man of confidence.

pensation, and confirm it by a fresh bull. The honest Mendoza believed in the sincerity of Gardiner, and did not suspect a trap. But he was too good a lawyer not to see that such an action would be an explicit recognition of a radical defect in the act of dispensation granted by Julius II., and that the queen would thus become involved in a fatal course. He therefore thought it bad advice, and persuaded the queen not to follow it.*

Snares were multiplying under the feet of the unfortunate queen. But it must have been a great consolation to her to receive the following encouraging and affectionate letter from Charles V.:—

"MADAME AND MY AUNT,

"Your letter by Francisco Phs (Philipps), bearer of this present, came duly to hand. I have perfectly well understood the verbal message he brought from you respecting the affair (of the divorce), and the reason why you sent him to me. After him came your own physician, Vitoria, with whom I had also a long conversation on the subject. You may well imagine the pain this intelligence caused me, and how much I felt for you. I cannot express it otherwise than by assuring you that, were my own mother concerned, I should not experience greater sorrow than in this, your case, for the love and affection which I profess to your serene

* See the same letter of August 16th, 1527, pp. 327, 328.

highness is certainly of the same kind as that of a son towards his parent.

"I have immediately set about taking the necessary steps for the remedy (of your case), and you may be certain that nothing shall be omitted on my part to help you in your present tribulation. But it seems to me that in the meantime your serene highness ought not to take this thing so much to heart as to let it impair your bodily health, for, if this is preserved, all other matters will be remedied, with God's help. I beg you to bear in mind this my recommendation, and I have no doubt that in this, as in other matters, your serene highness will act much better than I could counsel. As I do, however, presume that before the receipt of this, my letter, you will have heard my intentions through Don Inigo de Mendoza, I shall say no more here than to refer you to my letter to that ambassador, as well as to the message now conveyed by the above-mentioned Francisco, which is no doubt what your serene highness most wishes to know. Most earnestly entreating you to inform me as soon as possible of the course of this affair, that I may do all that is necessary for your protection, as well as of your health, I remain, &c.

"In the hand of your good nephew,

"CHARLES.*

"Palencia, the 27th of August."

---

* Gayangos, Calendar, vol. iii, part ii, p. 345.

Re-assured by such proofs of devotion and affection, feeling herself supported by Charles V. at a distance, and assisted by Mendoza at hand, Catharine thought she ought to appear both resigned and satisfied. On his side the king, though separated from her à *thoro*, saw her often, and treated her at least with apparent courtesy and kindness. He wished to delude the public and the queen herself, that he might pursue his intrigues and machinations unhindered. But Catharine, through Mendoza, learnt all the plots against her; she saw that Charles V. did not forget her, and did not cease to labour in her cause at the Court of Rome, and she sent him confidential messages as occasion served. During this time the king pursued and organised his attack, and the queen prepared and organised her defence. It was war continued under the guise of peace.

238

CHAPTER VII.

Cardinal Wolsey's Double Mission—His Splendid Train—
His Meeting with Archbishop Warham, and afterwards
Fisher, Bishop of Rochester—He works for the Divorce
and against Catharine—Wolsey's Prayer at the tomb of
Saint Thomas of Canterbury—Expedients proposed in
his Correspondence with Henry VIII.—Wolsey in France
—Charles V. seems to treat him gently—Wolsey at the
Court of Francis I.—The Hand of the Princess Mary is
promised to the Duke of Orleans—The other Clauses of
the Treaty of Alliance are also settled and signed—
Wolsey at last opens the Question of Divorce—But
Queen Louise of Savoy will not leave him any Hopes of
the Eventual Marriage of a Daughter of France with
Henry VIII.

A DOUBLE mission had been entrusted to Wolsey. By the first, official and ostensible, he was commissioned to explain and settle the clauses of the last treaty agreed upon in England; the other, semi-official and secret, lay in confidentially communicating to Francis I. his master's plans of divorce. Both on his journey through England, and during his stay in France, he had promised to inquire after the opinions of the clergy and the feelings of the people. Wolsey was also to inform himself of the best means of reaching the pope's ear, and to find out whether the imperialists, in whose power he was, had already extracted some promise from him, or even some decision in favour of Catharine. In that case, a protest would be laid against all the acts done by him during the siege of the castle of Saint Angelo, and during his captivity, because he had not been free. This would give him a chance of retracting in case of need. A suggestion might also be made to him to increase Cardinal Wolsey's powers of jurisdiction as his legate in England.

Anne Boleyn was not afraid of the great confidence reposed in Wolsey by Henry VIII.; she knew very well that, while the cardinal was promoting the divorce, he was going to France to work for interests that were not hers. But in his absence she reckoned on pleading her own cause freely and effectually. And, as she foresaw, all the efforts he made to advance the divorce would finally profit no one but herself.

Henry desired that Cardinal Wolsey, as his lieutenant and special representative, should on his mission be surrounded with all the state and marks of ceremony generally reserved for royalty. The cardinal is therefore unjustly accused of a desire to eclipse the most powerful monarchs in his pride.

Nine hundred horsemen composed his company. There were several lords, spiritual and temporal, among them Tunstall, Bishop of London. When he rode through the City, Wolsey was mounted on a mule with housings of crimson velvet and stirrups of brass gilt; before him were borne two crosses of massive silver, and two pillars or small columns of the same metal with a ball on the top, and between them the great seal of England. When he gave a banquet to the King of France, his gentlemen served him on the knee, hat in hand—a token of respect Francis I. himself did not exact. It is none the less true that all these honours showered on the son of the Ipswich butcher still more augmented the hatred directed at him; his rivals took advantage of it to mine the ground beneath his feet. The higher he rose, the nearer he drew to his fall. He had a presentiment of this, and felt he was surrounded by treacherous enemies, eager for his destruction.

The anxieties of this statesman, with his passionate and servile devotion to King Henry VIII., leak out in his correspondence with that prince. He begs him not to listen to calumnious insinuations, and to continue to his old servant the affection he had always condescended to extend to him.

He set forth quite determined to perform the delicate double mission entrusted to him with unimpeachable zeal. His first desire, on his journey, was to gain, or, at any rate, favourably prepossess, towards Henry's projects Warham, Archbishop of Canterbury, and Fisher, Bishop of Rochester.

The first night of his journey he lay at Sir John

Wiltshire's, and met Warham there. He himself, in his correspondence with Henry VIII., gives an account of his interview, saying,

" The first night I lodged at Sir John Wiltshire's house; where met me my Lord of Canterbury, with whom, after communication on your grace's secret matter, I showed him that the knowledge thereof is come to the queen's grace, and how displeasantly she taketh it, and what your highness hath done for the staying and pacification of her, by declaring to her that your grace hath nothing intended nor done, but only for the searching and trying out the truth upon occasion given by the doubt moved by the Bishop of Tarbes. And, noting his countenance, gesture, and manner, I perceive he is not much altered from his first fashion; expressly affirming that, however displeasantly the queen might take it, yet the truth and judgment of the law must have place." *

Wolsey afterwards went to meet the Bishop of Rochester. He was the most respected, the most revered member of the bench of English bishops. No Protestant authors have ever reproached him with anything worse than supposed excesses in personal mortification. He had the queen's entire confidence, and she had sometimes confessed to him. The importance to Henry VIII. and his abettors of

* Miss Strickland, vol. iv, p. 122, 1st edition, 1842. From State Papers and Letters, Brewer, vol. iv, p. cclxiv.

detaching such a man from Catharine's cause may be understood. Besides, his example and authority might have influenced Sir Thomas More and several others. Fisher was old and weak, not suspicious; an admirable and charitable fault. So he could not contend with equal arms in a discussion or diplomatic encounter against the clever and astute cardinal. Wolsey began, very dexterously, by talking to him of the sorrows of the papacy and the calamities of the church—" and what things were devised, as well in prayer and fasting as other good deeds, and at your grace's commandment, by me indicated for the same. After which communication, I asked him whether he had lately heard any tidings from the Court, and whether any man had been sent unto him from the queen's grace. He answered, how truth it is, that of late one was sent unto him from the queen's grace, who brought him a message only by mouth, without disclosure of any particularity. He made answer, likewise by mouth, that he was ready and prone to give unto her his counsel in anything that concerned or touched only unto herself; but in matters concerning your highness and her he would nothing do without knowledge of your pleasure and express commandment." The cardinal answered— "Ye may be plain and frank with me, like as I, for my part, will be with you."* He said that "the

* Brewer, Calendar. Introduction, vol. iv, p. cclxvi, ix. The

queen was of a suspicious character, and quick to take offence. That she had wrongfully supposed that the king wished to divorce her, and had entertained unjust intentions with regard to her; that the Bishop of Tarbes must be answered, who had asked the hand of the Princess Mary for a French prince. It was impossible to avoid an inquiry whether Catharine's marriage with her brother-in-law could be considered valid, although contracted contrary to divine right. Instead of filling the world with her complaints, the queen ought to have had confidence in the king's sincere attempts to discover the truth, and procure a decision from competent authorities in this difficulty. It was certain that this would all come to good, if the queen would act differently, and be confiding and submissive where she had sworn confidence and obedience. It seems as if she had suggested the idea that the cardinal legate was desirous of seeing the king prosecute the matter ! ! ! It was clear that the queen, by her ill-considered proceedings, was paralysing the king's kind intentions towards her, and might perhaps prejudice her daughter's legitimate claims."

Thus Wolsey transformed the innocent into the guilty, and the guilty into the innocent. He cast upon Catharine the responsibility of all the scandal

expression about Wolsey, severe and just as it is, is taken from the same.

which was beginning to arise. Fisher, having no doubts of Wolsey's sincerity, and believing his dexterously arranged version, declared himself as disapproving of Catharine's spirit of presumption and disobedience, and expressed an intention of blaming her for it. But this would have brought on explanations and betrayed everything.

"Howbeit, I have so persuaded him that he will nothing speak or do therein, or anything counsel her but as shall stand with your pleasure; for he saith, 'although she be queen of this realm, yet he knowledgeth you for his high sovereign lord and king; and will not, therefore, otherwise behave himself in all matters concerning or touching your person than as he shall be by your grace expressly commanded.'" *

Thus Wolsey contrived to alienate from the unhappy queen the only adviser on whose sincerity and honesty she could implicitly rely, the most worthy member of the English bench of bishops, who could be of the greatest use in guiding her steps, and giving her most precious consolation.

When concluding his conversation with Fisher, the cardinal slipped in some objections to the validity of the bull of dispensation granted by Julius II., but Fisher made no direct reply. In this scene Wolsey, too much excited by the success of his dexterous confidences, had perhaps overshot his mark, and

* Brewer, Calendar. Introduction, vol. iv, p. cclxix.

thus unintentionally had opened the eyes of his too trustful senior.

Amid these diplomatic artifices and inextricable snares, what could be the fate of Catharine? Attempts were made to isolate her completely; it seemed as if she must soon find herself without counsellors or friends, ignorant of the formalities of law, and not knowing what steps to take in vindication of her rights. She still had Mendoza; but even his rare opportunities of communication with her had to be involved in mystery, in order neither to compromise her nor himself.

Wolsey, on the day succeeding his conversation with Fisher, at once astute and craftily hostile to the queen, went, if we may believe it, to Canterbury, to the feast of Saint Thomas à Becket. He officiated there as cardinal, joining the procession in full dress.

By his order the monks of Christchurch chanted litanies commencing with these words, *Sancta Maria, ora pro papâ nostro Clemente.** The calamities of the church seemed to interest him to the highest pitch. He failed not to pray for the pope at the shrine of Saint Thomas. How was it that the devotion then paid to this distinguished saint did not lead him to reflection on the contrast? What an example of independence, noble frankness, and heroic resistance to the impious requisitions of tyrannical power ought not Wolsey to have drawn from his

* Cavendish, Life of Wolsey, p. 151.

meditations over the relics of this archbishop, confessor, and martyr! But it was not till much later, in the ruffled school of adversity, that he came to regret and disavow his base complaisance for a king whose passions and errors he should have combated from the first.

Then he went on his way, and soon reached Calais. In his correspondence with Henry, he always expressed a hope that, if the deliverance of Clement VII. from his captivity could be accomplished, the pope would make use of his liberty to settle the king's business agreeably; he thought that, if this captivity were indefinitely prolonged, the cardinals might be called together to meet in a place affording complete security, such as, for instance, Avignon; and then these princes of the church might decide in the pope's absence* on the king's secret matter, and perhaps he himself might be made president of this august assembly.

But the cardinal did not know that at this very time the emperor, at Mendoza's request, had already written to the pope to beg him to withdraw his legatine authority in England from Wolsey, and even take from him all cognisance and authority to judge in the divorce suit, because he entertained an unjust and freely-expressed prejudice against the queen.†

* State Papers, Introduction, p. ccxxx.
† Letters and Papers, Brewer, vol. iv, pt. ii, p. 1502. Letter of Charles V. to Mendoza.

The cardinal was received with the greatest honour as he travelled all through Picardy. When he left Calais, he found an escort of cavalry on the frontier, sent by Francis I. to meet him. The people received him everywhere most favourably, for it was known that he was the herald of peace.

It is very curious that Charles V., who greatly dreaded an alliance between England and France, now made advances to Wolsey, and assured him that he was just about to give orders for the instant payment of the arrears of his pension, and another of six thousand ducats to be secured to him.*
Mendoza, indeed, was desired to exhibit a splendid bait for his seduction—that is to say, to dazzle his eyes with the hope of the pontificate. The emperor would now have every means of effectually promoting his election, for the chair of Saint Peter was in his hands. Wolsey, wise by experience, turned a deaf ear.†

"God forbid that he should allow himself to be influenced by such motives. It was enough for him that the emperor intended to replace the existing pope upon his seat in the plenitude of his power, and was desirous of restoring its ancient splendour to the church."

* Gayangos, Calendar, vol. iii, pt. ii, p. 24.
† When Clement VII. was made pope, Wolsey had thought he could reckon on Charles V.'s influence, from the promises before made to him, but it was turned in quite another direction.

Thus the emperor and the King of France were bidding against each other for Wolsey's favours. The ambitious cardinal may almost be said to have seen the greatest monarchs of Europe at his feet, and he was himself encircled with royal state. But the intoxication of the present was controlled by the fears of the future.

However, the emperor was desirous of concluding a treaty of peace with England, and, in order to gain over Henry VIII., he even went so far as to offer the hand of the Princess of Portugal for the Duke of Richmond. But Francis I. was ready to go to more expense for Wolsey than could Charles V., and he proposed terms still more favourable for England; so his alliance was preferred.

Whilst Charles V. was still endeavouring to win the cardinal by fair promises, he was doing all he could at Rome to obtain the withdrawal of the legatine powers. Thus did the greatest princes of the sixteenth century pay their tribute to the machiavelism of the time.

Meanwhile, Wolsey reached Abbeville,* and waited there several days for Francis I. At last the king met him at Amiens on the 4th of August, 1527. It is no part of our subject to describe the magnificent reception of the cardinal, nor the banquet given by the French Court, nor the more sumptuous one

* He arrived there on July 24th, and waited till August 3rd. The king had been detained in Paris by a bad leg.

still that Wolsey himself returned. It is notorious that diplomatic interviews and meetings have always been supplemented by splendid feasts.

When Wolsey was able to obtain audience of Francis I., the first conversation was about Princess Mary's marriage. Francis briskly interrupted him by saying that nothing in the world could suit him better, and that this marriage would be the cornerstone of a new alliance between France and England.

Wolsey continues his account of the interview in his correspondence with Henry VIII., by saying that he asked the king, if he was to marry Mary, what was to become of Eleanor, and how were his children to be recovered? "Vous dictes vrai, Monsieur Cardinal," was the answer; then, after a pause, "I pray you, therefore, show me your advice." * It was arranged, on Wolsey's advice, supported by that of the queen-mother and the chancellor of France, who were present, that Mary should marry the Duke of Orleans, the king's second son.

The other point related to the harsh conditions imposed by Charles V. in the treaty of Madrid. After reference to Queen Louise and his council, the king, hesitating between two conflicting and equally sacred sentiments, paternal love† and devotion for his country, consented, with tears in his eyes, to the

* Brewer, Calendar. Introduction, vol. iv, ccxciii.
† We have mentioned that his two sons were kept as hostages in a fortress until the signature of the treaty.

whole of the clauses, when some of them were odious to him. This involuntary token of feeling greatly astonished the veteran Wolsey, broken and hardened to business as he was. This statesman, in the days of his great reverse, was to discover that no one is exempt from paying his tribute of tears. Happy are they who, before they weep over their own fate, have known how to compassionate the fate of their friends, their relations, and their country!

After discussing all the questions of peace and war, Wolsey had not ventured to touch that of the divorce. He recoiled through a secret and involuntary repugnance at this part of the commission imposed on him.

Wolsey wrote to Henry VIII. to ask him if it were not advisable to wait till the matter was in better train at Rome before mentioning the divorce; he had commissioned Ghinnuci, Bishop of Worcester, the friars Casale of Bologna, and Salviati of Florence, to carry on the suit before the pope. For the management of this delicate business in the midst of soldiers and imperial agents, Wolsey had no confidence in any but Italian agents, as more supple than the English, and especially more insinuating and adroit. Henry VIII. for himself had sent Knight, his private secretary, to try to see the pope, and converse with him in private. The cardinal, first minister, knew nothing of this. Like other absolute monarchs, Henry VIII. carried on a counter-diplomacy parallel to that of his official government, and without any previous understanding.

In answer to his anxious and pressing letters on the business of the divorce, Wolsey received a diplomatic reply from the King of England that the only reason he had so far caused examination of the validity of his marriage was for the sake of forestalling objections that might be afterwards made against the legitimacy of the princess.

It was by insisting on this official version that Wolsey persuaded Francis I. to adopt the four treaties he had prepared. The first confirmed the perpetual alliance between the two kings of France and England. In the second it was agreed that the Princess Mary should marry the young Duke of Orleans, if she did not marry Francis I. himself. The third settled the rate of the pecuniary subventions that England was to furnish to France for the continuance of the war in Italy. By the fourth and last it was agreed that, as long as the pope remained a prisoner in the Castle of Saint Angelo, the two kings would consider as void and of no effect all briefs and bulls emanating from that pontiff; that during such time the churches of France and England should be governed by their own bishops; and that Wolsey's decision in quality of legate should be put into execution, notwithstanding the prohibition and interdict of a pope who could have no authority nor power, because he was not at liberty.*

* Rymer, Fœdera, xiv, pp. 200, 203, 227.

A short time afterwards, Wolsey went to Compiègne with the Court of Francis I. There he received a letter from his master expressing great satisfaction at such advantageous treaties. It was then that he ventured to write to the pope, in concert with four French cardinals, to supplicate His Holiness to appoint a vicar-general to represent him, and make his authority respected on this side of the Alps. Moreover, he informed Louise of Savoy of the scheme of divorce conceived and pursued by Henry VIII. If Catharine's marriage was annulled, he confided to her that he should ask the hand of Renée of France, daughter of Louis XII., for his king. Now while Francis' sister, the Duchess of Alençon, was marrying the King of Navarre, Renée had been promised to the Duke of Ferrara. That was what Louise told Wolsey. Francis would not much have cared to give the King of England contingent rights to the Duchy of Brittany by this marriage.* Thus Wolsey, in making this imprudent step, had uselessly compromised his master's honour, and thus spoilt the diplomatic success he had just obtained.

* As daughters of Anne of Brittany, Claude and Renée might claim to be heirs of the duchy, although it had been annexed to the crown of France.

CHAPTER VIII.

Wolsey in England—Henry VIII.'s Theological Treatise against the validity of his marriage—Clement VII. a Prisoner in the Castle of Saint Angelo—Henry sends him his secretary, Knight, who fails in his Mission—Wolsey resumes the conduct of the business, and gives Instructions and a fresh Commission to Casale living in Italy, and then to Fox and Gardiner; they go from England, and find the Pope escaped from the Castle of Saint Angelo and gone to Orvieto—Destitution and Isolation of Clement VII.—Curious Letter given by Wolsey to Fox and Gardiner—Violent scene between Gardiner and the Pope—He obtains the Conditional Dispensation he had requested, but the terms of the Commission are reviewed, and do not give an absolute power without appeal to two Legates sent to determine the matter of the Divorce—Cardinal Campeggio, as Legate and Member of the Commission or Ecclesiastical Court, is united to Wolsey—Wolsey protests before Fox that he will judge conscientiously whatever may happen.

WHEN the cardinal returned to England, the king gave him a private audience, and no longer concealed from him his intention of marrying Anne Boleyn. Wolsey would never hitherto believe this; he had hoped that this vehement passion would not be of long duration and would have no serious results, for it seemed to him that the daughter of the Boleyns had merely such qualities as shine and attract for the moment, but do not inspire a serious attachment. It is asserted that he then made fresh and ardent efforts to wean Henry VIII. from this fatal attachment condemned by true policy,* but he yielded at last and tried to cover his opposition by his zeal. Some think he could now have retired from public affairs, but he did not even think of a course that would have done honour to himself and restored him in public opinion. This statesman of vast ambition, and intoxicated with his greatness, did not even conceive the idea of falling back into private life. To retain his power, he was ready to sacrifice his most legitimate repugnance, and so at the moment he thought of nothing but blindly assisting his master's senseless passion. He laboured to destroy Catharine of Aragon whom he esteemed, for the benefit of a frivolous woman whom he despised, and by whom he knew he was hated. Nevertheless, there were some remains of the bishop in the courtier and statesman occupied with earthly cares. This was to re-appear one day when Wolsey had been pitilessly banished from the field of politics.

Henry VIII. was now leaning more than ever upon theology itself for the preparation and justification of his divorce. The author of the *assertio septem sacramentorum* wrote in support of his own cause

* As we have said before, we believe, in despite of Cavendish, that was the time he threw himself at the king's feet.

more zealously still than he had done in defence of the church against Luther. He took his stand chiefly on the prohibition in Leviticus, looking upon it as divine law utterly forbidding a marriage between brother and sister-in-law. When this little treatise was communicated to Wolsey, that prince of the church seemed to adopt the principles of it, and make it the absolute rule of his conduct. However, he submitted it to Fisher's examination who dared to pronounce against the king's conclusions, and consequently against the divorce. As to Sir Thomas More, he excused himself as not being a divine.

At this time the notion of a synod, a council, or meeting of cardinals was given up. All the efforts of Henry VIII. and Wolsey tended to obtain the voiding of the dispensation of Julius II., and granting of the divorce by the juridical omnipotence of Pope Clement VII.

"Strange to say," observes Professor Brewer, "on this occasion the English monarch and his minister were the most uncompromising advocates for the personal infallibility of the pope, and pronounced the divine commission of Saint Peter a sufficient justification for any act that his successor might do. Clement himself took a more mitigated view of his own authority. He was not convinced when they urged him to reverse the official decisions of previous pontiffs by an extrajudicial determination of his own, and to declare that determination irreversible and infallible. Nor were they more successful when, in their anxiety to secure their own ends, they went so far as to assert that, without the possession and exercise of such an authority, the pope could not be the father of his people, nor the head of that church which Christ had founded for the good of mankind. If Henry had obtained his divorce, he and Wolsey would have ranged themselves among the most unqualified supporters of the pope's personal infallibility. In these views they did not wholly want the support of more than one Roman lawyer and ecclesiastic." *

This plan of the campaign did not permit the English ambassadors to make an attack upon the bull of dispensation granted by Julius II. as contrary to divine and natural law. The very time when they were asking Clement VII. to perform an act of sovereign authority was not the moment for contesting his predecessor's power. They were thus compelled to content themselves with asserting—and this was their last expedient—that the bull had been obtained upon a false statement, and was, therefore, revocable. The reasons alleged in this view for demanding the revocation, or declaration of nullity, may thus be summed up:—

1. It was asserted that Prince Henry had requested a dispensation from the pope for marrying

* Letters and Papers, Brewer. Introduction, vol. iv, p. cccii.

Catharine; that was false. The prince was only twelve years old, and could not act with knowledge of the matter.

2. The dispensation was asked of the pope for the maintenance of peace with the Catholic sovereigns Ferdinand and Isabella. This was an untenable allegation; for the prince was much too young to have these statesmanlike views, and contract a marriage for political reasons.

3. The bull stated that this marriage was necessary for the maintenance of peace between England and Spain; but that was an erroneous idea. The pope had been led to suppose that some great calamity would ensue, if the two kingdoms were not again united by this alliance. Whereas, even if the marriage had neither been proposed nor concluded, the two kings would not have gone to war; and there was at that time no reason to apprehend any rupture between them.

But there were traditions in the management of ecclesiastical business which the papacy had no desire to transgress. The sovereign pontiff, Clement VII., being then separated from his chancellerie and ecclesiastical advisers, was very much disinclined to do anything, or take a single measure entailing important consequences, within the scope of his spiritual government.

Also the pope was so closely watched and guarded by the imperialists that Knight met with insurmountable obstacles in his attempts to reach him. Cardinal Wolsey also made a pressing demand that, as it seemed to be the pope's desire that the suit of divorce should be prosecuted and determined according to the requisite formalities, all might be done honourably and legally.

Some proposal had been made of obtaining from Clement, in consideration of his want of personal liberty, a commission extending Wolsey's powers in England, and giving him such a jurisdiction in that country as would give him sovereign powers of judging the divorce case by himself or his delegates. Well! Is it credible that, however anxious Henry VIII. was to expedite the determination of the suit in the most favourable manner, he was jealous beforehand of the immense spiritual power that would be conferred on Wolsey, and offended at the idea of thus finding himself face to face with a sort of English pope in his own kingdom? Not even for the sake of marrying Anne Boleyn did he choose to be in the power of one of his own subjects.

Knight was sent to Rome in order to diminish Wolsey's overweening importance. Perhaps, also, Henry VIII. thought, at Anne Boleyn's instigation, that Wolsey was not working quite honestly for the divorce, since all hope of a royal alliance for his master had failed. The cardinal, on hearing of Knight's journey, had written to Protonotary Gambara, and he succeeded in obtaining an interview with the pope, and informing him of the mission given to Knight, who managed to reach Rome through dangers and difficulties of all kinds,* only to be prevented from entering the Castle of Saint Angelo by Alarcon, the commander of the Spanish forces.

He had, however, brought from England a draft for brief or bull, containing both the declaration of nullity of marriage of Henry VIII., and the dispensation necessary for his marriage afterwards to Anne Boleyn. He sought for a cardinal who was not of the imperial party, and who might be willing to convey it to the pope, and procure the sanction of his seal and signature. The cardinal of the Quattro Santi† was mentioned as a safe man, so the draft was submitted to him. The cardinal saw that the document was the work of a novice's unaccustomed hand; he stated his objections to Knight, who consented to the amended draft of the bull as perfectly answering the end proposed. The cardinal, when pressed by Henry VIII.'s agent, consented to carry the papers given him to the pope. They were signed after correction, and Knight wrote to Wolsey: "At all events, I do bring a commission with me, and a dispensation, which I trust the king and your grace will like well." ‡

* He was stopped by brigands twelve miles from Rome, and very nearly lost his life.
† The Quattro Santi, or Four Martyrs, is the name of a church at Rome that always gives one of the cardinals his title.
‡ Letters and Papers, Brewer. Introduction, vol. iv, p. cccxviii.

Knight offered a fee of two thousand crowns to Cardinal dei Quattro Santi, whose palace had been pillaged by the imperialists at the sack of Rome,* but the noble Prince of the Church indignantly returned this kind of bribe; he also refused gifts of hangings, plate, and horses, attempts made to triumph over his probity by flattering his tastes. Such specimens of disinterested conduct were not rare at the Court of Rome, for there was much less corruption and venality there than has been supposed.

When the commission and dispensation reached England, neither the one nor the other was found to be regular. Both were declared to be of none effect. Cardinal dei Quattro Santi had altered the words of the commission and dispensation, "extracting its teeth and rendering it inoffensive" (Brewer). The drift of these changes made by him from the original minutes was not understood at first, so Knight was quite triumphing in his speedy and facile success,† and was greatly humiliated at the check and disappointment due to his ignorance of the forms of the Roman chancellerie.

These are the words of the draft commission given to Wolsey by Henry VIII. An attempt had been made to get the pope's signature to it by surprise,

---

* Strype, Ecclesiastical mem. Appendix, vol. i, p. 74.

† Knight said, in his letter, "Sufficient, though not like the minute." Letters and Papers, Brewer. Introduction, vol. iv, p. cccxviii.

taking advantage of his being alone, without his servants and ministers, reduced, indeed, to a harsh captivity:

"Clement VII., to our beloved, health and apostolic benediction.

"Whereas, eighteen years ago, our dearest son in Christ, Henry VIII., King of England, etc., was induced by the persuasion of those about him, and a pretended apostolic dispensation, to contract marriage with Catharine, his brother's widow; and whereas it has been found, upon further examination, that the said dispensation was granted on false pretences, and is faulty and surreptitious—that thereby the king's conscience is troubled; and that, in full confidence of our plenary power as supreme ruler here on earth, he has required etc., etc. In consideration of the premises, we appoint you, our dear son, the Cardinal of York, of whose virtues, love of justice and equity, we are well assured, to exercise our authority in your own person for the trial of this cause. We also appoint you —— as assessor, enacting that the decision of either of you shall be valid in the absence of the other. You are to proceed summarily and *de pleno*, without the publicity or formality of judicial proceedings, and inquire into the validity of the said dispensation. And, if you jointly or severally are satisfied of its invalidity, you shall pronounce the marriage between Henry and Catharine to be null and void, allowing the parties to separate, and contract marriage *de novo*, all appeal or challenge set aside. Also by this our authority we empower you to over-rule all canonical defects or objections, and declare the issue of the first as well as of the second marriage to be legitimate, if you think fit. And whatever is done by you in this cause, judicially or extra-judicially, we ratify and confirm in the fullest manner, without revocation."

"Never was a more extravagant demand made on a pope's good nature, and never was a stranger proposal submitted to the highest spiritual authority of Christendom."* It really was a suggestion to the sovereign pontiff to abdicate his functions of supreme judge, and basely lend a hand to a gross iniquity. The terms of the draft commission also prejudged the question of the invalidity of the dispensation, and implied the delivery of the sentence without any judicial examination of the truth. As Cardinal dei Quattro Santi said, "A commission so drawn, and with such clauses, could not pass without perpetual dishonour to the pope, the king, and the cardinal."

Though Clement VII. was partial to Henry VIII., he had too much dignity to yield to such injurious suggestions. No doubt he would have been very glad if the fatal suit could be decided far from him and without him. Catharine's acquiescence in a regular sentence delivered on the spot might, to a certain degree, have set the pope's conscience at

* Letters and Papers, Brewer. Introduction, vol. iv, p. cccxxiv.

THE POPE'S DIFFICULTIES. 263

rest. But the moment she appealed to the court of Rome, the pope felt very sure he could not refuse this appeal without committing an unpardonable and scandalous injustice.

And though he might have some reason to dread the possible extremities to which Henry VIII.'s wrath might carry him, there was also Charles V. to be dealt with, and his influence was exactly contrary to that of the King of England. While Knight and Wolsey's agents were trying, in the midst of the ruins of Rome, to circumvent the suffering pope, a prisoner in the Castle of Saint Angelo, and to prepare him to consent to the nullification of Catharine's marriage, the emperor did not fail to support the cause of his unfortunate aunt; under the pretext of an ecclesiastical mission, he sent the general of the cordeliers to the sovereign pontiff with a commission to beseech His Holiness to retain cognisance of this matter, and to prevent its being tried, and more especially to hinder judgment being given in England. Thus, in the very midst of his personal troubles, Clement tried to study this difficult question, and arrive at an accurate and learned solution. He ordered Sanga, his confidant and private secretary, to make him a report of the means employed in the case by both parties, and their respective systems. Meanwhile Henry VIII., seeing that his own diplomacy had not been successful, had again committed the conduct of his interests and his cause before the pope to the hands of Wolsey. Perhaps also, before giving him the entire direction of external affairs, he had been awaiting the issue of a matter wherein Wolsey was personally concerned.

Stafileo, dean of the court of Rota, and much famed for his deep learning, had been begged by the Kings of France and England to propose a vicar-general of the Holy See for the whole time that Clement VII. might be kept in captivity, or remain in dependence on the emperor. The cardinals were to meet at Avignon, or some other neutral territory, and proceed to the actual nomination of a vicar-general to manage the affairs of the church. Stafileo was to bring to the notice of Clement VII. that the person entrusted with this duty, strong in the support and the favour of two powerful kings, might, by his skill and courage, restore to its former greatness, the power of the popes that Charles V. had broken and trodden under foot. Clement VII. was much shocked at this proposal; he saw in it an indirect attack upon the rights of his pontificate; he easily perceived that Wolsey pointed to himself in the list of qualities and advantages of position that this coadjutor of the Holy See ought to possess; he knew that the ambitious cardinal had formerly entertained ambitious hopes of the triple crown, and did so still. Was it possible that he was not contented with labouring to secure the succession to Clement VII. when dead, but with feverish impatience desired to supplant him while yet alive.

This, therefore, made the pope very ill-disposed towards Wolsey, who, in complete ignorance of this, sent minute and urgent instructions to Casale, his diplomatic agent resident in Italy, and these show how much importance the cardinal attached to success, especially through the personal authority of the pope, in procuring the declaration of the nullity of the marriage of Henry with Catharine of Aragon. Perhaps even in his impatience to obtain a speedy decision, he injured the cause he desired to serve.

After communicating to his correspondent the theological reasons mentioned above against the validity of the bull of dispensation, he continues saying that the king considers the deaths of his children as a judgment of God, and that for the avoidance of fresh curses he had recourse to the Holy See. He asks permission to marry another person, from whom he might hope to have male children by the grace of God. A very pressing letter is sent from his majesty to the pope in his own hand. The pope was to be told, on the king's behalf and in Wolsey's name, how much they lament the unworthy treatment inflicted on His Holiness and the college of cardinals, he is to be assured that nothing in the world would be neglected to set him speedily at liberty. Then he was to be informed of the nature and circumstances of the marriage the king is bent on. Descriptions were to be given of the remorse* that a delicate con-

* Shakespeare, in his play of "Henry VIII.," several times de-

science must feel, and the calamities that must ensue upon a disputed succession; the prayers of the lords and wishes of the people were to be added. Nothing was to be omitted that might conduce to the annulling of the dispensation of Julius II. The present state of Italy and Christendom was to be held up before the pope's eyes. And he was to be made to understand how important it was for the Holy See that the king should never be at variance with the pope, and that, if the king were satisfied in this business, he would be pledged always to support the interests of the Church. Wolsey added that the pope might perhaps consider it more conformable to his dignity to do everything for the king without refer-

rides the pretended remorse of the king. Thus in Act II, Scene I, he introduces first the Lord Chamberlain, then Norfolk and Suffolk.

SUFF. How is the king employed?
CHAM. I left him private, full of sad thoughts and troubles.
NOR. What's the cause?
CHAM. It seems the marriage with his brother's wife has crept too near his conscience.
SUFF. No; his conscience has crept too near another lady.

The king afterwards joins in the conversation, and expresses some hypocritical regrets for Catharine.

"Would it not grieve an able man to leave
So sweet a bed-fellow? But conscience, conscience,
O, 'tis a tender place, and I must leave her."

Thus Henry is always acting his part, and keeping on his mask with his most intimate friends. Shakespeare understands and depicts this singular character most admirably. This theologian of a king was both a Tartuffe and a Nero. These are the features that Shakespeare has seized and beautifully illustrated.

ence to the sacred college, and to sign the enclosed commission with his own hand, it being formal, and only wanting the pope's sign-manual. The king begs that by this commission Wolsey may have power to examine into the nature of his marriage, and to judge of it with the persons he should think fit to associate with himself. There was also in the packet a dispensation quite ready for the pope's signature to be attached. If the pope had any suspicions of a leaning of Wolsey to Henry VIII., as he was his first minister, all possible endeavours were to be made to dissipate his suspicions. If he was found inflexible on this point, Stafileo, Dean of Rota, was to be proposed, now in England. The pope was to be told that delay would have as bad an effect as refusal.*

Together with the instructions for Casale, Wolsey had written an autograph letter to the pope, insisting vehemently on the need of success in his request, and saying, "If the pope is not compliant, my life will be shortened, and I dread to anticipate the consequences." In that he was nearer the truth than he fancied. A refusal from His Holiness would cost the loss of the king's friendship; and, under the present difficult circumstances, the necessity of favouring Henry's views for the dissolution or nullity of his marriage with Catharine would be felt. "There are

* These instructions are written in Latin, and are given here from the continuation of Henry's Hist., book xxx, p. xix.

secret reasons which cannot be trusted to writing—for which, and other causes, the king will never live with her as his wife."*

When these instructions reached Casale at his residence in Florence, Clement VII. had just escaped from the Castle of Saint Angelo, and taken refuge at Orvieto. But when this Italian emissary was setting out on his journey to go to the pope at his new residence, other instructions reached him with a second draft commission. The proposal was now no longer to make Wolsey sole judge of the divorce question, for fear of their making the queen's appeal inevitable; but the request was that an Italian cardinal of the party in opposition to the emperor should be associated with him, such as Campeggio, Trani, Farnese, or Stafileo, the Dean of Rota;† if the pope displayed any intention of selecting the second judge outside the cardinals, from the anti-English party, the first commission was to be adhered to.

It is supposed that Wolsey was very glad himself to get another person to share the unpopularity of his actions with regard to Catharine, and his perilous responsibility to Henry VIII.

* Letters and Despatches, vol. iv, part ii, p. 1638. Introduction, pp. cccxxxi, cccxxxii. The letter is in the Record Office, Wolsey to Sir Gregory Casale. It is not to be handed to the pope. The expression is, "In this I will state what I wish you to lay before the pope." The letter is in Latin, and is not stated to be in Wolsey's hand.

† But this name was rejected at first sight by the pope.

When Casale arrived at Orvieto, the pope was nearly alone there, and without any regular chancellerie; he was sad, dejected, and discouraged.. Nothing was more painful to him than to be thus discovered, and, it may be said, hunted in his new retreat by the English agents, leaving him no time to breathe. After eight days of entreaties, pushed almost to importunity,* Casale extracted the grant of the commission from the holy father, with the condition, it is true, that it should be amended by Cardinal Quattro Santi; and yet Clement could not give it to Henry VIII.'s secretary without shedding tears. It is easy to imagine the pope's misery in his cruel position. One way Clement VII. had a timid conscience and hesitating character, and seemed as if he did not yet know on which side was the right in the business of Catharine of Aragon. Another way, both in the interests of the Church and of himself, he must be afraid of entirely turning his back either on Henry VIII. or on Charles V. For the moment he had escaped from the imperial armies, but they were on his traces, and his restoration to the Vatican seemed more distant than ever. In truth, France and England had just declared war against the emperor, and Lautrec, at the head of a powerful army, proclaimed that he would soon be in Romagna. Meanwhile, Clement thought he ought to proceed cautiously, and not take an irrevocable

* December 30th, 1527.

decision. At the same time, he recommended Henry VIII. and his agents to preserve the most absolute secrecy on the concessions he had made them, for fear of annoying and irritating Charles V.

Cardinals Simonetta and Quattro Santi, who were at Orvietto, wished that the suit should be entirely concluded in England, and that Henry, after his divorce had been decided on the spot, should marry whomever he would, if he thought he could conscientiously do so. But in order to do this, Catharine must renounce the appeal to Rome, and take the veil.

In the draft commission the name of the cardinal, to be appointed to join with Wolsey to examine into the validity of the marriage of Henry VIII., had been left in blank. Among the cardinals named one had a bishopric in Spain, another was detained as a hostage at Naples; as for Campeggio, he was available, and was accepted by Casale, but they did not dare to let him depart before the arrival of Lautrec, so that he might travel in safety. Besides, when the French army was at the gates of Rome, the emperor would perhaps make proposals of accommodation to the pope. Clement VII. secretly cherished this hope, as then he would be more independent of the King of England.

But during this time the dispensation and commission, corrected by Cardinal dei Quattro Santi, had been examined at the Court of London. This time they were found correct in form, but insufficient in matter; and two fresh ambassadors were sent to the pope—two Englishmen—Fox, the king's almoner, and Gardiner, Wolsey's secretary.* Doctor Gardiner, a distinguished lawyer, owed his fortune to the cardinal of York, who loved him well, and called him his own half (*dimidium mei*). The king and his first minister thus each had their own representative. Doctor Gardiner had the precedence of Fox, and was named the head of the embassy.

The two ambassadors received their instructions and despatches early in February. Passing through Rome, they were to see Gregory Casale, and to act in concert with him, telling him the new position taken up. They were commissioned to thank the pope for his good intentions, and to make him understand that the dispensation and commission, as His Holiness had thought he ought to word them, were not sufficient for the good and stability of the realm. Henry VIII., also wishing to know the pope's intentions from his own mouth, had sent him Doctors Gardiner and Fox, who would be commissioned to tell him all they thought necessary to explain the cause of divorce. "Secondly," continues the despatch, "as Wolsey finds that the pope has been labouring under some misapprehension, as if the king had set on foot this cause, not from fear of his succession, but out of a vain affection or undue love

* Some authors say Stafileo was joined with them.

to a gentlewoman of not so excellent qualities as she is here esteemed, the ambassadors are to assure the pope that the cardinal would not, for any earthly affection to his prince, or desire of reward, transgress the truth, or swerve from the right path; nor would he have consented in any way to have reported to His Holiness otherwise than his conviction of the insufficiency of the marriage, nor have been guilty of any dissimulation. If God has given any light of true doctrine to the greatest divines and lawyers of this realm, and if, in this angle of the world, there be any hope of God's favour, Wolsey is well assured, and dare put his soul that the king's desire is founded upon justice,* and does not spring from any grudge or displeasure to the queen, whom the king honours and loves, and minds to love and to treat as his sister with all manner of kindness; and, as she is the relict of his dearest brother, he will entertain her with all joy and felicity. But as this matrimony is contrary to God's law, the king's conscience is grievously offended. On the other side, the approved excellent virtuous qualities of the said gentlewoman (Anne), the purity of her life, her constant virginity, her maidenly and womanly modesty, her soberness, chasteness, meekness, humility, wisdom, descent right noble and high through regal blood, education in all good and laudable qualities and manners, apparent

* How could a man be proposed as judge who had given his opinion so openly in favour of one of the parties?

aptness to procreation of children, with her other infinite good qualities, more to be regarded and esteemed than the only progeny, be the grounds on which the king's desire is founded, which Wolsey regards as honest and necessary."*

How could Wolsey, who makes such an ostentatious parade of his sincerity, ever dare to speak seriously of the remorse of this poor Henry VIII.? How could he manage to write this long eulogy of the virtues of Anne Boleyn without burning his fingers? We must be deeply grieved at the sight of a bishop, a prince of the Church, who prided himself on still having some feeling of sacerdotal dignity, demeaning himself to such concessions. Co-operating with the intrigues of Henry VIII. and his favourites, lending himself to their machinations, he was drawn to the top of a precipice, and could not stop. The historian must tell the truth about public men, whose character he has to discuss, whoever they be.

Gardiner and his colleague left Dover on the 11th of February, 1528, and were driven by storm to Gravelines, only landing with great difficulty; they also were nearly drowned in Romagna, while crossing a torrent swollen by recent storm.† Thus both in the beginning and ending of their journey they lost their baggage and most of their clothes. These difficul-

---
* Letters and Papers, Brewer. Introduction, vol. iv, p. cccxxxviii.
† They crossed the torrent at a ford on tall horses, and the water came up to their girdles.

VOL. I.   T

ties delayed them so long that they only reached Orvieto on March 25th.

There they found that the pope could not be said to have fully and truly recovered his liberty, "for hunger, scarcity, bad lodgings, and ill air keep him as much confined as he was in Castel Angelo."*

"The air of this city is very contagious, and the weather so moist that, except there be some change of the inhabitants soon, it will be of little consequence who are lords of this country, unless for penance you would wish it to the Spaniards as being unworthy to die in battle."†

The ambassadors found no chance of repairing their wardrobe at Orvieto. The townsmen said they had no more clothes than they wore; so there were none to be borrowed or made new in the place. This was also a cause of delay. When the ambassadors at last thought they were presentable, they asked an audience of His Holiness.‡ They were taken to a dilapidated palace, belonging to the bishop of the place; and on their way to the pope's presence they had to pass through three rooms, "all naked and unhanged, the roofs fallen down, and, as we can guess, thirty persons, riff-raff and other, standing in the chamber for a garnishment." The pope received them in his bed-chamber. When Gardiner had ex-

* Letters and Papers, Brewer, vol. iv, pt. ii, p. 1809.
† Letters and Papers, Brewer, vol. iv, pt. ii, p. 1812.
‡ This was Monday, March 25th, 1528.

plained the cause of their coming, and directed the pope's attention to the defects in the dispensation and commission, the pope replied that, notwithstanding his promise to amend them, he must dissemble until Italy was pacified.

Then the ambassadors protested against further delay.

"And whereas it was declared how your grace (Wolsey), being advertised that His Holiness somewhat stayed in expedition of the king's desire, for that it was showed him that the matter (the divorce) was set forth without your consent or knowledge, and you begged us to protest of your sincerity and mind concerning the merits and the qualities of the gentlewoman (Anne Boleyn), the pope said all such protestation was needless, for he could not believe that the king would be led by any undue (improper) affection, and he desired to see the king's labour and study in the matter. He added he did not believe the report that you were not privy to it, or that anything of so high consequence would not be set forth without your advice. But he confessed that the report had made him waver until he had ascertained the truth."*

Next day the ambassadors presented the king's book to the pope. He began to read it standing, then sat down on a form covered with an old coverlet not worth twenty pence; he read the pre-

* Letters and Papers, Brewer. Introduction, vol. iv, p. cccxlii.

liminary epistle and the latter part of the book touching the law with great attention. As he turned the leaves he made reflections and comments on the question, then he commended the talent used in its preparation, and said he would like to keep it, and read it at leisure. And as the preliminary epistle was addressed to Wolsey and the other English bishops, the pope asked what they had answered. The ambassadors replied that "there was none; but he might infer the answer from Wolsey's letters." Then he demanded whether the king had ever broken the matter to the queen. They told him it had been done, and there was reason to believe she would be content to abide by the judgment of the church. We may, in passing, observe that this was a more than hazardous expression. Then he asked them whether Wolsey might not be objected to as a suspected judge. "For that, by answering the king's epistle and delivering your mind, you had given sentence beforehand, and could not be considered indifferent." This was an objection they had not anticipated, and it was not very easily parried.*

In the evening they had an interview with Cardinal di Quattro Santi, and thought they had persuaded him that a commission meeting in England, and composed of English bishops, would be most in conformity with canon law. Next day, when they had

* Letters and Papers, Brewer. Introduction, vol. iv, p. cccxliii.

another audience of the pope, they found him in his study with three cardinals. He had seats brought, took one himself, and asked them to be seated by him. The commission to be appointed for the judgment of the divorce was discussed. Gardiner, as leader of the embassy, sustained this discussion in Latin for several hours. These debates extended to several other days. The pope urged on the ambassadors to accept a general commission at common law to take the evidence, instead of one or two commissions clothed with powers both extraordinary and definitive. Gardiner and Fox * complained that the pope and his advisers were objecting merely on a point of form. They said that, if the king could obtain no more favour from them than an ordinary person, he would take the remedy into his own hands, and not suffer his cause to be decided by men whose hearts had already prejudged it.†

It seems that this threat, so sharp and unexpected, intimidated Clement VII.; for he protested that he would do all he could for his majesty's satisfaction as soon as he had consulted two other cardinals, the Cardinal of Monte and the Cardinal of Ancona.

When these fresh counsellors of the sovereign pontiff had come the discussion was resumed in their presence. Then (it was the 1st of April) the pope,

---

* It seems Stafileo, a partizan of Henry VIII., was also present at this discussion.

† Letters and Papers, Brewer. Introduction, vol. iv, p. cccxliv.

who seemed justly terrified at the immense responsibility they wished to lay on him, declared that he was no canonist, and that he must have the advice of his cancellaria and of his lawyers; that, in a suit of so much importance, it was not enough for him, the head of the church, to be considered justified in England; that he must be justified before the whole Christian world. Gardiner answered that there was no reason to fear what the world would say; that the suit must be tried on its own merits, and judged according to equity and justice. In fact, the discussion was reduced to the point of determining whether the commission should be given exactly in the terms of the draft brought from England (giving Wolsey power to judge summarily, and finally), or whether it should be a general commission at common law, only giving the judges a power of first instance. Gardiner and his colleagues obstinately adhered to Wolsey's draft. The pope and his advisers said that the commission asked for was contrary to law and custom, and returned to the incompetence of Wolsey, which was said to be alleged by the queen herself.

This proposition was strongly contested by Gardiner with a boldness of language to which the pope was certainly not accustomed. According to the audacious ambassador, " If they could not point out the right way to the wanderer—a task entrusted to them by God—specially to a prince from whom they had received so many obligations, the world would exclaim against their cunning and dissimulation, for they promised much, and performed nothing." That His Holiness had no need of his canonist; that the whole canon law was in himself, in the sanctuary of his conscience, inspired according to the well-known adage,

"Quod Pontifex habet omnia jura in scrinio pectoris."

The pope replied, with ingenious modesty, that he had not the key of this sanctuary. Thus, in two words, he routed the learned and pressing arguments that Gardiner had urged in a discussion of four long hours.

Despairing of their cause, Gardiner and his colleagues consented to the appointment of a general commission in rather wider terms than had been drawn up in England. "We were always told that it should be of our own devising. But when it was drawn and submitted to them, everyone had some fault to find. One thought the matter was good, but the style was too ornate; another that the whole was inadmissible; another complained of the beginning, and proposed to substitute a different one of his own composition." In Gardiner's homely phrase, "they praised the present flavour of the meat, but blamed the cooking." *

At last it was agreed to entrust the composition

* Letters and Papers, Brewer. Introduction, vol. iv, p. cccxlvi.

of the document to the cardinals present, and they promised not to make too many alterations in the original draft. But when the form they had drawn was submitted to Gardiner, he found so many changes—and changes that certainly, to his mind, were not improvements—that he broke out into violent protestations, and declared that it was a complete deception. The two parties made recriminations of dissimulation and deceit. Gardiner especially accused the nuncio Gambarra of having lured the ambassadors to Rome by captious promises. Gambarra replied that he had done no more than his commission required. Gardiner exclaimed that, "when he should have to report what sort of friends the king found in the Papal Court, he would abandon it, and the Apostolic See, now tottering, would collapse entirely, to the applause and satisfaction of all the world." [*]

Hearing this insolent proclamation of revolt against the Church made in the name of England, Clement VII. could not contain himself. He raised his arms to heaven with exclamations of indignation, surprise, and scandal ("bade them put in the words contended for"), quitted his seat, and walked up and down the room with all the marks of great agitation.

According to Gardiner's own account, "after all these tempests, they came into still water." He does not tell us, as is most likely, that, in order to

[*] Brewer, p. cccxlvii.

get into this still water, he had to retract his too hasty words, and excuse himself to the noble pontiff, whose sacred character he had so grossly ignored. Whatever happened in consequence of this incredible scene, evidently the pope and the ambassadors came to a final understanding. A commission without exceptional clauses was granted for Wolsey and Campeggio to try the divorce case in England. The pope, delivering it to the ambassadors, expressed a hope that it would give satisfaction to the king. Gardiner was not quite contented with it, but he thought it better to take it as it was.*

Fox was immediately sent to England to carry the commission with the contingent dispensation to marry Anne Boleyn. He was delighted that the latter document had been sent back correctly copied from the draft, without any alteration. But, as the dispensation was not to become effective until the marriage was annulled, it did not signify much by itself; its importance was only accessory, and it could only become of value if the sentence of divorce was finally pronounced. The terms of constitution of the commission had much more significance, and had an essentially different bearing.

Reaching England about the end of April, Fox

* As there was no transfer to common law, the appeal was implicitly reserved.

It is to be remembered that Gardiner was the sturdy, rough Englishman of Queen Mary's time—the only one of her ministers found incorruptible by foreign influence or gold. (Ed.)

hastened to Greenwich, where he expected to find the king and Wolsey. As the king could not immediately give him audience, he ordered him to be introduced to Anne Boleyn's chamber, " who at that time, for that my lady princess and divers others the queen's maidens were sick of the small-pox, lay in the gallery in the tilt-yard.* And so, admitted unto her presence, after declaration made unto the same in generality, first, of such expeditions as were obtained, and sith, of your singular fidelity, diligence, and dexterity, used, not only in the impetration thereof, but also in hastening the coming of the legate with your most hearty and humble commendations, which she most thankfully received, and seemed to take the same most marvellously to heart, oftentimes in communication calling me Master Stevens,† with promise of large recompense for your good acquittal in the premises."‡

As they were talking the king came in, and then Fox made him a detailed report of everything that had passed at Orvieto. He presented the dispensation, then the commission, telling him that this last document could only be obtained after long debate, and could not be got in the form arranged in England; the ambassadors were obliged to content them-

* So at this time Anne Boleyn was one of the queen's maids of honour. Fox no doubt means the Princess Mary. The date of the letter is May, 1528.

† *I.e.*, Stephen Gardiner, mistaking Fox for him.

‡ Letters and Papers, Brewer. Introduction, vol. iv, p. cccxlix.

selves with the draft settled by the Roman cardinals; but its deficiencies were in some sort supplied by a promise made by the pope, as he said, not to transfer the suit, and to confirm the sentence, whatever it might be.* The king gave way to warm expressions of pleasure and thankfulness, and showed much satisfaction at the successful issue of the diplomatic negotiations.

Fox thought it right to attribute the success in great part to Wolsey, owing to the excellent instructions the cardinal had given to the ambassadors, and also the letters written to the pope even before their arrival, as he had proved that, when the king expressed his wish for a divorce and fresh marriage, he had not yielded to childish caprice, that his proceeding had been derived from conscientious reflection, and the person on whom he had fixed his choice was worthy of his affection.

Then the king desired Fox to wait upon Wolsey, and inform him of what had passed at Orvieto. The minister was not so well satisfied as the king with the terms of the commission; nevertheless the next day he seemed to be contented with it, when he found himself in company with Lord Rochford, Anne Boleyn's father. It was generally allowed that Gardiner had managed the negotiation well, but, as he had allowed himself to make use of violence and intimidation, Wolsey blamed him in that respect, and

* Did the pope really say this? It may be doubted.

said that, in treating with the pope, he ought never to have failed in the respectful behaviour due to the head of the Church.

A little later, as it was supposed by the lawyers that the queen might refuse to appear, or might appeal against the sentence, Gardiner was instructed "to make secret inquiry at the Court of Rome when it could be done; and, in such a case, how such a refusal would affect their proceedings, what was the remedy, and whether, during the appeal, it would be lawful for the parties to marry again. In minor points connected with the process he was to obtain the opinions of learned men, chiefly with the view of obviating any objections which might arise on the queen's part, of whose line of defence the cardinal had contrived to obtain some information. Gardiner was also to "inform himself how far, in a case of this high consequence, for the conservation of his honour, or else immortal ignominy and slander, and the damnation of his soul, Wolsey, for the discharge of his conscience, might rest the king's cause on the fact that he was wholly unacquainted with the granting of the bull for the dispensation of his marriage with his brother's wife, and whether the said ground be so justifiable, and of such sort, as his grace might well build his conscience upon it, without grudge or scruple hereafter."*

What argument of any weight could have been

* Letters and Papers, Brewer. Introduction, vol. iv, cccliii.

drawn from the establishment of this fact? No bishop or priest would have married Henry VIII. to his sister-in-law without having the bull of dispensation laid before him. Besides, the validity of this bull had been recognized by the king's council at the time of his marriage, after a discussion, when the contrary had been affirmed. Since Henry VIII. not only had made no opposition to this dispensation, but had taken advantage of it, he could not come forward to assert its nullity. Besides, this nullity was covered by his silence during eighteen years of nuptial cohabitation with Catharine of Aragon.

Fox recognized, in his correspondence with Gardiner, that, however broad were the powers granted by the commission, the queen could always exercise her right of appeal to the pope, and would at least, as a final resource, require that the decision of the business should be given at Rome, and this at the very end would disconcert the hopes of Henry VIII., and make all his plans of campaign abortive.

"Insomuch," writes Fox to Gardiner, "that yesterday, to my great, and no less joy and comfort, his grace openly, in presence of Mr. Tuke, Mr. Wolman, Mr. Bell, and me, made protestation to the king's highness that, although he was so much bound unto the same as any subject might unto his prince; and by reason thereof his grace was of so perfect devotion, faith, and loyalty towards his majesty that he could gladly spend goods, blood, and life in his just causes;

yet sith his grace (Wolsey) was more obliged to God, and that he was sure he should render an account *de operibus suis* before Him. He would, in this matter, rather suffer high indignation, yea, and his body jointly to be torn in pieces, than he would do anything in this cause otherwise than justice requireth; in that his highness should look after other favour to be ministered unto him in this cause on his grace's part, than the justness of the cause would bear. But, if the bull (*i.e.*, of Pope Julius) were sufficient, he would so pronounce it, and rather suffer *extrema quæque* than do the contrary, or else *contra conscientiam suam.**

Thus Wolsey's Christian conscience seems sometimes to awaken. In accepting the office of judge, he evidently sometimes tries to be serious. It seems as if he were trying to pledge himself by this energetic and independent language, and sort of profession of faith.

Wolsey felt that he was surrounded with enemies and ambuscades. Public opinion was turning against him, and the king's favour threatened to desert him. Failing men, he was tempted to turn to the God who never fails His servants. But Cæsar was to be his real god on earth for some time longer.

* Letters and Papers, Brewer. Introduction, vol. iv, p. cccliii. Letter, May 11.

CHAPTER IX.

The Two Kings' Defiance, and the Emperor's Reply—
Policy and Attitude of Wolsey before the Arrival of
Cardinal Campeggio—The Appointment of the Abbess of
Wilton—Discontent of Henry VIII., and his Correspondence with Wolsey on this Business—The Sweating Sickness—Henry's Momentary Return to Catharine—His
Letters to Anne Boleyn, and hers to Wolsey.

IN the month of January, 1528, at Wolsey's instigation, the English ambassadors were recalled from
the emperor's court, and the two Kings of France
and England sent a formal challenge to Charles V.
This was placed in his hands by Clarencieux and
Guyenne, kings-at-arms. The challenge contained a
long diatribe against the imperial policy. Among
other things, vehement reproaches were made against
Charles V. for the sack of Rome and ill-treatment of
the pope. The payment of the emperor's debts to
the English crown was claimed; and, according to
the terms of the defiance, these debts were increased
by the stipulated forfeit for having failed in the
promise to marry the Princess Mary.

Charles V. made a triumphant reply to all these

complaints. In the note he gave Clarencieux for the King of England, he acknowledged his debt to that prince of the sums lent him, and declared he would free himself in proper time and place, but he denied that he owed any indemnity for the suspension of the pension during the war, and asserted that, by the treaties of Paris and London, this debt was charged on Francis I. As to the claim made for the alleged forfeit he was accused of, this reproach was not serious, because Henry himself had objected to the celebration of this marriage with the Princess Mary, and had afterwards given his consent to the alliance Charles V. had contracted with Isabella of Portugal. As to the sack of Rome, and the profanations committed there, the emperor had been as much distressed and scandalised as any other Christian prince, and he would afterwards try to find a remedy. He winds up,

"Should not I have much more reason to send a defiance to King Henry than he has to me, if, as is reported, he wishes to separate from the queen my aunt, and marry another? I cannot believe this, having in my hands the pope's dispensation in favour of this marriage, so ample and so entirely free from subterfuge that I cannot see what can give cause for such a separation. How can the king's wish that I should marry his daughter be explained, if he endeavours to make her out to be illegitimate.* All this

* Some English authors have asserted that a junta at Toledo

is done by the evil and sinister instigation of the Cardinal of York, whose ambition I would not gratify, and who has boasted that he would put the emperor's affairs into such an entanglement that nothing of the sort had been seen for many centuries. And I protest before God and the whole world that all the damage and all the evils resulting from the said wars shall be laid to the charge of whoever is the author of them." *

The people, and especially the merchants and workmen, were much enraged against Wolsey for this declaration of war; the cessation of commercial relations with imperial dominions closed the ordinary channels for English manufactures through Flanders.†

Attempts at insurrection were repressed in the county of Kent with unheard-of severity; the minister directing was held chiefly responsible, though he did not take the most active share in it.

There was a little Lutheranism mingled with this

had objected to this marriage on the pretext that the legitimacy of the Princess Mary might be contested. Would not Charles V. have alluded to this in the document quoted? No Spanish author mentions it. And the editors of the two collections have not found any trace of this protest in the various archives they have searched with so much success.

* Histoire du Divorce, par Joachim Legrand. Pièces Justificatives, vol. iii, pp. 44-47. This very long protest is greatly analysed and abridged.

† In London itself there was a disturbance, called the apprentices' rising.

agitation. Wolsey wished to stifle the heresy in its birth; he was rigorous against the innovators, looking on them as rebels, both in a temporal and spiritual light.

In another direction, in order to meet a certain tendency to which Henry VIII. himself began to yield, the cardinal was working at the suppression of the smaller monasteries, and his agents took the opportunity of speculating and making severe exactions. Thus he made himself unpopular both with Catholics and Lutherans.

Nevertheless, till now Wolsey seemed as if he could console himself for everything with the king's favour. And behold! he found he was just getting into disgrace with that prince. Some retrospective details are here necessary. It was in an essentially religious view, said Henry VIII., that Wolsey was endeavouring to reform the larger monasteries, and when the abbesses or superiors of religious communities caused scandal, he thought it his duty to judge and depose them. Especially he would not consent to the nomination of persons of doubtful character to these exalted positions.

Now the Abbess of Wilton was recently dead. John Carey, whose brother had married Mary Boleyn, Anne's elder sister, begged for the post for his sister Elinor. His request was backed by Anne Boleyn and the king himself. Wolsey replied that he could the more easily give effect to their recommendations because the nuns of the monastery had placed the choice of the new abbess in his hands. But, on the customary inquiry and examination, it appeared that Elinor Carey was notoriously guilty of misconduct and immorality,

As soon as Wolsey was informed of this by his commissioner, Doctor Bell, he referred to the king, who did not insist, but apparently only desired his minister, in case Elinor was not appointed, not to select as abbess the person who stood in the convent as the representative of the opposite party, one Isabella Jordan; and immediately afterwards the king, in order to give a half-satisfaction to Anne Boleyn, wrote to her: "I would not for all the world cloy your conscience nor mine to make her ruler of a house which is of so ungodly demeanour; nor I trust you would not that, neither for brother (Carey) nor sister, I should so disstain mine honour or conscience. And as touching the prioress (Isabella Jordan), or Dame Elinor's oldest sister, though there is not any evident case proved against them, and that the prioress is so old that of many years she could not be as she was named, yet notwithstanding, *to do you pleasure*, I have done that neither of them shall have it, but . . . . some other good and well-disposed woman." *

* Letters and Papers, Brewer. Introduction, vol. iv, p. ccclxxxvi.

However, Wolsey, perhaps misunderstanding the intentions expressed by the king, and desirous of confuting the scandalous outrages and scorn unjustly heaped by Elinor's party upon the worthy prioress, Isabella Jordan, declared that it was according to the counsel of the best nuns of the convent that he nominated the latter as abbess. He sent Doctor Bell to announce this nomination to Henry VIII., and asked him to ratify it. The king received the message with much vexation; he displayed the greatest indignation at Wolsey's proceeding, saying that he had given his royal word to several of Elinor Carey's friends that, if their *protégée* could not be appointed, neither should her rival; that on these terms he had left the decision of the matter to Wolsey with perfect confidence in his wisdom and loyalty; "and surely," says Doctor Bell, "for my duty and true heart toward your grace, I would rather than part of my small substance you had elected some other."

Wolsey was much alarmed when he heard how strongly the king had expressed his displeasure, and hastened to write to him, and make the best excuses he could. Henry answered him in a letter which still shows some good feeling; there is to be seen in it the cordial tone he used with his friends, even when he was angry. And yet in this letter there is already a feeling of the blind workings of anger that make one shudder.

"The great affection and love I bear you causeth me, using the doctrine of my master, *quem diligo castigo*, thus plainly as now ensueth to break to you my mind, ensuring you that neither sinister report, affection to my own pleasure, interesse parts, nor meditation of any other body, beareth place in this case; wherefore, whatsoever I do say, I pray think it spoken of no displeasure, but of him that would do you as much good, both of body and soul, as you would yourself.

"Methinks it is not the right train of a trusty, loving friend and servant, when the matter is put, by the master's consent, into his arbitre and judgment (specially in a matter wherein his master hath both royalty and interest), to elect and choose a person which was by him defended (forbidden). And yet another thing, which much displeaseth me more— that is, to cloak your offence made by ignorance of my pleasure, saying that you expressly knew not my determinate mind in that behalf."

Here the king recalls the expressions he had three times before used and adds,

"Ah! my lord, it is a double offence both to do ill and colour it too; but with men that have wit it cannot be accepted so. Wherefore, good my lord, use no more that way with me, for there is no man living that more hateth it.

"These things being thus committed, either I must

have reserved them *in pectore*, whereby more displeasure might happen to breed, or else thus roundly and plainly to declare them to you; because I do think that *cum amico et familiari sincere semper est agendum*, and especially the master to his best beloved servant and friend, for in so doing the one shall be more circumspect in his doing, the other shall declare and show the loftiness that is in him to have any occasion to be displeased with him.

"And as touching the redress of religion (*i.e.* of the nuns), if it be observed and continued, undoubtedly it is a gracious act; notwithstanding, if all reports be true, *ab imbecillis imbecilla expectantur*. Howbeit, Mr. Bell hath informed me that her age, personage, and manner *præ se fit gravitatem*, I pray God it be so indeed, seeing that she is preferred to that room. I understand, furthermore (which is greatly to my comfort), that you have ordered yourself to Godward as religiously and virtuously as any prelate or father of Christ's Church can do; when in so doing and persevering there can nothing more be acceptable to God, more honour to yourself, nor more desired of your friends, amongst the which I reckon myself not the least."[*]

He then proceeds, in a very friendly way, and with some delicacy, to inform Wolsey that there were

---

[*] Letters and Papers, Brewer. Introduction, vol. iv, p. ccclxxxviii.

strange reports current about him. That it was said in the religious world that the monasteries were giving the cardinal considerable sums of money,* either to buy off suppression, or to obtain from his spiritual authority as legate some immunities or other favours they would have no chance of obtaining without making use of this means of corruption.

Notwithstanding these fine protestations. Wolsey was terrified; he vaguely felt the talon hidden beneath the velvet. He had a prevision that the devotion and the services of a whole life would not always prevail against even the least cause of displeasure. And, if the king failed him, what was left?

He alleged in excuse that the fear of the prevailing epidemic, which will be described immediately, had caused his secretaries and chief officers to leave him, that he had not his usual advisers with him when, on pressing entreaties, and himself weakened by the malady, he had a little too hastily come to the determination of appointing Isabella Jordan Abbess of Wilton, but that this nomination was conditional, and only to be definitive if the king confirmed it. Lastly his letter gave a very plausible explanation of his employment of the subsidies from the monasteries,

* When the king in need had demanded a contribution from the religious communities, they had treated him very shabbily. But with Wolsey they showed great liberality, and this made him give them a squeeze.

namely, on the religious and scientific foundations with which he was endowing the University of Oxford.

The king accepted this explanation, and showed his satisfaction at his remarks having been so well received; he desired Wolsey for the future to require no contributions from the monasteries for any purpose whatever, so as to deprive his enemies of any cause of complaint.

"Thus I end this rude yet loving letter, assuring you that at this hour there remains no spark of displeasure towards you in my heart."*

Wolsey's reply is full of exaggerated expressions of personal devotion and thankfulness to the king. It begins thus:

"SIRE,—Your gracious, loving letters, whereby I do perceive that no spark of displeasure remaineth in your noble heart towards me, hath, on my truth, so letificate and re-comforted me, being so replenished with heaviness and sorrow, *ut videar ex morte ad vitam restitutus.*"

He also declares at length that the money received by him from the convents was all employed in endowments for learning at Oxford, and that he had not diverted one single penny for his own use or that of his family.

* Letters and Papers, Brewer. Introduction, vol. iv, p. cccxciii, pt. ii, p. 1970

About this time Wolsey had a severe attack of an epidemic illness that was prevailing in London. This malady, causing quite a panic in the city and the English Court, was called the sweating sickness. Jean du Bellay, recently appointed French ambassador to England, describes it thus:

"This sweat, which has made its appearance within these four days, is a most perilous disease. One has a little pain in the head and heart, suddenly a sweat breaks out, and a doctor is useless; for, whether you wrap yourself up much or little, in four hours, and sometimes in two or three, you are dispatched without languishing, as in those troublesome fevers. However, only about two thousand have caught it in London. Yesterday, going to swear the truce, we saw them as thick as flies rushing from the streets and shops into their houses to take the sweat whenever they felt ill. I found the Ambassador of Milan leaving his lodgings in great haste because two or three had been suddenly attacked." *

The malady raged principally in the counties of Kent and Sussex, and had rapidly swept over London and the neighbourhood. At Court, the first person attacked by the disease was Anne Boleyn. Then there was a panic and general rout. Everyone fled. The king moved to Waltham in great

---

* Letters and Papers, Brewer. Introduction, vol. iv, p. ccclxxii.

haste. Anne went to her father's house at Hever. The king had only kept very few persons with him; and the number diminished every day. Two of the king's favourites died of this malady, William Compton, to whom he was much attached, and William Carey, the husband of Mary Boleyn. The king, constantly fleeing from the malady, left Waltham for Hunsdon, and at last retreated to Tittenhanger, a little house belonging to Wolsey, twenty miles from London. He took every precaution not to be surprised by death, and thus escaped the complaint.

At this time—it was a little before the episode of the Abbess of Wilton—he was very anxious about Wolsey's health. He even sent him a copy of his will,* and told him that the queen was always inquiring after the cardinal. For now the king seemed to have returned to Catharine, and lived with her with all the external signs of intimacy, and when, in prospect of speedy death, as daily imminent by the sweating sickness, he thought it necessary to take the sacrament, Catharine went to the altar, and received the holy communion with him.

Some persons were deceived by these appearances, perhaps even Catharine herself, and conceived a

* Lingard, vol. vi, p. 140. " He (the cardinal) made his will, and sent it to Henry for his approbation." The text is taken from Brewer. (Ed.)

hope that Henry would know how to understand the warning of Providence sent him, and that he would give up the project of the divorce;* but, in reality, through these strange vicissitudes of terror and devotion, he had hardly relaxed in his prosecution of his secret designs.

First, it is just the very time when he suppressed the household assigned to the Princess Mary and her private establishment at Ludlow on the score of expense. No doubt, in view of the growing unpopularity that attached to his attempt at divorce,† he wished to put down this little court, as it was hostile to him, and might have become a nucleus of opposition, if opportunity served. And he did not see that public opinion would be more strongly pronounced than ever when the parsimonious treatment of the Princess Mary was contrasted with the prodigal expenditure still lavished on the Duke of Richmond, who looked forward to inheriting the crown.

When Henry had ceased to fear any danger of the

* Lingard, vol. vi, p. 140. Letters and Papers, Brewer. Introduction, vol. iv, p. ccclxxvii.

† The Milanese ambassador confirms Mendoza's opinion; for he writes to his Court, "Many persons apprehend that, should this marriage take place, the population here will rebel." Letters and Papers, Brewer. Introduction, vol. iv, p. ccclxxvii. From Venetian Calendar, vol. iv, p. 252; and the French ambassador, Jean du Bellay, says the same.

contagion to himself, and when Anne Boleyn was not quite recovered from the succession of troubles which had vexed her greatly, the interrupted correspondence between them was resumed—no longer in the language of a king, like the letters to Wolsey.

"He came to me last night," he said to Anne, "with news as sad as possible. I was vexed, for three reasons: firstly, for having made known the continuation of the illness of my beloved mistress, whose health is as dear to me as my own, and whose sufferings I would willingly share. Secondly, because I fear having to suffer yet longer from this absence, which is so trying to me. Thirdly, because the doctor in whom I should have the most confidence is staying at some distance. I therefore send you my second physician, Doctor Butts, praying God that He may restore to health as soon as possible her who is worthy of all my affection. Be governed, I pray you, by his advice, and, thanks to him, I hope to see you soon return convalescent." *

We might extract a number of other passages illustrating the king's violent passion, and extra-

* State Papers, p. 1921. Introduction, vol. iv, p. ccclxxviii. See also the collection of Henry VIII.'s letters to Anne Boleyn, published by Crapelet, Paris, 1828, and Audin's Vie de Henri VIII., vol. i, p. 462. We do not think it possible to reproduce all that Audin quotes.

ordinary is the want of delicacy, even sometimes grossness of his expressions.*

Anne Boleyn's letters to Wolsey seem more interesting. They are evidently much laboured and carefully written under the inspiration of Henry VIII. She addresses very exaggerated professions of affection to the cardinal. "In my most humblest wise that my poor heart can think, I do thank your grace for your rich and goodly present, the which I shall never be able to deserve without your great help; of the which I have hitherto 'had so great plenty, that all the days of my life I am most bound of all creatures, next the king's grace, to love and serve your grace." †

She also says she flatters herself that the cardinal is convinced, and that she is very impatient to hear news from him of the legate Campeggio; as they would be sure to be good if they came from him. She knows that he is as impatient as she is, and would be more, if it were possible. But it is necessary to wait and hope.

The king wrote to congratulate Wolsey on the restoration of his health, and betrayed the secret of his greatest interest, "being grieved at not hearing

* As, for instance, a letter sent with a bit of "hart's flesh." They give a melancholy notion of the lady they were intended for, who could be pleased with such language. Vol. iv, pt. ii, p. 1932.

† Letters and Papers, Brewer. Introduction, vol. iv, p. ccclxxxii, and pt. ii, p. 1960.

of the legate's arrival in France, but hoping that the difficulties will soon be cleared away by the cardinal's pains, through God's help."

Protestant writers are in ecstasies over the pious sentiments of the king, only endeavouring to accomplish his wishes by the most lawful means.

In another letter to Wolsey, Anne Boleyn says she is eagerly longing for Campeggio's arrival, for, if it be God's will that the business is to be pursued, she prays for a speedy conclusion.

"Now, good my lord, your discretion may consider as yet how little it is in my power to recompense you, but all only with my good-will; the which, I assure you, that, after this matter is brought to pass, you shall find me, as I am bound in the meantime to owe you my service; and then, look what things in this world I can imagine to do you pleasure in, you shall find me the gladdest woman in the world to do it."*

A most edifying expression! The fervent prayers of Lady Anne had no truly lofty and disinterested aim, but they may be considered more sincere than the indications of good-will she showered on Wolsey. Certainly the cynicism of her promises to the judge, of a great reward if she ever became queen, were remarkable. It is bribery and corruption in a flagrant form, it must be acknowledged.

* Letters and Papers, Brewer. Introduction, vol. iv, p. ccclxxxiii.

And, after this, can anyone venture to blame Catharine for suspecting the cardinal's justice, and thinking it her duty to refuse him? The understanding of this upright judge with the other side is evident. A creature of Henry VIII., loaded with benefits, he could not give an impartial decision in his master's suit.

www.ingramcontent.com/pod-product-compliance
Lightning Source LLC
Chambersburg PA
CBHW030734230426
43667CB00007B/715